The West Front, drawn by
F. Mackenzie and engraved
by J. Le Keux, from Britton
1836, pl. V.

SALISBURY CATHEDRAL
THE WEST FRONT

The west front with scaffolding in place for G.G. Scott's restoration, 1869. NMR, Gerald Cobb Collection.
© Crown Copyright.NMR.

SALISBURY CATHEDRAL
THE WEST FRONT

A History and Study in Conservation

edited by Tim Ayers

PHILLIMORE

2000

Published by
PHILLIMORE & CO. LTD.
Shopwyke Manor Barn, Chichester, West Sussex

© The Contributors, 2000

ISBN 1 86077 152 1

Printed and bound in Great Britain by
BIDDLES LTD.
Guildford, Surrey

Colour printed by
ST RICHARD'S PRESS
Chichester, West Sussex

Contents

v

List of Illustrations

COLOUR PLATES

ST. JAMES'S PALACE

In May 2000 the West Front of Salisbury Cathedral, after being shrouded in scaffolding for almost five years, was unveiled in a great festival of light and music. The beautiful pale stonework of the West Front, with its ranks of statues, has now been spectacularly revealed after a monumental programme of cleaning and repair. Their conservation seems to me to be a particularly fitting way to celebrate two thousand years of Christianity.

This book records the work and achievement of the many people involved in this important project. It is also a history of this magnificent Cathedral and of its significance to those who have worshipped there down the ages.

It has given me enormous pleasure to have been involved in the project to restore Salisbury Cathedral, which has been funded jointly by the Cathedral Trust and English Heritage, and I am delighted to recommend this fascinating book to anyone who cares about both the past and the future of one of our great cathedrals.

List of Subscribers

Maureen E. Atkinson
Lt Col R.C. Ayers OBE
David Azzolina
Betty and Gordon Bagley
Leslie and Susan Baker
Clare P. Barker
Kusuma Barnett
Mrs Raymond Barton
Beatrice Bathe
Miss B. Battye
Corinne G. Bennett
Sir Christopher Benson and Lady
   Benson
Graham T. Beresford
Dr John Birch
Joan Blacklock
P.S. Boden
Jennifer Bowen
John W. Briggs
David A. Brown
Sarah Brown
John F. Bushell
Cathedral Architects' Association
Catharine Chandler
Bridget Cherry
Timothy N. Chick
Columba Cook
David J. and Jennifer A. Cooke
Janet Corps
Ralph W. Daniel
Dr Jonathan M. Daube
The Dean & Chapter of Salisbury
   Cathedral
Dearle & Henderson Ltd.
Mr and Mrs C.A. Dew-Jones
Major General R.L.C. Dixon
Canon Bruce Duncan MBE
Richard Durman
Canon David Durston
Mr and Mrs K.S. Eckett
Rupert Edwards
Mr Øystein Ekroll

John Elliott
James Farquharson
R.A. Farquharson
B.W. Ferris FCIOB
Freeland Rees Roberts Architects
Felicity Gardner
Dr John A.A. Goodall
Warren F. Goodell
The Greville-Heygate family
Dr and Mrs Richard Hamber
Margaret Hardiman
Tim Hatton Esq. OBE
David Heath
Sir Edward Heath KG MBE MP
Janet M. Henderson
Mrs Hatty Hillier
John H. Jacob
Michelle Johnson
Dr James F. Johnston
Brian Jones
Nicola Jones
D.C. and J.A. Kennedy
Robert Key, MP
Philip J. Lankester
Michael and Hazel Lee
Stephen J. Linard FRICS
Dr Øivind Lunde
Peter and Deirdre Luton
William Peter Mahrt
The Ven. and Mrs J.S. Maples
Richard Marks
Peter Marsh
Dennis Martin
Janet and Joseph McGrath
Dr Linda Monckton
Dr Richard K. Morris
Marjorie Nelson
W.S. Oglethorpe
The Revd Canon June Osborne
   and Mr Paul Goulding QC
Brig. Kit Owen LVO OBE
Michael Paraskos

Howard C. Parker, FAIA
Howard G. Perkins
Ann Philp
Mr and Mrs S. Ponting
Purcell Miller Tritton
Ronald P. Radley
T. Redding
David Richards
Marion Roberts
Dr Warwick Rodwell
Mrs Mavis Rose
Salisbury Cathedral Trust
John Schofield
Mr T.J. Searle
Dr and Mrs Colin Smith
Roy and Jean Spring
Mark and Dilys Spurrell
Nancy D. Steele
Neil Stratford
Sumthing.co.uk
Priscilla Tapley
Mrs. W. Mary Thomas, LRAM
Pamela J. Travers
Oliver D. Tregoning
The Lord Tryon
Nigel J. Tucker
Bynum Ellsworth Tudor, Jr
Donald and Noreen Tyson
Andrew Waring
Colin Watts
Donald and Peggy Webb
Miss Susan M. Webb
Jeffery Weeks
Roy Whitehead
E. John Whiteley
William Wilks
Dr Paul Williamson
Keith J. Woodbridge
Guy A. Woodworth
Christine M. Woodworth-Batho
Mr and Mrs John W. Yago

Preface

by The Very Reverend Derek Watson, Dean of Salisbury

I am delighted to commend this book as a valuable record of an important piece of work.

Our West Front is an inspiration to many, and there is a great deal here to stimulate and inform their appreciation. This major project has involved such a high quality of expertise and skill that it deserves proper attention.

We are indebted to those who have contributed both to this book and to the work itself. It has taken talent, time and money, and it would not have been possible without the support of the Cathedral Trust and English Heritage. We are most grateful to all who have played their part.

Acknowledgements

The authors would like to thank the following for help and advice Dr Ron Baxter, Annie Brodrick, Sarah Brown, Dr Spike Bucklow, Dr Paul Crossley, Peter Draper, Anna Eavis, Dr Lindy Grant, Catherine Hassall, Helen Howard, Peter Mactaggart, Dr Christopher Norton, Dr David Park, Prof. Marion Roberts, Roy Spring, Dr Christine Stevens, Prof. Malcolm Thurlby, Philip Ward-Jackson, Chris Weeks and Dr Paul Williamson.

For their help in providing information about conservation, carving and masonry processes: David Henson (senior conservator), Christina Kaye (sculpture conservator), Jason Battle (carver), Chris Sampson (head mason), all of Salisbury Cathedral Works Department. For her help in providing information about the statue of St Augustine: Jane Erith (Secretary, Friends of Salisbury Cathedral). For their support in helping us to develop specific conservation techniques during the west front programme: Jeanne Marie Teutonico and Bill Martin (English Heritage Building Conservation Research Team). For his continuing support and interest during the west front programme: Peter Burman (Director, Centre for Conservation, York University).

We also acknowledge with gratitude the permissions granted by many institutions to reproduce photographs for which they hold the copyright. They are named at the end of each caption. Peter Marsh, who has taken many of the photographs in the Catalogue, is also acknowledged for colour plates IIIa and d, IVa and main photograph, Va, c and d.

ABBREVIATIONS

Biblical references are to the Douay version (Turnhout, 1935 edn).

BL   British Library, London
Bodl. Bodleian Library, Oxford
CI   Courtauld Institute of Art, London University (Conway Library)
NMR   National Monuments Record Centre (English Heritage), Swindon
RIBA   Royal Institute of British Architects, London

Introduction

TIM TATTON-BROWN

Nearly forty years ago, Sir Nikolaus Pevsner described the west front thus:

> The façade of Salisbury Cathedral is a headache. There is so much in it which is perversely unbeautiful. There are also far too many motifs, and they are distributed without a comprehensible system.[1]

This is rather a harsh judgement, and one that I hope this book will reassess, after a detailed study of all the new evidence gained from the programme of cleaning, recording and repair that has been carried out in the last five years.

The west front or façade of Salisbury Cathedral is, in fact, a series of decorated layers that were built up around the west end of the cathedral at the time when the nave was being built, almost certainly in the years between the mid-1230s and the mid-1250s. In this introduction I want to look briefly at the building sequence of the whole cathedral to see how the west front fits in.

William de Waude's *Historia* tells us that on 18 April 1220 the foundation (*fundamentum*) of the new church of Sarum was laid and on that day Bishop Richard Poore and a large group of clergy and laymen laid a series of stones at the place of foundation (*locus fundationis*).[2] It has been presumed that this was at the extreme east end of the cathedral, as within five years the three low eastern chapels were complete and in use. However, a study of the plan and of the fabric of the lowest parts of the walls suggests that the foundations of the outer walls of the whole cathedral, all the way to the west front, were laid out at about the same time, and that the lowest part of the external wall plinth, and the internal wall bench were built from west to east. Only after this had been laid did the walls of the east arm start to rise up.

The evidence comes from both the plan and from the constructional sequence exhibited in the lowest masonry. The building was very carefully laid out on the ground with an exact north-south and east-west alignment. The plan has been studied by Dr Peter Kidson.[3] He established that the nave was the most regular part of this, and that the eastern arm plan was built up from a series of north-south base-lines on the west side of the two transepts. The original setting-out lines for the cathedral may have

---

[1] *BoE, Wilts*, p.398.
[2] W.H. Rich Jones, *The Register of St Osmund*, II, London, 1884, p.13.
[3] P. Kidson, 'The historical circumstances and the principles of the design', in RCHME 1993b, pp.62–79.

been the *c.*460ft long east-west axis and the *c.*230ft long north-south line, drawn through the west part of the greater transept.

Soon after a papal licence for the new building was obtained in 1218,[4] work probably began on digging foundations 4-5ft deep, down to the natural bed of river gravel that lies on the Upper Chalk. This was a huge undertaking for a building over 460ft long. It was to have 6ft wide foundations for the main outer walls, and a whole series of large external buttresses (also having massive foundations). Once the rammed foundations had been put in, their top surface was very carefully levelled, and lines were probably marked out on them for the first courses of masonry. Externally this was to be two courses of plinth masonry (a lowest chamfered course, and a course topped with a large roll-moulding), while inside a wall bench was created, which had a small roll-moulding beneath the seat. Both the external and internal masonry came to the same height, 1ft 4½in (42cm) above ground level, and between them the rubble core of the wall, about 4ft wide, was rammed in.

The roll-moulding below the bench is a very distinct feature around the inside walls of the whole cathedral, continuing as far as the north and south returns for the west front (fig. 1). In the nave and western part of the greater transept the wall bench and lowest courses of the plinth, described above, are in synchronisation (i.e. at the same level), but the internal bench is made to step up progressively as it moves eastwards because of the steps in the floor in the greater and lesser transepts (fig. 2). This perhaps suggests that the building work for the lowest two courses started in the western part of the cathedral and moved eastwards, so that the slightly raised floors of the eastern arm could be constructed by infilling eastwards of the two principal steps (fig. 2). East of the presbytery step, the floor level was almost exactly 1ft higher than in the nave and outside of the building. Quite a large amount of rubble infill would, therefore, have been needed.

Only after this initial building work to establish the floors and the outer walls in the whole of the cathedral would the builders have turned their attention to the higher walls of the eastern arm. Once again, however, the uniform coursing of the masonry of the plinth, and the plain wall above it, suggest that this outer wall for the whole of the eastern arm, as far as the second bay of the nave, was all built at the same time. Moulded stone discs, with inset bronze consecration crosses, were very carefully set into the top of the wall, at the required height, 7½ft.[5] Is it possible that these were the 'stones' (i.e. the stone discs with inset consecration crosses) that were laid on 28 April 1220, as described by William de Waude?[6] If not, the stone of the lowest plinth courses

---

[4] The plan of the churchyard and close had probably been laid out in the 1190s, and it is just possible that the work on the cathedral was started at this time as well. An appendix to the *Statutes of Bishop Martival* reports that 'the church of Sarum was begun in the time of King Richard' (i.e. 1189–1199): see n.17.

[5] Dewick 1908, pp.1–34, esp. p.11.

[6] See my 'The Salisbury Cathedral consecration crosses', *Transactions Monumental Brass Society*, XVI, pt. 2, 1998, pp.113–16.

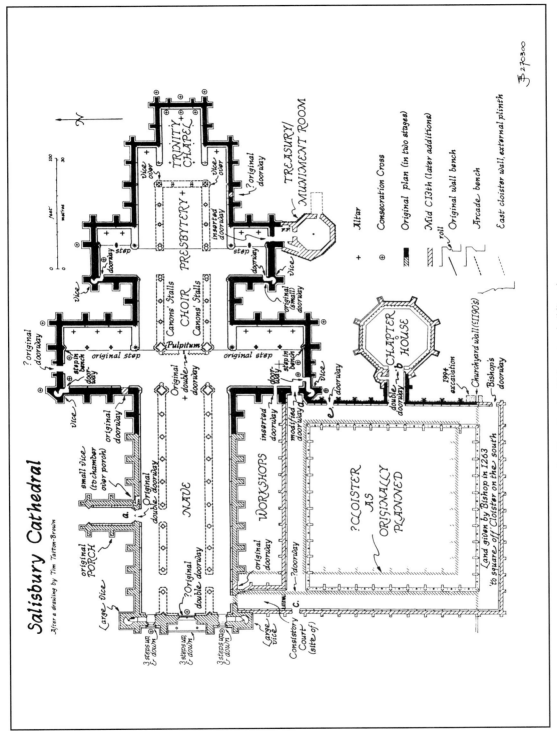

1 Plan, showing 13th-century building phases.

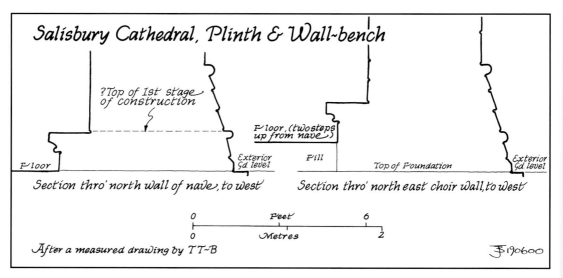

Salisbury Cathedral, Plinth & Wall-bench

?Top of 1st stage
of construction

Floor, (two steps
up from nave)

Floor

Exterior
Gd level

Pill

Top of Foundation

Exterior
Gd level

Section thro' north wall of nave, to west   *Section thro' north east choir wall, to west*

| 0 | Feet | 6 |
| 0 | Metres | 2 |

After a measured drawing by T T~B   Æ190600

2   Sections through the lower wall in the nave and presbytery.

was presumably meant. Whichever is correct, it seems very likely that the foundations and lowest levels of the outer stair-turrets of the west front were in place by 1220. The inner wall bench (with its roll-moulding) just turns the corner in the extreme north-west and south-west corners of the nave, and the floor-level in the passages leading to the stair-turrets is exactly that of the top of the bench. The coursing of the external moulded and battered plinth continues unchanged around the outside of the corner stair-turrets, dying out only when it reaches the aisle doorways. This suggests that the plan of the projecting stair-turrets, at least, was laid out at the very beginning.

All of the original doorways in the eastern arm of the cathedral, as well as the great north door of the nave, are carefully defined by having the roll-moulding on the bench turn into them. This is not, however, the case with the three west doorways, because here three steps rise up to the thresholds, which are level with the top of the internal wall bench.[7] The roll-moulding at the west end of the nave aisles does not turn in either. The wall bench in the west wall of the nave proper has a plain chamfer beneath it, a feature that it shares with the arcade bench or stylobate for the piers. All of this perhaps suggests that the plan and design of the main part of the west front, with a series of three steps leading up to the west doorway thresholds is secondary, perhaps worked out at the time when the arcade benches were being designed. This must have happened at the east end of the cathedral by 1225, at the latest, when the

[7]   The wall bench, with the roll-moulding, continues into the north porch, showing that this too was planned from the start. There is also a short section of roll-moulding below the wall bench outside the doorway from the south transept into the north-east corner of the cloister. The cloister was also planned from the start and was not a later addition, as has sometimes been suggested. See my 'The cloisters of Salisbury Cathedral', *Spire*, 65th Annual Report of the Friends, 1995, pp.6–10.

arcade bench at the west end of the Trinity Chapel was in place and work on the upper walls was about to start.

The construction of the whole eastern arm must have taken about a decade, and was probably complete by 1236, when timber was being supplied for the canons' stalls.[8] Within eight years, the first services in the choir had presumably started, as a new pyx was given by the king in 1244, and vestments were being made.[9] In November 1246, a new bishop, William of York (1246-1256), a royal chaplain and Provost of Beverley, was forced on a reluctant chapter by the king. In the following year, a new *custos fabrice*, Master Ralph of York (a canon from 1239 until his death in 1262) and a new 'engineer', Master Nicholas of York, the bishop's official and later a canon, who was probably also the *magister operis*, were appointed.[10]

This group of men from York must have been responsible for the main work on the west front, though it is possible that the building of the three groups of tri-gabled porches at the base of the west front was already complete by 1246.[11] Conclusive evidence is lacking, but it is noteworthy that the two side porches incorporate in their central gables a stone disc, on which was originally fixed a bronze consecration cross. A third consecration cross was placed on the inside above the trumeau of the central doorway.[12] It is very likely that the external crosses were fixed at an early date, well before the completion of the eastern arm. It is worth noting that at the famous council, held in 1237 by the papal legate, Cardinal Otho, at St Paul's Cathedral in London, the first statute of a new set of ecclesiastical constitutions decreed that, with no exceptions, all cathedrals and conventual or parish churches 'whose walls had been completed must be consecrated within two years of that time', even if the structure remained unfinished after the stipulated two years had elapsed.[13]

The work that the 'new men' from York were completing from 1247 onwards would almost certainly have been the nave and west front. They probably followed a design already drawn up by Elias de Dereham ('*rector*' of the fabric from 1220 until his death in 1245).[14] While this was going on, Masters Ralph and Nicholas of York had probably seen the radical new French style of architecture being built at Westminster Abbey from 1246, and it was no doubt these two men who were responsible for the design of the new Chapter House and the enlarged rib-vaulted cloister, which closely followed the Westminster style. Each stage of the building

---

[8] On 18 June 1236, the *Calendar of Close Rolls* (1234–37, p.277) records the giving, by the king to the canons, of 20 'good oaks' from Chippenham forest 'to make stalls in their church'.

[9] *Calendar of Lib. Rolls* (1240–45), pp.222, 291.

[10] D. Greenway, *John Le Neve, Fasti Ecclesiae Anglicanae, 1066–1300, IV, Salisbury*, London, 1991, pp.61, 69–70.

[11] See below, p.22.

[12] In the eastern arm there were three groups of external crosses on stone discs on each of the cardinal faces (north, east and south), and three groups of internal crosses cut into the masonry. We might, therefore, have expected the full complement of six crosses in the west front.

[13] Quoted in Blum 1991, p.21.

[14] I believe that Elias de Dereham was the designer of Salisbury Cathedral. See discussion in Hastings 1997.

work on the west front terminates in a prominent string-course, which ultimately ties the work back into the main levels in the nave: aisles, triforium, clerestory, and parapet. I would suggest that all of the four main upper levels were being built in the decade or so from *c.*1240 and that only the central high gable and the spirelets were still being built in the first half of the 1250s, once the roof had been completed. In the early 1250s large numbers of oaks were being given by the king.[15] Felling dates in the winter of 1251-52 have recently been obtained by dendrochronology for the timbers in the triforium roof west of the north porch.[16]

The cathedral was consecrated on Michaelmas Day (30 September) 1258 and seven and a half years later the building work on the cathedral was finally said to have been completed. This comes in a marginal note in Bishop Roger Martival's *Book of Statutes* (written 1315-19), which says that 'the church of Sarum was begun in the time of King Richard, continued through the reigns of three kings, and was completed on the 8th Kalends of April [25 March] in the year 1266; the whole expense of the fabric up to that time having been 42,000 marks'.[17] We can be certain that the whole of the west front was complete by this time at the latest, though without its proposed statues. I would also suggest that the bell-tower, Chapter House and cloister were finished as well.[18]

Early in the 14th century about 275 ft of masonry were added to the top of the lantern tower over the crossing. This is more than twice the height of the whole west front, and the spectacular tower and spire has dominated the cathedral ever since. The tower and spire are covered in ballflower decoration, and the quality of the masonry is superior to that in the rest of the cathedral. The style of decoration is also completely different and, as I have tried to show elsewhere, the tower and spire, though undocumented, were almost certainly built during the time of, and at the expense of, Bishops Simon of Ghent (1297–1315) and Roger Martival (1315–1330).[19] It is possible that the adding of statues to the west front was also being undertaken at this time, and it is likely that, with the succession of Robert Wyvil as bishop (he remained at Salisbury for 45 years, 1330–1375), all work on the cathedral had been completed. Wyvil himself was a royal clerk, 'provided' by the Pope, who was probably less involved with his cathedral, though his magnificent brass was formerly placed at the centre of the presbytery between the tombs of his two predecessors. Wyvil was, however, much

---

[15] These grants are listed in full in Simpson 1996, p.11. Leland reports that Bishop Giles of Bridport (1257–1262) paid for the lead roof.

[16] By Daniel Miles, September 2000.

[17] Quoted in W.H. Jones, *Salisbury (Diocesan Histories)*, Salisbury, 1880, p.94.

[18] Most earlier works suggest a much longer chronology for the building of the Chapter House and cloister – see also Blum (n. 13), but I believe that the bell-tower was built by the 1240s, and that the Chapter House and cloisters were constructed in the 1260s.

[19] T. Tatton-Brown, 'Building the tower and spire of Salisbury Cathedral', *Antiquity*, 65, 1991, pp.74–96 and 'The tombs of the two bishops who built the tower and spire of Salisbury Cathedral', *Wiltshire Archaeological and Natural History Magazine*, 88, 1995, pp.134–137.

concerned with military affairs as his brass shows, and during his time, the bishop's palace (and all the bishop's other manors) were given a licence to crenellate (in 1337).[20] It is therefore possible that it was this bishop who added the final crenellations to the top of the west front and to the top of the Chapter House (they were removed again in the early 19th century), though his predecessor, Roger Martival, had obtained the first licence to crenellate the close walls in August 1327.[21]

The recent cleaning, recording and conservation work on the west front has now produced a mass of new information about the constructional details, the statuary and, above all, about the polychromy, particularly that used in the west porch. It is this new information which forms the bulk of this book, and perhaps allows us now to think of the west front as more than just a 'perversely unbeautiful headache'. It is instead a magnificent screen for statuary, over one hundred feet square, which still dominates the western churchyard and close.

---

[20] *Cal. Pat. Rolls* (1334–38), p.498. Work on building the eastern close wall continued in the early 1340s, but must have ceased during the Black Death.

[21] *Cal. Pat. Rolls* (1327–30), p.159. See also Coulson 1982, pp.69–100.

3 West front. CI.

The Middle Ages

TIM AYERS AND JERRY SAMPSON

INTRODUCTION

The recent conservation of the west front has offered an opportunity to reassess a part of Salisbury Cathedral that has attracted little attention in recent studies (fig. 3). The present chapter begins with a consideration of this art-historical literature and then brings together the new information on the building, sculpture and polychromy, to give a view of the front as it changed through the later middle ages. The following chapter reviews the evidence for the period from the Reformation to the 20th century and a survey of the conservation itself brings the history up to date. There are also separate chapters on polychromy and early photography, as well as an illustrated catalogue of the sculpture.

The front has attracted few followers on aesthetic grounds. For Britton, the 'formally square outline … cannot be considered either beautiful, picturesque, or pleasing'.[1] Pevsner thought it 'perversely unbeautiful' and 'a headache'.[2] Yet its importance in other ways is obvious. As Dodsworth wrote (1814): '… the west front was the part in which the architect has chosen to display his taste and fancy … A comparison of this front with the other parts of the structure will prove that the design of the builder was to exhibit his power of combining grandeur with elegance and simplicity; and that, if he was elsewhere sparing in his ornaments, it was from taste and judgement, not pomposity of imagination.'[3] Quite simply, the front demonstrates the most elaborate use of architectural decoration anywhere in the 13th-century cathedral, in a building distinguished by its careful use of architectural vocabulary.

The front has been approached by architectural historians in a variety of different ways. Formally, the design was placed in relation to other English façades by Webb in his survey of medieval architecture in Britain.[4] The sources for the design have been explored by McAleer, presenting it as the culmination to a line of development in late

---

[1] Britton 1836, p.69.
[2] *BoE, Wilts.*, p.358.
[3] Dodsworth 1814, p.129.
[4] Webb 1956, pp.105–106. See also Kowa 1990, pp.134–36.

Romanesque buildings.[5] As Wilson observed, subsequently it exerted 'no influence whatever'.[6] Aspects of function and meaning have also been explored. Webb commented upon access, in relation to the splendid north porch.[7] The liturgical use of this and other fronts was examined by Blum and has been pursued by others.[8] Draper has stressed the place of the liturgy in the determination of architectural forms across the whole cathedral, including the west front and other doors.[9] This poses questions about authorship and design procedure, the respective contributions of patrons, their representatives and master masons. For Salisbury, there is relatively good documentary evidence for those involved, although it has been interpreted in contrasting ways.[10] Erlande-Brandenburg has drawn attention to the wider context of the façade within its close and in relation to the town.[11]

The west fronts of Wells and Salisbury promote sculptural display, yet assessment of the surviving sculpture has been cursory. This is common to the surviving Gothic sculpture on other English west fronts, whether for reasons of quality, illegibility or incompleteness, by comparison with continental examples. A deeper cultural unfamiliarity with three-dimensional sacred images has possibly inhibited investigation from other points of view. At Salisbury, the surviving medieval figures are of good but not outstanding quality, and some have long been in poor condition. Recognised as additions to the front, they have also contradicted the canonical qualities of completeness and coherence in design often attributed to the architecture of the building. If the west front of Wells is usually held up as a relatively complete English screen façade, to compare with French monuments, Salisbury has been in the shadow of them all. The restoration of the old and the creation of many new figures by James Frank Redfern, under George Gilbert Scott, between 1866 and 1869, has not helped. The uncertain extent of his restorations, and the sheer number and physical presence of Redfern's sculptures has made assessment of the medieval remains difficult.

In his book on the sculpture at Wells, published in 1851, C.R. Cockerell devoted space to the iconography of the Salisbury figures, which stood then alone on the front and were easier to read.[12] Writing in the late 1860s, Armfield touched again upon such matters, in setting out the scheme of Redfern's works.[13] This Victorian array gave new identities to several medieval figures and Armfield's description has been perpetuated in cathedral guides down to the present day.[14] The dominance of

[5] McAleer 1984, ch. V; McAleer 1988.
[6] Wilson 1990, p.175; McAleer 1988, p.150.
[7] Webb 1956, p.105.
[8] Blum 1986; McAleer 1988, pp.147–49; Kowa 1990, p.136; Sampson 1998, pp.169–73.
[9] Draper 1996, esp. pp.28–29.
[10] *EMA*, see 'Dereham, Elias of' and 'Ely, Nicholas of'; Blum 1991, pp.10–11, 20–21, n. 34; Jansen 1996; Hastings 1997.
[11] Erlande-Brandenburg 1994, pp.166–74.
[12] Cockerell 1851, pp.96–98.
[13] Armfield 1869a and b.
[14] Fletcher 1927; Cochrane 1971; Spring 1987, pp.32–40.

the 19th-century scheme was demonstrated in recent discussion of how to replace two medieval images (nos. 19a, 26a) that had changed their identity in Redfern's restoration of them – the Victorian identity has been maintained. Little attempt was made to interpret the medieval subject matter further, until Blum's brief overview in the *Macmillan Dictionary of Art* and Brown's recent book on the cathedral furnishings.[15]

The art-historical literature has been concerned, rather, with style and date. Cockerell describes the large-scale Salisbury figures in terms of the Pisani, making comparisons with nationalistic pride to the schools of Florence and Pisa.[16] In this century they have also been discussed in relation to schools, represented on the one hand by the west front at Wells, and on the other by sculptors working for King Edward I in the years around 1300. Prior and Gardner's monumental survey of 1912 found that the statues were different in style from those at Wells[17] and suggested that those 'first executed for the front have all disappeared, while what have chanced to survive may be the later additions to the niches.'[18] They were compared with the documented figures of *c.*1291–93 by William of Ireland for Edward I's Eleanor Cross at Hardingstone, Northants, and placed in the vanguard of a new style.[19] Stone's influential survey of British sculpture in the Pelican History of Art series concurred broadly, attributing one of the figures to Ireland himself.[20] Ireland's style anticipated work of the following decades and, against it, according to Stone, a London or court school consciously reacted. In general, this thesis of stylistic development has stood largely unchallenged until the recent publications of Phillip Lindley.[21] For the Salisbury figures, a dating at the end of the century has continued to prevail,[22] although some have had reservations.[23]

There has been confusion as to the extent of the original scheme of sculpture, but many of the questions posed by the surviving figures can now be answered with greater certainty. The architectural fabric has also been thoroughly recorded. This presents opportunities both to resolve old questions and to address new ones. What was the original extent and chronology of the sculpture and what does it reveal about changing priorities over time? Given the elaboration of the front's design, what can be concluded about its relationship to the rest of the cathedral? What is the relationship between form, access and liturgical function?

[15] Blum 1996a; RCHME 1999, pp.179–81.
[16] Cockerell 1851, p.95. He cites J.-B. Séroux d'Agincourt and L. Cicognara. Cockerell also praised the large-scale figures in a lecture to the Archaeological Association, meeting at Salisbury in 1849: *Archaeological Journal*, vi, 1849, p.300. Earlier, Dodsworth (1814) had been generally complimentary, p.129.
[17] Prior and Gardner 1912, pp.319, 345–46, 642.
[18] *Ibid.*, p.345. In his shorter handbook, Gardner glossed over this problem of later additions: Gardner 1937, p.162.
[19] Prior and Gardner 1912, pp.345, 642.
[20] Stone 1955, p.144.
[21] On the Eleanor Crosses: Lindley 1991, pp.69–92.
[22] Williamson 1995, p.211; Blum 1996b, p.76, n. 25, pl. XLID.
[23] *BoE Wilts.*, p.358; Hirschhorn 1977, p.79, n. 282; Blum 1991, p.22 n. 79; also Blum 1996a, p.629.

THE THIRTEENTH CENTURY

The façade of the great church offered a field for architectural ingenuity and display, often playing with familiar components in unfamiliar combinations. The Salisbury front was conceived as a screen façade, concealing the transverse elevation of the nave and richly decorated with zones of arcading (fig. 3). This combination was favoured for a number of Romanesque façades in western France and England, but the Salisbury design was probably inspired directly by that of the important Benedictine abbey of Malmesbury, which lay within the diocese (fig. 4).[24] Here was enshrined St Aldhelm, the first bishop of the see of Sherborne, to which Salisbury was a successor. In both places, a richly decorated screen is flanked by turrets, although these are over the nave aisles at Malmesbury, rather than beyond them. Both churches also have ornate lateral porches, although these are perhaps in the tradition of a building even closer to Salisbury, its predecessor cathedral church at Old Sarum.[25]

The design also responds directly to that of another neighbouring church, at Wells, newly elevated to cathedral status and consecrated in 1239 (fig. 5), in adopting the screen format for the display of sculpture, in the three great lancets lighting the nave and in the arrangement of niches that flank them. Similar, too, are the polychromatic use of Purbeck marble shafts, the particular nature of the passages that run within the thickness of the front and, again, the prominent nave porch. Unlike Wells, however, the Salisbury design has shallower niches and turrets instead of towers, and emphasizes rather the importance of the west doors by giving each a triple gabled porch. These reveal an awareness of developments in northern French façade design at the end of the 12th century, deriving ultimately from Laon Cathedral.[26] The feature has been borrowed with no understanding of its original architectural context and the porches are on a modest scale, in the English tradition of small west doors.[27] The earlier rebuilding of the west front of St Albans Abbey, begun under Abbot John de Cella (1195–1214), seems also to have included three porches, one before each doorway.[28]

The visual and symbolic importance of the west front in the architecture of the cathedral's exterior makes it inconceivable that the cathedral authorities, the bishop, the Dean and Chapter and their representatives, were not closely involved in the design. The oddly hybrid and obvious borrowings from great churches locally perhaps reflect this; they were yardsticks by which the patron could define the design and status of their own new building. The omission of west towers follows other buildings in the period and region, but contrasts with the apparent intention at the cathedrals of

---

[24] Webb 1956, p.105; McAleer 1984, ch. V; McAleer 1988, pp.125–26, 131, 137.
[25] Stalley 1971, p.75.
[26] Kowa 1990, p.134, makes a comparison with the façade of Saint-Nicaise at Reims.
[27] Blum 1986, p.149 argues for a liturgical motive, but see McAleer 1988, p.149, n. 80.
[28] T. Walsingham, *Gesta Abbatum Monasterii Sancti Albani*, ed. H. T. Riley, I, London, 1867, pp.218–20; E. Roberts, *The Hill of the Martyr, An Architectural History of St Albans Abbey*, Dunstable, 1993, pp.77–80.

4 West front, Malmesbury Abbey, Wiltshire.

Coventry and Wells, which are roughly contemporary.[29] Old Sarum, identified as important for other aspects of the cathedral's design, had also had a western block.[30] The decision is perhaps in keeping with the desire of the patron for simplified forms, which is a principle in the building as a whole. It is apparent also in the low stone lantern that was erected over the crossing.[31] The practical need for such towers for the hanging of bells was removed by the building of a separate detached belfry. Salisbury did not proclaim its status with towers, but chose instead to make a feature of the west doors. These have emerged also as central to the front's original decoration.

[29] For Coventry, see Morris 1994, pp.52–54.
[30] Stalley 1971, p.74, n. 2; RCHME 1993b, pp.72–73.
[31] Simpson 1996, pp.17–18.

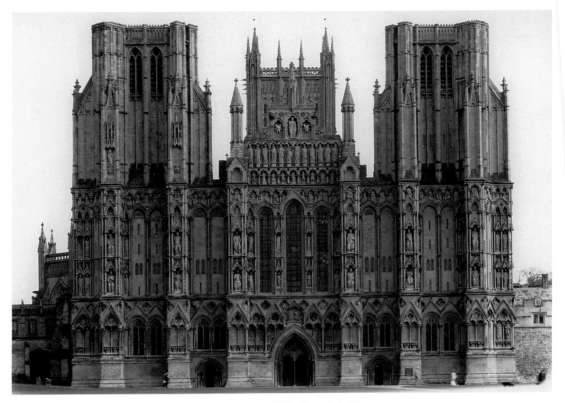

5 West front, Wells Cathedral. CI.

Scholars have wrestled with the problem of attributing authorship to the architecture of the cathedral.[32] This is complicated by the fact that the building provides evidence for particularly careful planning and choices in design.[33] The documentary evidence for those who may have been involved, both patrons and masons, is relatively rich. Bishop Richard Poore (1217–1228) transferred the cathedral from Old Sarum and is stated by Matthew Paris to have summoned noble craftsmen from distant parts.[34] A mason or 'cementarius' called Nicholas of Ely was the beneficiary of a grant of land by the bishop, to the east of the cloister.[35] The remarkable career of Elias of Dereham has been much discussed.[36] At Salisbury, he was described in the cathedral's lost martyrology as 'rector' of the fabric, 'a prima fundatione', according to John Leland.[37] He was also a prebendary of the cathedral by 1220 and until his death in 1245.

[32] Blum 1991, pp.10–11, 20–21; Jansen 1996, pp.34–37.
[33] Draper 1996; Jansen 1996, p.37.
[34] M. Paris, *Chronica Majora*, III, ed. H. R. Luard, London, 1876, p.391: ' … consilio nobilium artificum, quos a remotis convocerat, amplum jecit fundamentum …'.
[35] *EMA*, s.v.; Blum 1991, p.11.
[36] *EMA*, s.v.; Blum 1991, pp.10–11; RCHME 1993a, pp.8–9; Jansen 1996, p.34; Hastings 1997.
[37] Leland, I, p.266.

Elias's career is circumstantial evidence for his personal involvement in the cathedral's design. By 1220, he was a man experienced in creative enterprises of the most sacred kind and for the greatest patrons, as the 'incomparabilis artifex' of the shrine of St Thomas Becket.[38] In the realm of architecture, he is documented to have designed his house in the cathedral close as an 'exemplum' or model.[39] It is impossible to define a personal contribution to the design of the front but, as the steward of Bishop Jocelin of Bath and Wells (by 1229),[40] perhaps he facilitated access to designs there and to the masons' yard. Not only does Salisbury respond directly to the neighbouring cathedral, but the borrowings descend to measurements: some of the dimensions for the distinctive internal wall passage above the west door are taken almost unchanged from one building to the other.[41]

CONSTRUCTION

The relationship between the fabric of the west front and that of the west nave strongly suggests that the two were erected together (figs. 1,6). It has been suggested that there is a possible break in the construction at a high level, in the seventh bay west from the crossing.[42] However, careful examination of the internal fabric both from ground level and within the triforium and roof spaces has failed to identify any clear indications of a break in this vicinity, so that for the present it is probably best to consider the nave as a single campaign of building.

Of the various features of the fabric which could be indicative of a building break – changes in the design of elements of the architecture or the horizontal coursing, changes in the height of the original scaffolding lifts, consistent changes in the mortars or the source or bed of stone used in the construction – none is sufficiently consistent to suggest that there is a major break in the building within the western three bays. The horizontal coursing of the fabric west of the north porch is, in general, not consistent enough for minor breaks in the line of the bed joints to be considered reliable indicators of breaks in the progress of the construction – indeed on the lower fabric of the interior of the west front, for instance, it is common for the coursing to change on the internal angles, and it would clearly be impossible for there to be so many discrete episodes in the building history.

As a general principle it is to be expected that the west front and west nave would have been built up as a unit. It is good building practice, in that the thrust of the arcade has to be stabilised by the end wall, and was normal elsewhere in cathedral building in both the middle ages, and in the 19th and 20th centuries. As a possible

---

[38] M. Paris, *Historia Anglorum*, ed. F. Madden, II, London, 1866, p.242.
[39] Wordsworth 1917, p.441; RCHME 1993a, pp.8, 234, 238.
[40] HMC, I, p.36.
[41] Sampson 1998, pp.171–72.
[42] Jones 1995, p.17.

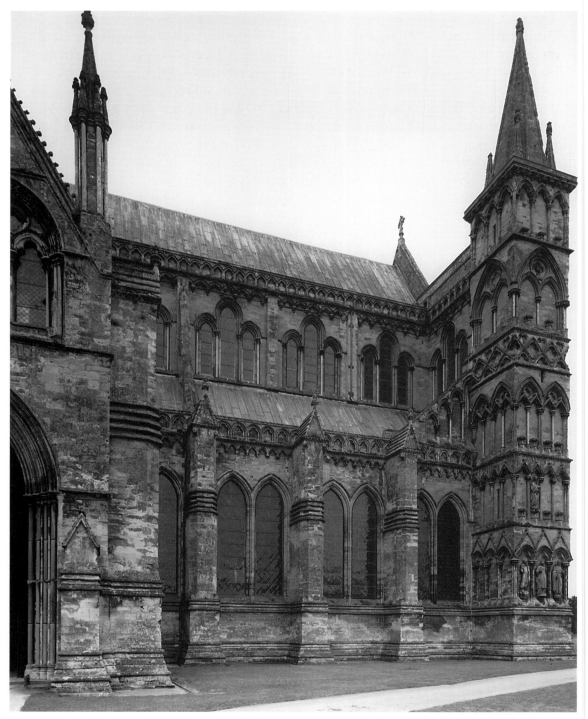

6   The north side of the nave. CI.

indicator of this, all of the major external string courses pass seamlessly on to the stair-turret of the west front. On the interior, the horizontal divisions of the nave elevation are largely abandoned (fig. 12). However, the design of the west wall appears consciously to imitate the triple division of this. The clerestory windows throughout the church consist of triple openings under a single relieving arch, the shafts between the inner openings being tied back to the outer skin with metal stays. The triple lancets of the west wall are of the same general form, although here each set of triple shafts between the windows is locked to the outer skin with three through-stones. In both clerestory and west windows the lower jambs are pierced by a walkway. Just as the western lancets are an amplification of the clerestory, so the form of the west gallery beneath them echoes the double cusped openings, crowned with blind quatrefoils, of the triforium level. Piercing the west wall with three galleries, two of them open to the interior, and imitating the double-skin construction of the clerestory means that the west wall is of a much lighter build than the comparable west wall of Wells Cathedral.

A comparison with other sites suggests two possible building sequences: either the erection of the whole façade as a unit to the tops of the flanking stair turrets and the apex of the gable (as at Truro Cathedral, at the turn of the 19th century); or the closing off of the nave and aisles structurally, followed immediately afterwards by the building of the link-walls (between the turrets at the top of the front) and the upper parts of the stair turrets above the aisle roofs (as at Wells Cathedral, upon which the design of Salisbury's façade is partly modelled). Although the west front of Salisbury is wide (a little over 110 ft or 33.5 m), and possesses link-walls between the stair turrets and the side walls of the nave clerestory, it is nowhere near as wide as that of Wells (150 ft or 45.5 m), where the western towers are placed outside the aisles. For this reason it is less likely that the sequence of construction found there would have been repeated at Salisbury. In addition the wide stairs at Salisbury,[43] with north-south passageways across the full width of the façade at three levels (whereas Wells has only one) and a parapet wall-walk at the top, would have provided the medieval masons with excellent access to the rising fabric throughout its construction.

The greater part of the fabric of the cathedral as a whole, and of the west front in particular, is remarkably homogeneous. As in the west nave, those changes in the source of the building stone or the form of the mortar mix used that often indicate breaks in the sequence of construction of a building, are also absent from the west front. While some breaks in the coursing of the stonework – the other major signature of a hiatus or change in the progress of construction – can be identified, it is likely that these reflect the method of building as much as its chronological sequence.

The coursing breaks that are commonly found in the angles of the lower masonry of the internal elevation seem to be no more than the medieval workshop's response

[43] With a 3 ft 8 in (1.11 to 1.12 m) radius.

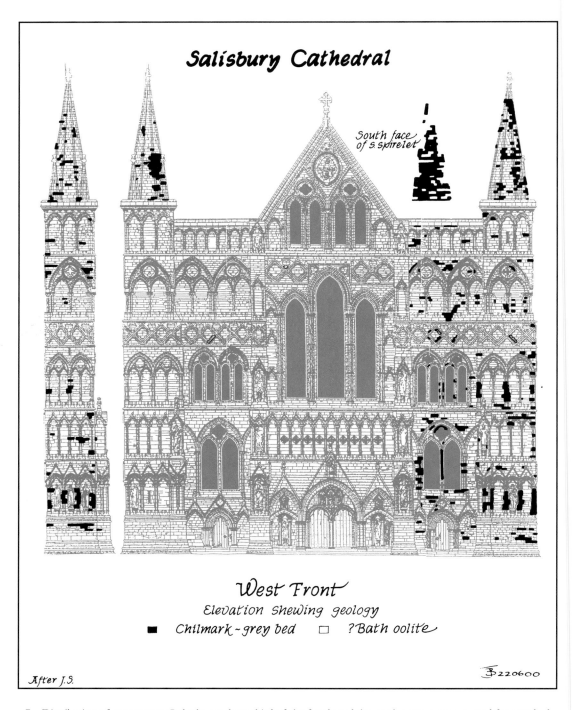

Salisbury Cathedral

South face
of s spirelet

West Front
Elevation shewing geology
■ Chilmark ~ grey bed   □ ?Bath oolite

After J.S.   ₿220600

7 Distribution of stone types. Only the southern third of the façade and the north turret were surveyed for grey-bed Chilmark stone.

to such major changes in the plane of the wall; while the most obvious coursing breaks higher up the façade relate to causes inherent in the structure. For example, there are numerous instances on the two stair turrets where the horizontal lines of the courses will step up or down slightly – usually by no more than one to two inches (2.5–5 cm) – particularly towards the centres of the elevations. These changes, generally small and not forming any coherent pattern, are very probably the result of the consistent interior coursing of the stair-drums being passed through the wall to the exterior.[44]

The building stone is almost entirely from the Chilmark/Tisbury group of sandy limestones and, while the beds are fairly variable, trial plotting of the distribution of these different varieties has revealed no coherent distribution suggestive of changes in the pattern of building (fig. 7).[45] The only significant distribution isolated so far has been the consistent selection of a hard grey bed for exposed mouldings, exemplifying the way in which the different beds available from the quarries were being exploited for different purposes by the medieval masons, and indicating a high level of expertise based on long experience of the stone. Very occasionally a block of a paler stone with a similar texture to Portland stone has been found, and there are a few blocks of a coarse oolite similar to the coarser varieties of Bath stone.[46] It is interesting to note that the whole distribution of the coarse oolite is restricted to a narrow horizontal band centred on the quatrefoils of Zone B.

As elsewhere in the cathedral, colour contrast was achieved by the use of Purbeck marble for shafts, bases and capitals, as well as the cusping of the doorways.[47] The shafts were fixed with iron cramps let into the top bed beneath the capital, and it seems likely that it is the rusting of these fixings which has been responsible for the destabilisation and loss of the majority of the shafts.

The mortar used in the medieval fabric is a hard white lime mix containing stone dusts and occasional flecks of coloured aggregates (red and orange rounded quartz sand grains), charcoal flecks and small unmixed lime or chalk lumps, the wall cores using chalk and flint nodules and broken Chilmark/Tisbury stone rubble. No significant variations in this mix, suggestive of changes during the course of construction, have been identified.

---

[44] Consistent because predicated upon the height of the treads.

[45] For the stone, see pp.145–49 and Tatton-Brown 1998.

[46] Stones of very similar geological types are found in Wyatt's work of the 1790s at the east end of the cathedral, repairing damage to the exterior of the Trinity Chapel caused by his removal of the flanking chantry chapels, and perhaps reusing stone from them; both types of stone are also present in the original fabric (c.1500) of the Poultry Cross in the centre of the city, where the 'Portland' type block would appear to be a variety of Chilmark/Tisbury stone.

[47] Above the Purbeck trumeau and capital of the central west door the abacus and necking of the capital are of a copper alloy – this appears to be an original medieval feature.

Scaffolding.   In the absence of coursing breaks and major changes in the stone types or mortars, the main evidence for the sequence of the construction of the façade is to be derived from the reconstructed form of the original scaffolding and the slight off-sets found in the fabric of the gable, which suggest adjustments to the wall-face at the beginning of a season of building.

The putlog holes, which originally accommodated the horizontal members of the medieval scaffolding, seem to have been left with loose blocking stones in their outer openings at the end of the building campaign, so that they could easily be reused later to erect small cantilevered scaffolds for maintenance. They have clearly been employed in this way on a number of subsequent occasions, and many of the closing stones have been more permanently fixed using a variety of different mortars and cements indicative of when they were last used (see p.88). Because the stone blockings have often been renewed in the process, it is not always certain that the putlog holes which they close are part of the original pattern, so that independent checks on their authenticity have sometimes to be made.[48]

Two classes of such holes can be shown to be almost certainly medieval: those which pass right through walls or buttresses (since these must have been constructed in the course of making the original wall-core); and those which have severe 'scoring' of the stone beneath the lower lip of the hole and (when this can be examined, where a blocking stone is absent) on the horizontal sill of the hole. This scoring appears to be the result of the mechanical erosion of the surface of the stone by the claws of nesting birds landing on the sill of the open holes over several hundred years.[49]

Using the distribution of original putlog holes (fig. 8), it quickly becomes evident that the positions of the horizontal lifts of the medieval scaffolding are remarkably consistent across the whole of the façade, suggesting in turn that the building was erected as a unit in a consistent series of horizontal layers, the whole probably being under scaffold to the same height at the same time. Had the scaffold been stripped from the centre screen and then erected on the stair turrets there would be very little likelihood of the horizontal lifts lining up in the same positions.

The vertical relationships of the putlog hole system are also generally consistent, so that the holes usually line up vertically over the full height of the building, indicating the positions of the standards which supported the lifts (fig.9). It was common practice even into the 20th century to tie in the horizontal putlog beams to alternate sides of the standard — in order to load it evenly — and this is commonly seen here. This

---

[48] A number of the holes are now concealed by 19th-century figure sculptures, while others have been obscured or destroyed by later repairs.

[49] In more than one instance (as for example Zone D, aisle wall, northern spandrel above aisle window) putlog holes were found to be filled with old nesting material. Jackdaws still nest regularly in the open putlogs of the south cloister at Wells. It is of note that this phenomenon is also found in the internal putlog holes above the west windows of the nave, suggesting that birds have had access to the interior of the west front over a considerable time (perhaps through the quatrefoils of the singers' gallery).

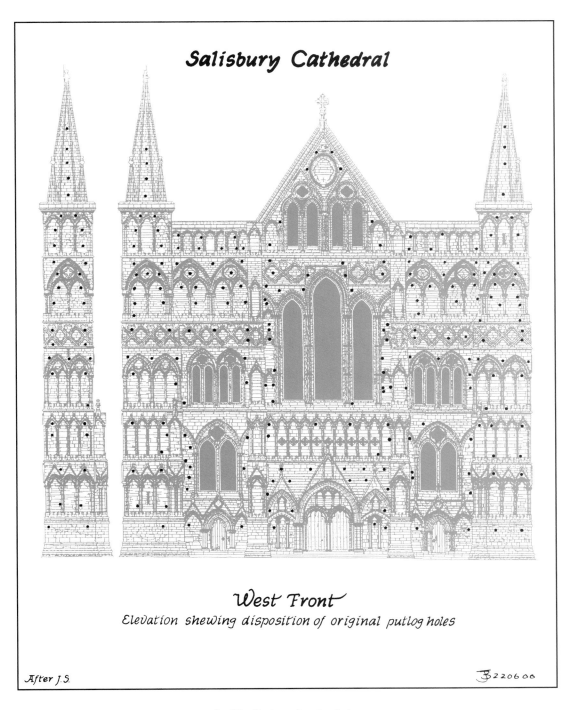

Salisbury Cathedral

West Front

Elevation shewing disposition of original putlog holes

After J.S.

ℬ 220600

8   Distribution of putlog holes.

vertical relationship also suggests that the scaffold was probably not stripped and re-erected during the course of the building works, since it is unlikely that all of the standards would have been replaced in the same positions. The putlog holes in the side walls of the nave have not been explored over their whole height, but those that survive on the clerestory suggest that the lift heights are consistent between the façade and the west nave and, therefore, that the two parts of the structure were erected together.

There are two places, however, where this consistent pattern breaks down, one probably at the start of the construction process, the other right at the end. The projecting part of the central west porch has putlog holes which appear to be arranged on a slightly different grid to those of the west wall above, both vertically and horizontally. This part of the porch projects a considerable distance beyond the face of the wall above and it would appear, as a result, that it was erected from a discrete scaffold either before the rest of the west wall above was constructed or, by leaving the open scar for its junction, at the end of the campaign. The scaffolding for the porch appears to have been lighter in structure, since the surviving evidence suggests that it had fewer standards. The outer standards of the main scaffolding for the rest of the central west wall would have been positioned only a little to the west of the porch wall, and an increased number of standards would have been necessary to support the ninety feet (27.5 m) of gridded timber-work above.

The undesirability of having to build up the inner standards of the main scaffolding from the tops of the newly built porch gables might suggest that the builders left the junction of the porch with the main elevation as an open scar and built the projecting structure after the main scaffolding was struck – a sequence analogous with that at Truro.[50] However, even at plinth level the lower parts of the wall on each side of the entrance to the porch project sufficiently far forward to have necessitated some seating of the upper scaffolding on the masonry of the porch, making it likely that this first light scaffolding for the porch was erected at the beginning of the building campaign and then superseded by the main scaffold for the rest of the façade. Whether this part of the building was actually erected at the end of the campaign or not its general design must have been fixed at the beginning, in order to accommodate its junction with the rest of the wall.

Belonging to the end of the building sequence are the two spirelets which crown the stair turrets. Here, too, the consistent positioning of the scaffolding standards breaks down, with the two standards on each face of the elevations moving inwards from near the corners of the turrets into the spandrels above the three tall niches of Zone A. This change is identical on both turrets and, occurring as it does immediately above the tops of the aisle link-walls, suggests that the main scaffolding was struck at this level to reveal the west front in its more or less completed state, while the

[50] Barham 1976 contains a remarkable series of photographs documenting the construction sequence at Truro.

Salisbury Cathedral

West Front

Elevation shewing disposition of medieval scaffolding

After J.S.

£220600

9   Reconstruction of the original scaffold.

construction of the two crowning spirelets continued from small independent cantilevered scaffolds.[51] Above the parapets of the turrets the spirelets have only single putlog holes on the cardinal elevations, indicating a light and, by modern standards, precarious scaffolding for such a height — though similar light structures were commonly used in such situations well into the present century (fig. 10).

The central west gable above the high vaults was also probably constructed from a lighter cantilevered scaffolding, the interior putlog holes (as is often the case in gables) not relating to consistent standard positions (fig. 11).

Seasonal Breaks. Two possible indicators of seasonal breaks have been found in the masonry above the top of the high vaults. The medieval building season ended in October, when the first frosts began to threaten the set of the lime mortars, and construction did not start again until the following March, when the weather began to warm up. Occasionally it is possible to identify a hiatus between two annual seasons on the basis of

10 Even in relatively recent times light cantilevered scaffolds were in use for work high on buildings, as here, where French tilers are perched precariously on platforms one plank wide. Compagnons de Devoir.

changes in the style or the form of the masonry. In the west gable this may be characterised by two very slight alterations in the thickness or alignment of the internal elevation of the wall: at the base of the passageway between the roof space and the stair, and part way up the internal elevation of the central gable (figs. 11, 13).

In the passageway this is clearest on the north side, where there is an offset on both east and west walls: that on the east wall being at the level of the passage floor; that on the west wall being one course higher. On the east side the wall face moves

---

[51] This would have been desirable for several reasons: to free up the forest of scaffolding for use on the next phase of construction in the cloister and Chapter House; to improve the lighting of the west end as it was taken into use; to allow freer access to the west doors for liturgical purposes; and simply to reveal as much as possible of the fabric. Otherwise the whole scaffold would have remained static for the further two to three seasons needed to complete the spirelets and gable.

Salisbury Cathedral

West Front

Section thro' passages to west

11 Interior cut-away view of the west front, showing wall passages and changes in the form of their roof-corbelling (their profiles marked in the key).

back by up to 2.5 cm above this level, while on the west wall the wall face moves inwards into the passage by a somewhat lesser amount (1–1.5 cm). This seems to have been a correction for a slight bowing of the wall, since sighting along the wall suggests that the lower part of the structure bows outwards. This realignment of the wall-faces probably took place at the beginning of a building season, perhaps correcting movement that had occurred over the previous winter; or (since this was perhaps the first time that the whole width of the façade could have been sighted across since reaching the height of the triforium passageway) correcting an error accumulated during the course of building the elevation below.

For the medieval builders a seasonal, or perhaps slightly longer, hiatus at this height would have been a logical option, since this is the level at which the nave would have been rendered weatherproof – being very slightly above the tops of the nave walls – and allowing the turning of the vaults. At this height the fabric would have provided a paved and waterproof top to the west wall, with access to the stair turrets along the paved base of the passage at the top of the link-wall, as well as to the nave parapets which are positioned at exactly this level. It seems likely, therefore, that once the wall had risen to this height, work would have concentrated on the completion of the nave vaults, with further effort continuing over the following winter towards completing the decoration of the nave so that the whole church could be brought into use.[52]

There is evidence that the next building season on the façade comprised the walls of the passageway to the stair turrets with the wall-walk above it, the turrets to near the base of the corbel table at the top of Zone A and the bases of the west gable windows, but not any large part of their superstructure. On the west wall within the roof space there is a stepped joint running down above the passageway doors in the gable at both sides,[53] suggesting that the masons completed the passageway and the structural work to the top of the link-walls before building the central part of the gable. This height of masonry represents approximately one-tenth of the overall height of the façade, which would be roughly in line with what might be expected of the annual progress of construction in the west nave/façade. It lies immediately below the point at which the scaffolding for the spirelets becomes independent, and may therefore represent the last season when the whole of the façade was scaffolded.

Conclusions. The existing evidence suggests, therefore, that the west front was built as a unit over more than a decade, almost certainly constructed together with (at least) the western bays of the nave, from a sturdy timber scaffolding, the height of the whole structure generally keeping pace north and south of the central elevation. Not only does general building practice and the configuration of the medieval

---

[52] The 13th-century high wood roof of the nave is lost, but by analogy with Wells it is likely that the full length was completed (with a temporary west wall), before the masonry gable was constructed.

[53] The stepped offsets over both passages are of approximately 1 cm in depth, or less.

12 Interior view of the west front. CI.

scaffolding suggest that this was so, but the identifiable seasons of work in the building of Zone A – with halts at the nave wall tops and the top of the link-wall parapets – shows that construction was taking place at a consistent horizontal level across the whole width of the building between the stair turrets. Organisationally this must always have been the preferred method, since the masons would be working only a limited number of templates for moulded blocks at any one time, and the numbers of moulded and carved elements – such as capitals and headstops – could easily be predicted, so that the fixing of stone was not held up waiting for odd pieces to be carved.

Different parts of the separate horizontal layers in which the façade arose may have been worked upon separately, rather than the laying of stone being spread right across the whole width of the façade at any one time. Thus the distribution of 13th-century repairs to moulded stones, executed using a hot mastic (see below and fig. 13), suggests either that for a brief period finances (or the supply of stone) may have run so short that broken stones were repaired rather than recut, or that a stockpiled cache of blocks was damaged in a large-scale accident, such as the collapse of a store. Whatever the cause, in the upper part of Zone B, in the northern stair turret and aisle link-wall, there is a sudden increase in the numbers of repaired stones, suggesting that the north side was being worked on at a time when the corresponding area to the south was not.[54]

The two seasonal breaks in Zone A bracket approximately ten feet (3 m) of walling in height, and the area of Zone B incorporating the mastic repairs is of about the same height, suggesting that this may have been an annual average for the builders. Indeed, it is unlikely that the pure lime mortars of Salisbury, even with the use of gallets in the ashlar facing, would have enabled much more than this to be erected in a single building season.[55]

It is likely that the lines of the annual construction targets during the building programme corresponded wherever possible with string-courses and the springing heights of arches (fig. 13). Occasional instances of extra-wide joints have been noted at the bases of string-courses, where the ashlar may have been capped off with a mortar coating at the end of one season, and the first course of the next season laid directly upon it. No off-sets have been observed at the springing points of the arcades

[54] A similar distribution pattern at Wells has been interpreted as reflecting the financial crisis of c.1242 (Sampson 1998, pp.103–107). At Salisbury, the northern section of Zone B, from the springing of the arches to the top string contains 40 of the total of 85 repairs for the whole façade. On the centre and south of the façade, Zone B also accounts for almost 50 per cent of the repairs in these areas.

[55] John Harvey has estimated that, under normal circumstances, only seven courses of walling could be erected in a season (pers. com.). Debate still continues as to the availability and knowledge of hydraulic limes in the middle ages (which might have allowed greater productivity because of their quicker set); however, at Salisbury it is probable that the almost pure calcium carbonate of the local chalk would have been burnt to provide the lime for the mortars, making the possibility of any natural hydraulic component in the mix very slight. Working back on the basis of 10 ft (3 m) of walling each season might suggest something like a 12-year programme for the construction of the west nave and west front, assuming that there were no major hiatuses in the work, and that the whole width of each 10 ft layer was completed in the season.

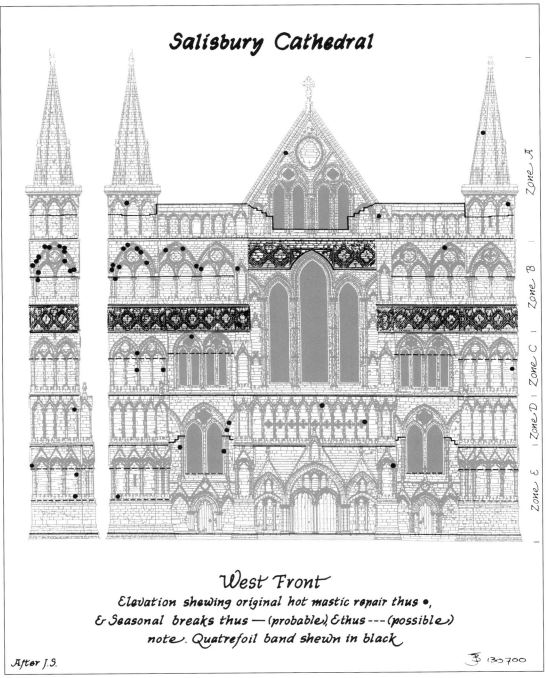

Salisbury Cathedral

(label, right margin top to bottom) Zone A | Zone B | Zone C | Zone D | Zone E

West Front
Elevation shewing original hot mastic repair thus •,
& Seasonal breaks thus — (probable) &thus --- (possible)
note. Quatrefoil band shewn in black

After J.S.

13 Distribution of hot mastic repairs and possible phases of work. It is possible to speculate upon the extent of work in the building seasons on the west front/nave, by applying the findings of the two identifiable 'season breaks' in Zone A and the top of Zone B. The lines of string-courses are the most likely temporary 'ceilings' for work, since the projecting blocks forming the strings need to run further into the wall than the general ashlar blocks and thus cap-off more of the wall-core. This would provide additional protection against frost and water penetration during the winter. The four major string-courses are at or near the positions of the floors of the galleries which cross the façade, and their paving would provide almost complete protection for the wall-core. There are also structural reasons for considering the whole of the quatrefoil band in Zone B to be contemporary, indicating that the centre-screen rose higher than the flanking masonry at this point. The projecting central west porch could have been constructed later, to a toothed joint left to receive it (see p. 22), but is probably contemporary with the rest of the lowest tier.

at Salisbury, but at Wells the upper part of the southern tower base has a one-inch (2.5 cm) off-set at this height on the middle zone of niches, which has been interpreted as the hiatus point for the shifting of the focus of construction to the north side of the façade.[56] On the basis of the evidence presented thus far, it is possible to hypothesise between ten and fourteen seasonal construction targets within the architectural framework of the west front, to which the masons may have worked. For this to be linked with a hypothetical chronology for the nave, however, it is necessary to know whether the whole of the nave was constructed together, or whether the west nave and façade were built as an independent second phase after the eastern part had been finished.

A possible sequence can be proposed for the succession of building seasons during the construction of the west front/nave (fig. 13). Above the foundation and lower plinth, the gabled porches of the west doorways (with their projection beyond the plane of the west wall) could well have taken more than a single season to construct, and might have preceded the lowest tier of niches on the turret phases by a season. Above this, Zone D (corresponding to the upper part of the nave aisle windows, and incorporating the singers' gallery) is an obvious candidate for a season's work. Its upper margin, terminating as it does at or just below the sills of the west windows at the floor of a passageway, must have been one of the most significant constructional objectives in the whole building campaign.

The building of Zone C could have spilled upward into the upper parts of the west windows, so that at this stage the central section of the façade was slightly in advance of the west ends of the triforia and the stair turrets. This is suggested by the disposition of the quatrefoil band of Zone B, which rises above the central west windows, but is probably contemporary with the lower sections of the band to north and south. Contributory evidence for the central west wall being slightly in advance of the flanking masonry at this point is provided by the change in the moulding of the corbelling of the clerestory passage roof, which changes from the form used in the lower parts of the façade to that used in the high-vault level passage as these passages return on to the façade from the nave (fig. 11).

It is probable that the full height of the west windows – sandwiched between the top of Zone D and the base of Zone B – would have taken two seasons to construct, suggesting a subdivision for Zone C at the level of the springing of the canopies and triforia windows (fig. 13). A similar subdivision at springing level appears from the evidence of the mastic repairs to have taken place in the niches of Zone B above, and could also have affected the lower niches of the stair turrets in Zone E. The upper line in the diagram marks the point at which the main scaffolding was struck and the cantilevered scaffolds for the gable and spirelets erected, while the high vaults (perhaps already substantially complete above the nave to the east) were turned against the east

[56] Sampson 1998, pp.31–32.

face of the west wall. Above this point a further two seasons would probably have been required to top-out the façade.

These suggested divisions represent only the nominal planned building objectives, horizontal lines in the architecture towards which the masons' yard would have worked during a given season of construction. There is no implication that work ever stopped for a significant period. Rather, it is likely that each represented a 'ceiling' towards which work across the whole façade progressed, and at which each level of construction temporarily terminated before building continued upwards toward the next 'ceiling'.

THE MASONS YARD

Banker Masons.   The hierarchy of the medieval masons' workshop, as today, must always have been somewhat blurred; so that a banker mason (one who worked at a 'banker' or bench, cutting the moulded blocks) could have functioned on occasion as a fixer mason (one who laid the stones in the wall), and the fixers would certainly have had enough skill to trim and adjust the worked stones which arrived on the scaffolding. Such versatility would probably have been encouraged by the training which must then, as now, have moved the young apprentices from workshop to scaffolding according to the requirements of the project. Furthermore, the banker mason would not necessarily always work at ground level, since there is plentiful evidence of stones being worked on the scaffolding or rising building, near to where they were to be fixed,[57] or after fixing on the building itself. Nonetheless, it is simplest to treat the evidence which can be gleaned from the stonework from the point of view of these two aspects of the mason's craft.

Unlike the Doulting stonework of Wells Cathedral, the Chilmark/Tisbury stone at Salisbury bears evidence of numerous different finishes. One of the characteristics of the western nave of Wells and the upper parts of the nave of Glastonbury Abbey is the re-tooling of the block to a fine finish bearing vertical striations, probably through the use of a drag; but in the Salisbury workshop no single type of finish seems to have been specified. The best preserved surfaces on the exterior of the façade are to be found in the protected stonework of the central west porch, in particular the upper parts of the north and south flanking walls above the blind arcades. Here the general finishes show that the axe and both the claw chisel and the broad flat boaster were in use side-by-side, so that plain vertically or diagonally tooled blocks occur together with the 'cross-tooled' surfaces left by the claw. Both coarse and finer grades of claw chisel were in use and, while some masons left the heavily tooled surfaces untouched,

---

[57]   For a modern instance, see the illustration in Kennerley 1991, p.47, where the Lady Chapel of the Anglican cathedral in Liverpool has banker masons working on the wall tops adjacent to the new vaulting. This would have made it much easier for the builders to make the final adjustments to the voussoirs. It probably accounts for the large deposits of stonedust which are often present in the vault pockets of medieval buildings.

others partly abraded the marks away or lightly boasted the surfaces, since in a number of instances cross- and vertical tooling are mixed on the same stone.

Position marks[58] and masons' marks have scarcely been encountered on the exterior fabric or the interiors of the stairwells and gable, though deep, roughly scored marks appear towards the top of the interior jambs of the main west windows. Even where it has been possible to examine the concealed beds of ashlar stones during cutting-out no certain marks beyond those used in setting-out the block have been identified. Since marks were usually required as a tool of quality control, or to tally an individual mason's output for payment purposes, it would seem likely that by the time the façade was under construction the masons yard was sufficiently cohesive and trusted not to require the consistent marking of block coming from the banker, or that its organization did not include payment by piece-work.

Another part of the expertise of the banker masons would have been the selection of stone for different requirements on the building. As mentioned previously, they were consistently selecting stone from a darker grey bed for moulded blocks that were subject to weathering in exposed positions (fig. 7). It is generally used for attached columns etc. on south and west-facing angles, and it can be proved to belong to the 13th-century campaign by the presence of both original mastic repairs and early 14th-century paint on a block on the north-east corner of Zone E. So successful has this selection been that where stone of the more common Chilmark/Tisbury type has been fixed adjacent to it, or in cases where the block itself is partly of the more common bed,[59] the ordinary stone may have weathered back by up to 1.5 cm leaving the grey block standing proud.[60]

Fixer Masons.   It would seem to have been the fixer masons who were responsible for many of the hot mastic repairs which appear on the west front (fig. 13).[61] In all

---

[58] A possible position mark appears on the sinister jamb of niche no. 165.

[59] In a number of instances a single block is partly composed of the grey bed, partly of the more normal yellowish bed – indicating that the grey stone is from the same quarry as the rest of the stone, and that the beds were contiguous. The use of such mixed blocks suggests that the stone was much sought after and prized for its weathering characteristics. It tends to be less glauconitic with a coarser and more crystalline structure, and is often shellier than the main building-stone bed, though generally less so than the 'trough bed' favoured by Scott (see below).

[60] On the southern spirelet the use of this stone has been so successful that the normal environmental weathering characteristics – that stone facing south and west will be more heavily eroded than stone facing north and east – has been reversed. The grey bed block on the south and west sides has remained less affected by the prevailing weather than the ordinary stone on the other elevations.

[61] First noted at Wells Cathedral by Roger Harris (Harris 1984), see Sampson 1998, pp.103–107. At Wells the technique was introduced in the first decade of the 13th century; the Salisbury workshop appears to have employed hot mastic repairs from the beginning of the work in the 1220s. In the Trinity Chapel, the first phase of the building (1220–25), no such repairs have so far been found; however, in the Choir (underway thereafter) the pier immediately west of the south door has a mastic repair in its southern elevation. This repair is very like those found at Wells, a smooth brown mix with some calcining of the stone, without the sandy or tile aggregates that are often found in the later repairs on the Salisbury west front, and in two noted on the north porch. This later variation suggests a developing tradition, in which the smoother early mixes are largely replaced by those with stone dust, tile and black grain aggregates by the 1240s to 1260s.

the located instances it is clear that the repairs were carried out before the parent stone was fixed and the great majority seem to be in places on the block which would most easily receive accidental damage whilst being moved from the banker to the building; it therefore seems likely that this was a fixer's technique to deal with blocks damaged in transit, the stones being repaired on or near the scaffold immediately prior to fixing.

These repairs were being executed with a great degree of skill, showing that the Salisbury fixer masons were accomplished stoneworkers. The vast majority consist of carefully cut and squared inserts very accurately fixed into the parent block, the joints often so fine that the jointing material is only visible under magnification. Few irregular breaks were fixed, suggesting either that the majority of accidental breaks were the result of crushing rather than clean fractures, or that very great care was being exercised to ensure as perfect a repair bond as possible. At Wells lead or leaded-iron dog-cramps were occasionally used to give additional security to the fixing of the larger repairs and this technique is also seen at Salisbury. However, there is little in the way of iron reinforcements in the 13th-century fabric: even where dog-cramps were used in considerable numbers on the upper parts of the spirelets, there does not seem to have been an iron core, the cramp relying solely on the strength of the poured lead.

The laying of stone often involved the use of gallets, small pieces of stone, usually lias, slate or flint, laid in the bed joint to prevent the mortar being squeezed out by the weight of the block before it could set. Oyster shell, a common material for such gallets elsewhere, has only been noted in the north spirelet and may be associated with later repairs, possibly executed as the result of a lightning strike (see pp.87-88). Flint gallets have generally been neatly knapped to form a thin rectangle.

The construction of the putlog holes would also have been the province of the fixer masons and it seems that where these passed through the wall-core they were carefully built, their sides being shuttered with narrow planking before the core was laid around them. Indeed the whole assembly, consisting of the horizontal scaffolding beam and the vertical shuttering boards at its sides, may have been laid on the wall top and the core built up beside and around it, since this would have allowed a loose enough fit for the beam to be withdrawn smoothly at the end of the work.

DATE

The close analysis of the west front has been possible only because of the erection of scaffolding. Without such access to the upper parts of the nave, especially, the construction sequence and chronology in relation to the rest of the cathedral can only be couched in the form of a working hypothesis, to be tested as the opportunity may arise.

The eastern arm of the church can be dated from documentary sources, as outlined in the Introduction. The foundation stones were laid on 28 April 1220 and the work was sufficiently advanced that the three altars of the eastern arm could be consecrated on 28 September 1225. The choir was complete enough by 1236 to warrant a grant of wood from the royal forests for the making of new choir stalls. The two years before this had seen other gifts of wood, totalling two hundred trees, which relate almost certainly to the roofing of the east end. Matthew Paris credited Bishop Robert Bingham (1229–1247) with the completion of the choir stalls and the lead roofing of the 'front of the church', or eastern arm. The consecration of the church took place in 1258 and the whole church was described as complete in 1266. Relatively small royal gifts of timber suggest that roofing was underway in 1251–53 and again in 1261.

Within this documented chronology the analysis of the fabric is open to a number of possible interpretations. The clearest evidence for a break in the physical fabric of the church occurs in the plinth of the second bay of the nave eastwards from the crossing (fig. 1), and there appear to be additional indications of this break in the form of the string-course above the arcade in the eastern bay of the nave and in the form of the aisle label stops. A building-phase break is also found in this position at Wells and elsewhere, and it must represent the extent of masonry shoring needed to support the crossing before the nave was built. It is likely, however, that the erection of Salisbury Cathedral was a more complex operation than a simple division into two main phases separated at the east nave, especially given the complexity of the architecture of the eastern end with its double transept.[62] The interpretation of the documented end-date for the building campaign on the church is also ambiguous. Was just the church or the whole complex complete by the dedication of 1258, or were one or both not finished until 1266? Further close analysis of the fabric, preferably from scaffolding, will be necessary before a definitive model for the more detailed phasing of the church can be proposed with any confidence.

Particularly useful in establishing firm dates will be the results of dendrochronology on the cathedral's doors and on the surviving 13th-century roof of the adjoining north aisle of the nave, upon which work is now underway.[63] The two great west doors and those giving into the aisles to north and south are of 13th-century manufacture and can be placed, for now, within a relative chronology in relation to the others within the cathedral.[64] They are all distinguished on the back by lattice bracing, with roves at all intersections. This method of construction is shared only by the pair that opens into the church from the nave north porch and one other, directly adjoining inside, into the staircase that leads up to the chamber over it. A similar

[62] Wells certainly has an additional break in construction at the eastern side of the crossing, defined on the basis of a change in the source of the building stone.

[63] As this volume was going to press, initial results gave felling dates of winter 1251-52 for timbers in the adjoining triforium roof west of the north porch (Dan Miles, September 2000), which fits in well with the previous analysis.

[64] The authors would like to thank Tim Tatton-Brown for the analysis that follows.

construction, but without the roves, was then employed for the door that leads from this chamber into the nave triforium space. This door is presumably later, therefore, and the same form would be used for other doors in the cathedral, including those into the cloister from the south transept and those in the vestry. The great west doors are therefore of the earliest form in the church.

THE CLOISTER

Had the original intention to construct a somewhat smaller cloister been carried through, the west front would have been unaffected by it.[65] A blocked doorway in the penultimate bay of the south aisle of the nave was intended to give access to the north-west angle of this smaller cloister. In 1263,[66] however, a grant of additional land to the south was made by the bishop, enabling the ground plan to be enlarged. As a result, the north end of the west range was made to butt up against the east elevation of the façade (fig. 14). No provision had been made for this in the architecture of the façade,

14 The south-west turret from the east, showing the junction with the west cloister.

suggesting that the fabric of the west front was already complete by this time.[67]

This change of plan led to the blocking of two east-facing windows, at plinth level and on the lowest circuit of the southern stair, and the creation of an access door from the east side of the southern stair turret on to the roof of the consistory court. As a result, a new window was broken through on the south side of the stair, in the Zone E niches, with a neat moulded head and plastered jambs. The new doorway providing access to the cloister roof, only 60 cm wide and 163 cm high, has been cut through the string course between Zones D and E, its head extending into the lower

[65] Blum 1991, pp.25–36; RCHME 1993b, pl. 59, pp.8–10, 40–43, 80; Tatton-Brown 1994.

[66] Blum 1991, pp.26–27.

[67] At Wells, however, where the cloister must always have been planned to run in between the southern buttresses of the south-west tower, there was also no provision made for accommodating it, and the pitched roof line has been brutally cut into the architecture on the east face of the south-western buttress: see Sampson 1998, pp.71–73.

courses of niche no. 160, and its sill cutting the line of the flashing groove for the lead of the cloister roof to the north, but coinciding with it to the south.[68]

SCHEMES OF DECORATION

The screen front is adapted at Salisbury, as elsewhere in the early 13th century, for the display of sculpture (fig. 3).[69] Across the façade and around the flanking stair turrets, the original plan was for 170 large-scale figures in shallow niches, as the original trefoil-section stubs for consoles survive. The central porch had three niches for images directly over the west door and one niche each on its three external gables. The survey showed that no statues of this date remain, but that some had probably been made. All of the surviving large-scale medieval figures were added at later dates and, as such, they are considered in the next section. There is, however, much small-scale decorative sculpture that is contemporary with the building, comprising stiff-leaf foliage for capitals and other features, and corbel heads and headstops.

The form and iconography of the 13th-century sculpture were obviously planned, in outline at least, before the front's construction. The triple porches may derive ultimately from those of northern France, but the concentration there of sculpture upon the doorways is not found at Salisbury. Important figures were intended for the central porch, it will be argued, but not in quantity. The main display was to range across the façade above, as at Wells. Narrative subjects, present on the façade of the neighbouring cathedral, were abandoned in favour of single figures, contrasting with the increasingly vigorous deployment of narrative in northern French portal sculpture in the first half of the 13th century, at Amiens (west front) or Reims (north transept).[70] It was recognised, perhaps, that narratives were hard to read at a height; an extended Old Testament cycle would be taken up shortly in the more visible spandrels of the Chapter House wall arcade.[71] Contrasting again with Wells, the buttresses at Salisbury are interrupted visually by image niches, angled across the corners, perhaps so that the tiers of figures could break up the verticals.

As elsewhere, these tiers formed part of a hierarchy focusing on a central vertical axis, which is apparent in the architectural design of the central bay, with its taller porch gables and giant lancets. This is also evident in the surviving decorative carving. While foliage is distributed across the whole façade, most of the decorative figure sculpture is concentrated in this bay. At porch level, the 19th-century gargoyles may replace medieval originals. Flanking the great lancets are three niches on each side, with canopies supported on two corbel heads each (some male, some female). On the

[68] At Wells a similar doorway was cut into the southern stair in the 15th century, when the 13th-century cloister was raised to incorporate a second storey.
[69] For the numbering of the niches, see p.190.
[70] Sauerländer 1972, pp.464–65 (Amiens, St Firmin portal), 481 (Reims, saints' portal), pl. 245.
[71] Blum 1969; Blum 1996b.

15 Bust-length figure, north angle, south central buttress, west front. CI.

buttresses to left and right appear the only contemporary figure sculptures to comprise anything more: three weathered bust-length figures, holding foliage stems or attacked by beasts (fig. 15).[72] On each buttress in Zone C, there are three little tonsured heads in high relief within quatrefoils (to north, south and west), in the gables above the niches. The band of quatrefoils in Zone B has foliage filling only on the central buttresses and the only niches on the front to be recessed, with a shallow curving back, also occur on these.

At the top of the hierarchy, the 13th-century vesica was to hold a figure of Christ. A Majesty may have been meant, as probably executed later. It is unlikely that a Last Judgement was intended, for there is nowhere to show the Dead Rising, so prominent at Wells. Further clues to the scheme may be provided by number symbolism. Lower down in the central bay, the eleven niches that run across the front above the porch gables could have been for a set of prophets or Apostles, either curtailed or spreading on to the buttresses. Alternatively, perhaps they were for angels. At both Salisbury and Wells there was a gallery within the thickness of the wall at this level, pierced with apertures for the choir to sing through – a choir represented at Wells by bust-length angels.[73] At Salisbury, however, traces of medieval paint have been found around these openings, suggesting that the statues were never installed (see p.112). This is confirmed by the lack of visible fixings in pre-restoration photographs (fig. 16).

The survey found no evidence that any large-scale sculpture had been executed for the screen, but that preparations had been made for it on the central buttresses. One very fragile 13th-century base survived to support figure sculpture. This was the console beneath the medieval figure of St Paul, on the south buttress (no. 95), which rose from stems of stiff-leaf type. It was repaired, presumably, in Scott's restoration, when it was copied for new figures in this tier. The console under the equivalent medieval figure on the north buttress was completely restored, but Fenton's pre-

[72] Shown by Carter, BL, Add. MS 29939, f.39.
[73] Blum 1986; Sampson 1998, pp.169–73.

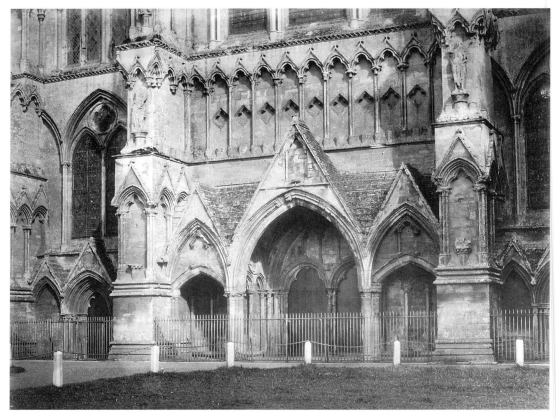

16   The central west porch, photographed by Roger Fenton, Albumen print, *c*.1858. Sotheby's.

restoration photographs reveal that it was similar originally (fig. 64). Located in prominent and complementary positions, these bases confirm that work on peopling the screen was taken a step further, but abandoned. The fact that they support later figures demonstrates that no figure sculpture was completed at this level in the 13th century. While the façade may have been incomplete in this respect, it is argued elsewhere that it may have been limewashed and lined with red paint, to imitate masonry (see p.124), as on the cathedral's interior and on the exterior at Wells.[74]

In striking contrast, a good case can be made for 13th-century sculpture on and inside the central porch (figs. 16). Among the most exciting findings of the recent survey has been the extensive evidence for painted decoration in this region. Within, up to sixteen medieval layers of paint were identified, representing perhaps six repaintings. These are discussed elsewhere (see pp.112-13). The sheer number of repaintings, alone, would suggest that the earliest layers go back to the completion of the porch in the 13th century, allowing a repainting every fifty years or so until the

[74]   Sampson 1998, p.125.

Reformation. On the exterior, substantial traces of paint were found also on the entrance arch and surrounding the niches in the two side gables. These were painted in a copper-green or copper blue, consistent with the earliest paint layers within the porch. At Wells, too, the area around the great west doorway seems to have been decorated with the most elaborate painting and pigments.[75]

If the stonework of the porch was painted by this time, it is likely that the niches were also filled with sculpture. Painting was an inherent part of the finishing of sculpture in this period, as can still be seen on the south portal of Lausanne Cathedral in Switzerland, for example.[76] At Salisbury, associated decorative carving on the tympanum and its surrounding arch, including heads, was completed and painted. There is also other evidence for sculpture in the form of fixings and supports. The six niches on the inside and outside of the porch had leafy supports built into the wall, as recorded in pre-restoration photographs (fig. 16). That beneath the central niche in the tympanum had been drastically cut away. On the two flanking exterior gables, pre-restoration photographs show the remains of off-centre fixings, different in type from those used elsewhere on the front. These may have supported the shoulders of figures, as at Wells.

The juxtaposition of the central niche in the gable of the central porch with the consecration crosses in the central gables of the lateral porches (see below) might suggest the presence here of the Virgin, as the dedication saint of the cathedral, or Christ. French High Gothic cathedrals of a similar dedication often show Mary in this position.[77] At Salisbury, the precise dedication was to the Virgin's Assumption, as at Notre-Dame in Paris, but this is a rare subject in the surviving sample of Marian images from 13th-century England. It may sometimes have been implicit in the Coronation of the Virgin.[78] While there is a Coronation over the central doorway at Wells (fig. 17),[79] at Salisbury there is no suitable place on either the interior or exterior of the porch. One possible location might be in the pair of niches in the gable of the north porch, another the tympanum over the entrance to the Chapter House, as Burges suggested.[80] On the west porch, the images on the two flanking exterior gables might have been censing angels, as the wall face has been cut away in a fashion consistent with kneeling figures (Catalogue, nos. 180a, 182a).

The only objection to the presence of the Virgin on the central gable is that she may have appeared within the porch itself. Redfern made the Virgin and Child group that now appears directly over the door in the central niche, flanked by angels, but the

---

[75] Sampson 1998, pp.131–32.

[76] Williamson 1995, pp.5–6, 58–59.

[77] Laon west front (Virgin and Child), Chartres south transept (Virgin and Child): Sauerländer 1972, pp.425, 435, pls. 68, 107.

[78] Morgan 1991, p.87, n. 56.

[79] Sampson 1998, p.252, no. 286.

[80] Burges 1859, p.110. It also appears on the surviving 13th-century common seal of the Salisbury vicars choral: RCHME 1999, p.71, fig. 53.

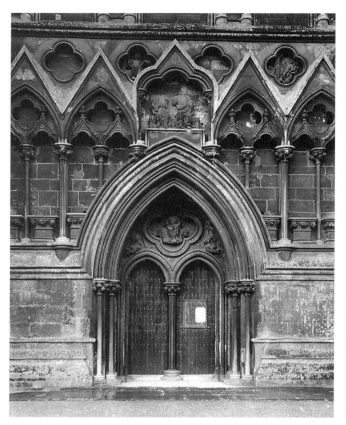

17   West doorway, Wells Cathedral. CI.   **18**   West doorway, Llandaff Cathedral. CI

canopy work and tympanum are substantially original (fig. 16). That the Virgin was the original subject is suggested by a will of 1468, which mentions an 'image of the blessed Virgin Mary adjoining and over the western doors of the cathedral church of Salisbury'.[81] She might then be the dedication saint, enthroned with the Christ Child, as on the cathedral's seal (fig. 19).[82] The dedicatee could be variously placed. The bishop in the tympanum over the great west door at Llandaff Cathedral, begun under Bishop Henry of Abergavenny (1193–1218), may be St Dyfrig, co-dedicatee, whose relics lay in the church (fig. 18).[83] At Westminster Abbey, it has been argued that St Peter was on the trumeau of the central doorway in the north transept.[84] The Virgin

[81]   Malden 1904, p.29; Salisbury, Cathedral Archives, Machon's Register, p.237: 'In primis lego animam meam deo omnipotenti beate marie et omnibus sanctis eius, et corpus meum honesto modo sepeliri cum lumine pulsationibus et aliis consuetudinibus coram ymagine beate marie virginis iuxta et super ostia ecclesie cathedralis Sar' in occidente.' We are indebted to Sarah Brown for drawing our attention to this and to Suzanne Eward in the cathedral library for arranging the transcription of the Latin.

[82]   Birch, I, nos. 2213 (1239), 2214. The surviving silver seal matrix of the church's seal 'ad peticiones et ad ca(usa)s' also shows the enthroned Virgin and Child: RCHME 1999, p.71, fig. 53; Birch, I, no. 2216.

[83]   *BoW, Powys*, pp.239, 246.

[84]   H. Westlake, *Westminster Abbey*, London, 1923, I, p.20; Binski 1995, p.71.

is also placed on the tympanum at the great west door of at least one English cathedral with another dedication, at Wells (fig. 17), and at the entrance to Chapter Houses (Westminster, York), acknowledging her central role and significance in the history of salvation, and perhaps her popularity in England.

Her prominence is matched in some regions on the continent, such as northern Italy in the Romanesque period,[85] but departs from the norms on the west fronts of French High Gothic cathedrals. Here the tympanum of the central portal usually includes a culminating image of Christ enthroned, whether in Judgement, in Majesty or crowning the Virgin, in the long tradition of Christ as the Door.[86] The Virgin and local or dedication saints were often represented in flanking portals.[87] At Wells and Salisbury, the screen front perhaps invited a more extended composition, with the en-

19 Seal of Salisbury Cathedral. CI.

throned Christ at the top, in the great gable. At Salisbury, he may also have appeared originally in the vesica over the doorway from the north porch into the church (fig. 20). There are remains of fixings in the quatrefoils, perhaps originally for metal images of the tetramorph, to accompany a Christ in Majesty. If the Virgin were over the great west door, there might then have been a deliberate distribution of iconographical emphasis between the building's two most elaborate entrances. This would be consistent with other evidence for careful planning in the cathedral's design.

On the western tympanum the accompanying features suggest that the central figure was shown as the Queen of Heaven. The lost figures were under canopies, indicating sacred space and perhaps the Heavenly City (see cat. nos. 183–85). Already common in other settings (all over the front), such canopies are not usual on the tympana of other 13th-century English portals, which usually centre quatrefoils or geometrical shapes, not only for the Majesty or Last Judgement, but also at Wells for the Virgin and Child. The tympana of the nave portals at Chichester also centre

85 Kendall 1998, pp.114–15, 118–19, 179, 182.
86 Kendall 1998, ch. 4.
87 As at Notre-Dame in Paris or Amiens: Sauerländer 1972, pp.454–56, 463–64, pls. 152, 161.

20 Doorway into the church, north porch. CI.

21   Detail of tympanum, west doorway. CI.

geometrical shapes. The arrangement at Salisbury perhaps reflects contemporary winged tabernacles in wood or precious metal, as represented in 13th-century Scandinavian wood sculptures.[88] Many stone Virgins under aedicules survive on French tympana from the mid-12th century, but these are usually set within a wider iconographical context, on jambs, lintels and archivolts.[89] Exchanges with metalwork in this period are well known and metal was actually used in the decoration of the porches.[90] Above and below the capital of the trumeau are bands of copper alloy, and a lead-set metal fixing seems to have been removed from the gable of the central niche on the tympanum.

Above the three empty niches are four relief heads within geometric shapes (fig. 21). They retain much medieval paint, including expensive azurite and ultramarine, as well as gold leaf, marking the importance of the location (see p.127 and pls. II, IV). The two larger heads have the distinctive tonsure and bald pate of SS Peter and Paul respectively, who may stand for all the Apostles and saints who rule with Christ in

[88]   Andersson 1949, pp.151–60; Williamson 1995, pp.114, 117, fig. 179.

[89]   Sauerländer 1972, pls. 6 (Chartres, west front), 35 (Bourges, north portal), 40 (Notre-Dame in Paris, west front), 69 (Laon, west front). K. Horste, '"A Child is Born": The Iconography of the Portail Ste.-Anne in Paris', *Art Bulletin*, lxix, 1987, pp.198–204.

[90]   Williamson 1995, pp.25, 47, 73, 76, 113.

Heaven. Heads within frames are found again on the external central buttresses and are a feature of the front's decoration. Such heads were relatively common by the mid-13th century and are prominent inside the cathedral as corbels for the vault shafts.[91]

The framing arch of the tympanum carried a deeply undercut band of foliage, which a photograph shows to have been almost completely destroyed before Scott's restoration (fig. 16). That it was filled originally with figures is suggested by the recent discovery of small fragments from the edges, of a figure and birds (fig. 22). A single band of deeply undercut female figures, perhaps Virtues, under canopies frames the Virgin and Child in the tympanum of the earlier west door at Wells, c.1220.[92] Within similar foliage are the figures surrounding the outer and inner entrances to the Chapter House at Westminster Abbey, c.1246–53 (fig. 23).[93] On the outer entrance, flanked by a pair of angels, the Virgin is framed by a band of Old Testament figures, including ancestors of Christ, within foliage (fig. 24). A Tree of Jesse forms the outer order on the north transept portal at Lichfield, c.1230–41, and the foliage frame at Salisbury might be consistent with a similar subject.[94] Virtues would shortly be taken up at Salisbury (with Vices) around the arch of the inner Chapter House entrance.[95]

The Salisbury tympanum was concentrated on the proposed image of Mary, just like that at Westminster on the outer Chapter House doorway.[96] Of the Westminster arrangement, it has been observed that the intention was not to create a programme, but rather to focus upon the single image. Appropriately, Abbot Ware's 13th-century Customary prescribes that the monks should pay respect to the Virgin when passing.[97] The relative simplicity of the sculpture at these doors might reflect then not the unimportance of their images, but the opposite. This is confirmed, rather, by the evidence of the polychromy, which reveals the importance of the west door, despite the more ornate treatment of west doors on the continent, with which they are often compared.

Another important feature of the 13th-century decoration remains visible, although decayed (figs. 3, 16, 25). The central gables of the two lateral porches were inlaid with metal consecration crosses, within circular Chilmark/Tisbury stone discs, from a group of ten marking the consecration of the cathedral; a variety of dates in the 13th century have been proposed.[98] As mentioned, metalwork may originally have enhanced the cathedral's portals in other ways. The importance of the two consecration crosses is

---

[91] Whittingham 1979.
[92] Sampson 1998, pp.83–86.
[93] Binski 1995, pp.15–16, 185–86.
[94] Thurlby 1986, p.122, fig. 3.
[95] Green 1968.
[96] Binski 1995, p.186.
[97] *Customary of the Benedictine Monasteries of Saint Augustine, Canterbury and Saint Peter, Westminster*, ed. Sir E. Maude Thompson, Henry Bradshaw Society, II, London, 1904, p.166.
[98] Meredith 1881; Middleton 1885, pp.458–60, pls. xxxv–xxxvi; Dewick 1908, pp.15–17; Blair 1975; Rogers 1987, p.11, n. 31; Tatton-Brown 1996; T. Tatton-Brown, 'The Salisbury Cathedral Consecration Crosses', *Transactions of the Monumental Brass Society*, xvi, 2, 1998, pp.113–16; RCHME 1999, pp.186, 188.

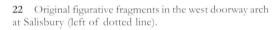

22 Original figurative fragments in the west doorway arch at Salisbury (left of dotted line).

23 Inhabited foliage band from the archivolt, inner Chapter House doorway, Westminster Abbey. © Crown Copyright. NMR.

24   Entrance to the Chapter House from the cloister, Westminster Abbey. CI.

emphasised by making them higher than the others, in the central gables of the lateral porches. One might have expected to find another cross within the central porch, as a set of twelve was required. Directly over the dedication saint on the tympanum, the metal fitting removed from the central gable might conceivably have been for such a metal cross, on a smaller scale. Alternatively, one might have been painted on the walls adjacent to the west doorway. The prominence of these potent signs, originally no doubt polished or gilded and shining, their carved frames richly painted, marked this very visibly as a consecrated building, with all that that involved. The wider significance of these and the proposed images of the central porch will be discussed below.

25   Drawing of one of the external consecration crosses, Salisbury Cathedral. John Blair.

Style and Date.   Of the minor decorative figure sculpture integral to the west front, a little can be said about style. Much is now extremely weathered, but it appears that several carvers were involved – hardly surprising across such a surface area. The heads on the tympanum were richly painted but carved relatively crudely. The headstops were finer. A group on the central bay and lower south turret is in the style of the larger corbels for the nave vault shafts, including those adjoining the interior of the front itself. In both places they are distinguished by broad square chins and wide foreheads, with slightly protruding lips and eyeballs undercut at the corners (fig. 26).[99] Women's hats, curls and wispy drapery under the chin are also comparable. Some heads have little smiles or show their teeth, typical of the interest in facial expression around mid-century, as illustrated by a famous headstop from nearby Clarendon Palace.[100] At Salisbury, the similarities between the exterior heads and the nave corbels confirm the evidence of the fabric that nave and front were completed at around the same time. There is no sign of the brilliant carvers responsible for the heads on the pulpitum or the Chapter House wall arcade.

The three slightly larger figurative subjects, the bust-length figures on the great buttresses to either side of the porch, represent human beings wrestling with nature, and are probably not by the same hand as the group identified above (fig. 15). The

[99]   Whittingham 1979, figs. 9, 11–15.
[100]   *Age of Chivalry*, cat. no. 295.

26 Headstops, exterior of the west front (above) and corbels to nave vault shafts (below). CI and © Crown Copyright. NMR.

drapery is in narrow vertical pleats, as found on many figures on the earlier west front at Wells;[101] or the Virgin of the Annunciation in the Chapter House at Westminster Abbey, probably datable to 1253.[102] The central overlapping fold is common to many images in English manuscript illumination from the beginning of the century.[103] It is

---

[101] Courtauld Institute Illustration Archives, Archive 1, *Cathedrals & Monastic Buildings in the British Isles, Part 2, Wells, North-west Tower*, 1977, Colchester nos. 290 (1/2/154), 294 (1/2/158); *Part 4, Wells, West Front, Central Section*, 1977, Colchester nos. 156 (1/4/105), 214 (1/4/121), 286 (1/4/163).

[102] Williamson 1988, pp.123–24.

[103] eg, Morgan 1982, cat. no. 28, ill. 100 (*c*.1210); Morgan 1988, cat. no. 126, ill. 138 (Lambeth Apocalypse, *c*.1260–67).

found in images of around mid-century, including the Missal of Henry of Chichester, probably painted in Salisbury by the so-called Sarum Master (fig. 27).[104] There is no sign on the west front of the new broad-fold style, which appears at Salisbury in the Chapter House (entrance doorway and spandrel reliefs);[105] and on the tomb of Bishop Bridport, who died in 1262. This tends to suggest an earlier date.

One may imagine that any larger 13th-century figures on the western porch would also have been in the earlier pleated, or trough-fold style, like the sculpted Virgin and Child on a boss in the Lady Chapel at Worcester (1224–32);[106] those in seals of the 1240s and '50s, such as that of Merton Priory, 1241;[107] or the illuminations of the Sarum Master. The latter are generally thought to be in the monumental idiom of wall painting and have been compared with the vault of the Guardian Angels Chapel at Winchester and, more tentatively, with those now recorded only in antiquarian drawings of the vault of the eastern arm at Salisbury, perhaps of the early 1240s.[108] For a fuller context in three-dimensional images of this period in similar styles one must look to the wood sculpture of Norway.[109]

27   Virgin and Child, with Henry of Chichester, Missal of Henry of Chichester, Salisbury, *c.*1250. John Rylands Library, Manchester.

[104]   *Ibid.*, cat. no. 100; *Age of Chivalry*, cat. no. 108.
[105]   Whittingham 1974.
[106]   Williamson 1995, fig. 175. On this and other contemporary images of the Virgin and Child in the west of England, see Thurlby 1986, pp.126–28.
[107]   *Age of Chivalry*, cat. no. 283.
[108]   Morgan 1988, pp.56, 57; RCHME 1999, pp.161–66.
[109]   Andersson 1949, pp.127–30 (Hove), 138–40 (Enebakk), figs. 49, 56; also *Age of Chivalry*, cat. no. 250.

THE LATER MIDDLE AGES

Additions of sculpture on two and probably more occasions represent the most important changes to the west front in the later middle ages. When the new figures were painted, they would have altered its appearance significantly and there is good evidence that previous paintwork within the west porch was also renewed up to the Reformation (see pp.128-29). At some uncertain date, the parapet was crenellated, which may be related to these additions. This feature was then removed in the 19th century.

THE PARAPETS

The original form of the high parapets which top the link-walls has been partly obscured by later alterations and additions (figs. 3, 28). On the nave and aisles, as elsewhere on the building, they consist of blind arcades rising above the wall-top walkways, and at high level this arcading returns to form a decorative frieze on the eastern faces of the link-walls of the façade. However, in order to accommodate the enclosed intramural passage at the level of the roof spaces, the link-walls here rise higher and are crowned by their own parapets (fig. 11). On the eastern elevation the top course of this is of 19th-century date (in at least two phases), and the next course down, consisting of very large blocks of Chilmark/Tisbury stone (up to 110 by 53 cm), appears to be a later medieval replacement.

There is no evidence on either stair turret that the original form of the western face of the parapet was as high. Indeed there is good evidence that the top moulding of the parapet on the western side was at its present height, since the block bearing this moulding that returns on to the south-central buttress appears to be a 13th-century survival. However, prints and drawings show crenellations rising to the corbel table of the turrets (fig. 48). It would seem, then, that an original low parapet was remodelled in the later middle ages, its extra height merely butting against the earlier fabric, and that it was returned to something resembling its original form in the period prior to 1853, when the front was photographed without crenellations by Sedgfield (fig. 60). There is a possible trace of the 13th-century eastern parapet at its junction with the north side of the nave roof, which suggests that the later medieval stonework is approximately 15 cm higher than the original – a height difference of the same order as the present difference between the eastern and western parapet walls.

SCULPTURE AND DECORATION

The survey revealed, on formal and stylistic grounds, that the larger figures surviving or recorded on the west front were added after its completion (pl. I). Eight remain (nos. 19a, 26a, 86, 95, 129, 145, 166, 169), now concentrated in the lowest zone of

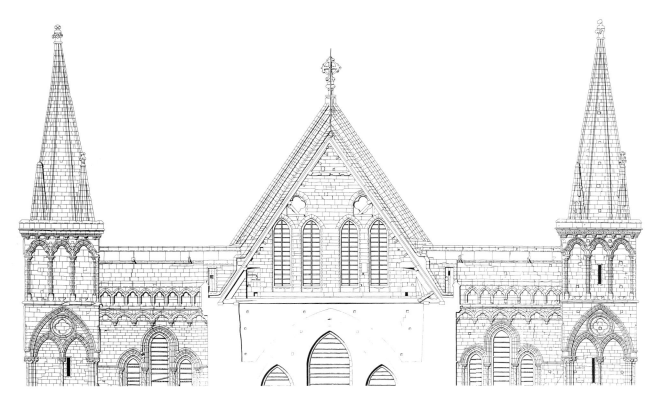

28   The parapets from the east.

image niches and on the west face of the two central buttresses, as well as a bird in the great gable (no. 23).[110] Within living memory, another figure stood in Zone D on the lesser north buttress, but this was lost in 1963 (no. 124). A second, in the equivalent position on the lesser south buttress, had been lost a century earlier (no. 150a). The present discussion is in three parts, the first focusing upon the evidence for the original extent of this sculpture, the second on its iconography and the third upon stylistic issues and dating. The catalogue illustrates the figures and deals with problems of identification.

1. *Extent and Coherence of the Added Sculpture*

Material. This section considers the sculptures as a group, from the point of view of their material, fixings, bases and subject matter. They are all of a face-bedded sandy limestone, probably the local variety known as Chilmark/Tisbury, and are sometimes of a slightly green or yellowish hue.[111] There are differences in the blocks used, some

---

[110]   For the numbering system, see p.190. Nos. 19a and 26a have been removed for safe-keeping and are now displayed in the nave roof space.

[111]   On the stone, see pp.147–48 and Tatton-Brown 1998.

29   Fixing system for the larger medieval figures.

having prominent calcite veins (nos. 86, 169), others chert inclusions (nos. 19a, 129) and yet others shells (no. 26a). These particularities are found again in the 19th-century work, but not in the 13th-century masonry or carving. The fact that they are spread across the whole front may suggest that they are from a similar bed, but that it had a variety of inclusions; alternatively the blocks could have been quarried at different times.

Fixings. There is material evidence of other kinds for the original extent of the scheme. Where it is possible to inspect the backs of the surviving large-scale figures, it appears that each was attached to the wall in a similar way: with two upturned iron hooks, one in the back of the figure at chest or shoulder height and the other at a similar height in the wall, both set in lead, with an iron ring then laid over the top to join them (fig. 29). The stone was recessed around the hook in the wall, to make this easier.[112] All of the visible surviving fixings are of this kind (nos. 19a, 26a, 86, 95, 129, 145). Two other figures (nos. 166, 169) are so close to the wall that they have probably been reattached. The 19th-century fixings follow a similar system, but are of copper.

This system was not used universally in England, but the recessed hooks were used elsewhere on the Salisbury front to support large-scale figures that are now lost.[113] The recent survey and pre-restoration photographs have provided evidence for a limited number of these fixings (pl. I). One was in niche no. 195. There were also two within the west porch, in the central niche of each triplet of blind arcading on either side of the door (nos. 201, 206). The figures probably stood on tall bases, as separate iron dog-cramps were let into the wall above the wall bench, presumably to hold these in place. There may have been a third figure in the southernmost niche, where there are remains of another dog-cramp, but the stonework above is disturbed (no. 207). Flanking the porch, on the west faces of the central buttresses in the lowest zone, there once stood two more figures (nos. 178a, 187a), whose fixings are visible in Fenton's photograph (fig. 16).

[112]   The exception is the niche containing a medieval figure of St Peter (no. 86), which has no recessing around the lead-set hook.

[113]   A very similar system was used in the later Lady Chapel, Gloucester Cathedral.

In summary, all of the figures surviving or recorded on the central buttresses, on the lesser north buttress and against the east walls of the central porch, probably had a similar fixing system. They could well, therefore, be contemporary.

Consoles. Bases or consoles offer another clue to the former presence of medieval sculptures, for the trefoil stumps left by the 13th-century builders required these before they could conveniently support figures. They were provided for all the standing figures, although the two seated figures were more clumsily supported, without them (nos. 19a, 26a). Early photographs confirm the presence of other consoles in the two niches at the foot of the central buttresses (nos. 178 and 187; fig. 16); one was repaired and survives in the northern niche. Carved with ballflower, it served as a model for many 19th-century consoles in this zone. That to the south was removed. Other bases were presumably taken down earlier, once the statues that they supported had been lost.

The known consoles are less consistent in form than the stone and the fixings. In the lowest zone (E, fig. 30), they are decorated with carving: ballflower (nos. 178, 187); foliage (no. 169) and a mask flanked by fish (no. 166). No two have the same or similar mouldings to their tops, and they vary slightly in height. In Zone D, however, the three surviving consoles are all similar, plain and clumsy, rising from trefoil neckings to a roughly semicircular (no. 124), a half-oval (no. 129) and a rounded-off rectangular top (no. 145). They vary in height from 8 in to a foot (20.5 cm to 30.5 cm). The bases in the lowest zone are more elaborate, perhaps because they were more visible from the ground. The consoles in the zone above are very similar and probably contemporary, confirming the evidence of the fixings. As discussed above, the consoles in Zone C, supporting SS Peter and Paul, were both originally of the 13th century.

Two further consoles provide evidence for later additions to the front. Early photographs show that the base beneath the lost figure on the lesser south buttress (no. 150) was substantially taller than the rest in its tier (fig. 64). There is also a rather different console inserted into the wall of the blind arch to the right of the south-west door (no. 208). Set high up, within the arch head, it has a polygonal top that is supported by a feathered angel and must have been for a small statue or group. It is of late medieval date. The sculpture was of distinctive form: to our right, the springing of the arch has been cut away slightly and an iron fixing supplied, suggesting a composition that spread across the arch head in this direction. There is no sign of a fixing in the wall above the console itself. As in other locations where sculpture is or was present, traces of colour have been found (see p.124).

Polychromy. By comparison with the west front at Wells, the traces of exterior polychromy at Salisbury are few, with the exception of the central porch (see pl. I).[114]

---

[114] Sampson 1998, ch. 3.

30 Consoles: (a) niche no. 166; (b) niche no. 169; (c) niche no. 178. CI and author.

What has survived, however, falls into a pattern that offers another tool in establishing the former presence of medieval sculpture. The traces are concentrated in places that retain, or probably once had, medieval statues: nos. 166 and 169 (statues), 178 (console and fixing), 195 (fixing) and in the vesica at the centre of the great gable (where the accompanying bird implies the presence of a Christ in Majesty). Polychromy was applied, perhaps, only where sculpture was added, while scaffolding was still in place.[115]

[115] Williamson 1995, p.5.

Paint has also been found around the other two niches on the north face of the north turret (nos. 167–68), which could well, therefore, have been filled with statues. That in the head of no. 167 is particularly rich. Several paint traces appear to have been laid over lichen growth, implying that the paint, and probably therefore the statues themselves, is later than the niches (see pp.114, 123).

Central Porch. There is evidence of another kind, in Hemingsby's Register of chapter documents, for an image of the Virgin outside the west door, presumably within the porch, by March 1341.[116] The context is a dispute between the Chapter and their Treasurer, Walter Wyvil, the bishop's brother,[117] over the possession of offerings of candles being made at two images of Mary, this one and a Virgin in childbirth, or 'gysyne'.[118] Five years earlier, in May 1336, Chapter had ordered that all offerings at the other image should be given to the fabric fund, but the west door image is not then referred to.[119] It may be mentioned again in two 15th-century wills, although one of these describes her image as being over (*super*) the west door and has been taken above to refer, therefore, to an earlier tympanum image.[120] The leaving of offerings would be more convenient at a lower level.

The recent survey located the site of a sculpture that might well have been such a porch image (fig. 31, pl. VI). To the south of the west doorway, on the north-facing wall, at chest height and above, there is an area of disturbed walling, with two associated features. The wall is filled with evenly coursed stones, forming tidy vertical joins with the original masonry, their upper extent obscured by later repairs. Beneath, there is a cut-back stone, probably a corbel block, which has been inserted into the 13th-century coursing. At the foot of this, there is carved a Lombardic letter C, followed by a three-dot word-spacer. To the right are the

31 Elevation of the wall to the south of the west doorway, showing site of sculpture, carved letter (a) and possible pricket (b).

---

[116] Chew 1963, no. 159: '... super perceptione cere ad ymaginem beate Marie que dicitur gysine, et alteram ymaginem ejusdem ad portam occidentalem, que est extra, ex devocione fidelium oblate ...'

[117] On Wyvil, see Chew 1963, pp.259–60.

[118] Wordsworth 1901, pp.305–306.

[119] Chew 1963, no. 275.

[120] Malden 1904, pp.29, 30; Salisbury, Cathedral Archives, Machon's Register, pp.237, 238.

remains of an iron fixing, lead-set into the wall. This must mark the site of a statue, probably within a niche, once inserted into the wall, standing on a corbel block and with an associated feature, perhaps a candle pricket. The letter C may have been either for an inscription that remained unfinished, or to show a painter where to supply one. Its Lombardic character tends to imply a date before the mid-14th century, when blackletter became more popular for monumental inscriptions. This would be in line with the proposed *terminus ante quem* of 1341.

As we have seen, statues were also added on the east walls of the recesses to either side of the west door (nos. 201, 206, 207). This may have occurred at the same time, although the remains have now no surviving features in common. The figures were very different in scale, so this is hardly surprising. Any architectural canopy over the smaller sculpture would have required integration with the wall. The larger figures had recessed lead-set iron fixings resembling those for surviving statues on the façade above, and were probably contemporary with these. If not directly contemporary, they may have been conceived in relation to these Marian images.

Conclusion. Apart from the two central buttresses, there is no evidence at all for large figure sculptures above the lowest two zones of niches (pl. I). There is also good evidence, of different kinds, for five more large-scale medieval figures in the lowest zone, giving grounds to support Hollar's view of further statues at this level, if not a full complement (fig. 48). There were a further two figures, at least, in the central porches, not counting the smaller niche figures. No evidence has been found for further figures in the second tier up, beyond the two that were lost in the last 130 years, on the lesser northern and southern buttresses. On the south face there never was any sculpture.

This then was a partial scheme. The evidence of the paint, laid over lichen growth, confirms the stylistic evidence (see below) that the larger figures were installed some time after the architecture was complete. All of the surviving full-scale figures and most of the lost ones could be of the same date, in terms of their material and/or fixings, although the consoles suggest some anomalies. The almost symmetrical arrangement of the known and surviving sculptures (pl. I) may indicate that this was, in fact, the full complement of figures by the end of the middle ages.[121]

2. *Iconography*

The subject matter of the surviving figures provides another litmus test for the coherence of the scheme, but one that previous writers have explored little, perhaps

---

[121] The asymmetrical arrangement of the figures in niches nos. 169 and 195 can be explained in two ways: first by the desire to relate no. 169 to the proposed three figures on the directly adjoining north face of the north turret; but also because the central niche of the northern triplet on the west face (no. 170) contained a window to light the stair within, making fixing difficult.

because it was assumed that so much had been lost.[122] In general, the known disposition of the sculptures makes formal sense. They were gathered around the central porch, complementing what it has been proposed existed already. They were also concentrated in the lowest zone, where people could see them, and there was a greater concentration of figures on the north, the main approach to the cathedral's nave north porch, and the town side. The upper figures on the central axis and buttresses reflect a hierarchical ordering of a simple and universal kind, which was predetermined by the 13th-century mandorla in the gable.

Detailed arguments for the identity of the figures are given in the catalogue, with illustrations, but the findings are summarised in the present section, with previous interpretations in brackets. John Carter's drawings of 1802 are reproduced here (fig. 32). In Zone E, the deacon may be St Stephen (not St Birinus; no. 166), but there is no good evidence for the identity of the mitred prelate (no. 169). In Zone D, the figures on the central buttresses were St John the Evangelist (rather than the Virgin of the Annunciation; no. 129) and St John the Baptist (no. 145). St James (not St Bridget, Roger of Salisbury or William Longespee; no. 150a) certainly stood formerly on the lesser south buttress and the lost figure on the north buttress was a priest (not St Augustine; no. 124). In Zone C stood the Apostles Peter and Paul (nos. 86, 95). In Zone A was a pair of enthroned prelates (rather than angels; nos. 19a, 26a), distinguished by their mass vestments. The bird over the vesica in the great gable is likely to have been the eagle of St John, with a scroll (rather than the dove of the Holy Spirit or a Pelican in Piety; no. 23).

Even in their diminished number, the images reveal coherence in arrangement. The figures on the central buttresses were clearly conceived and made as pairs. In the lowest zone, the two lost figures had matching ballflower consoles (nos. 178a, 187a). Perhaps they represented the Old Testament, to introduce the Marian image(s) in the porch and the hierarchy above. Within the porch, the larger added figures might also have been complementary to the Marian theme. The image to the right of the door was conceivably an amplification at a more accessible height of the image in the tympanum, to meet (or encourage) the demands of a public prepared by 1341 to leave candles in her honour. Within the church, there were several other images of the Virgin in the later middle ages, besides the patronal one associated with the high altar.[123]

The Baptist and the Evangelist, in Zone D, are commonly shown together. They shared a name, but the Golden Legend explains also that the Evangelist went to heaven on the feast of the Baptist's birth.[124] Evangelistic status is stressed by the left-hand figure's eagle attribute and arguably, originally, by a scroll. This may have carried the first words of St John's Gospel, 'In principio erat verbum'. Just as this John wrote of

---

[122]   The fullest accounts are Blum 1996a; RCHME 1999, p.180.
[123]   Wordsworth 1901, pp.160, 280 n. 1, 299; Frere 1898, pp.4, 6, 114 (high altar).
[124]   *Golden Legend*, I, p.335; *Lexikon* 1994, 7, cols. 111–12, 171–74; Réau 1956, II, 1, p.439; Réau 1958, III, 2, p.713.

Christ's life, so the Baptist had anticipated and proclaimed his coming. His words 'Ecce agnus dei' (John 1, 29) were manifest in the roundel that the saint held up, originally displaying the lamb. Both displaying attributes at their right shoulders, the St Johns therefore proclaimed Christ's life, as the word made flesh, and his saving Eucharistic message of physical sacrifice.

The Apostles Peter and Paul were the greatest of the Roman martyrs and appear together from an early date, distinguished by their facial appearance, as well as by their attributes of keys and a sword.[125] They shared a feast day on 29 June and their lives were closely linked in the Golden Legend.[126] If Peter was the rock upon which Christ built his Church (Matthew 16, 18), Paul was a dominant figure in its establishment and spread, as converter of the Gentiles. The two often flank the Crucifixion and Peter usually occupies the position of honour on Christ's right (our left), as here. The Apostles are turned towards each other and sway in complementary directions. All four surviving figures on the lower central buttresses were therefore universal, commonly paired, playing central parts in Christ's life and the establishment of the Church, but also ruling with him in heaven.

As the 13th-century designer had intended, Christ was the culmination to the scheme and his status in Majesty was confirmed by the associated Evangelistic symbol of St John. John's eagle and a scroll may therefore have appeared twice on the front. This would have set up a simple visual rhyme and evoked the fact that he was author not only of the Gospel, describing Christ's Incarnation and life, but also as it was believed in the middle ages of the Book of Revelation, which set out the Second Coming in its fullest form. The symbols of the Evangelists derive from the beasts described in Revelation, giving 'glory and honour and benediction to him that sitteth on the throne' (Revelation 4, 7).

It is harder to make sense of the other figures on the front, because they are now few and lack attributes, but general observations can be made. Those remaining in the lowest zone were presumably saints and certainly represent the Church – a deacon and a bishop or archbishop – and this may have been filled out elsewhere. Perhaps there was a churchman of special importance in the central niche on the north face of the north turret, next to the deacon, in niche no. 167; this received painted decoration of a more elaborate kind than that for the niches on either side (see p.114). Stephen was a universal saint, but it is tempting to think that Salisbury's local bishop saint, St Osmund (d.1099, canonised 1456) found a place somewhere on the front by the end of the middle ages. The lost figure on the lesser north buttress was also a cleric, wearing mass vestments. That on the lesser south buttress was an Apostle, but probably a late addition (see below).

---

[125] *Lexikon* 1994, 8, cols. 130–34, 161–65; Réau 1959, III, 3, pp.1038–40, 1083–85. In England, Norton, Park and Binski 1987, p.40.
[126] *Golden Legend*, I, pp.342–48, 351, 354.

166, 169

124, 19a

86, 129

26a, 145, 150a

95

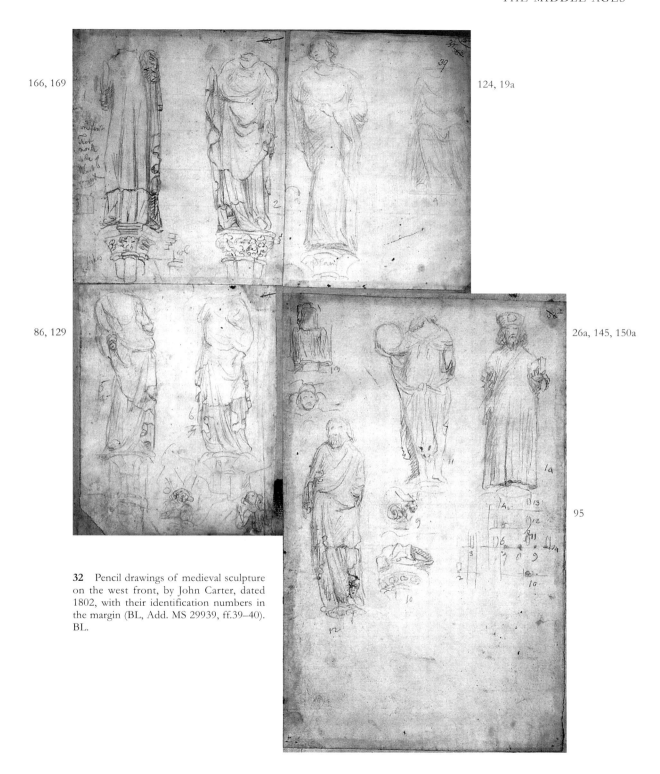

32 Pencil drawings of medieval sculpture on the west front, by John Carter, dated 1802, with their identification numbers in the margin (BL, Add. MS 29939, ff.39–40). BL.

The two enthroned prelates until recently at the top of the central buttresses form another pair and are vested for the mass (nos. 19a, 26a). They do not, therefore, fit into the hierarchy outlined previously for these buttresses, but again represent the Church. In particular, they may stress the episcopal order that had its seat here. The importance of bishops to the building has been stressed elsewhere, in continuities with Old Sarum;[127] in the promotion of Bishop Osmund's statutes as a standard and of Osmund himself as a saint;[128] in the promotion of Bishop Ghent's sanctity (by 1319);[129] and perhaps in the style of the architecture.[130] Bishops also played a key role in the building, from Poore, Bingham and Bridport in the 13th century, to (arguably) Ghent and Martival in the early fourteenth.[131] It is not known whether they played any part in the completion of the front in the 14th century, as Archbishop Melton (1316–1340) did at York,[132] but it is inherently likely, given the absence of a resident Dean for most of the 14th century.

Comparisons with other fronts reveal some common principles in their formal arrangement. The concentration of sculpture on the buttresses, as prominent features of the architectural design, is paralleled at York, c.1330–40, as is the emphasis on the great west doors, the symbolic and ritual entrance.[133] At Lichfield (fig. 34), there was a minor concentration of sculpture around the inner central porch vestibule. At Lincoln, a gallery of kings was added over the central door in the second half of the 14th century. In the concentration of figures across the bottom two zones, the added figures loosely resemble Exeter (1340s), with its very different two-tier screen (fig. 33). This marks a new direction in west front design, concentrating images again around the doorways, but also at a legible level. These similarities are determined by symbolic importance, structural prominence and legibility.

The wider interpretation of the Salisbury figures, as allegories of the church, is considered in the final section, but some similarities with other façades may be noted. The Marian focus in the central porch is shared with Wells, as discussed earlier. At Exeter, large-scale Marian images frame the front's southern door (Annunciation, Adoration of the Magi).[134] At Lichfield and Exeter galleries of kings may represent the Virgin's ancestors in the Old Testament.[135] Unlike Exeter, Lichfield, Wells (narratives and full-length figures) and, arguably, York (the heavily restored voussoirs of the great west door), there is now no Old Testament component at Salisbury, although possible

[127] RCHME 1993b, pp.72–73, 75.
[128] Greenway 1996; Stroud 1984.
[129] Wordsworth and Macleane 1915, pp.202–203.
[130] Jansen 1996.
[131] Blum 1991, pp.9–10, 14–15, 21–22; Tatton-Brown 1995.
[132] CVMA, GB, III, 1, p.3.
[133] *Romanesque*, p.50.
[134] Henry 1991, p.138.
[135] Henry 1991, pp.135, 136; Williamson 1995, p.222; Cobb 1980, p.140, fig. 223 and Morris 1993, p.106, pl. XXIXa, b.

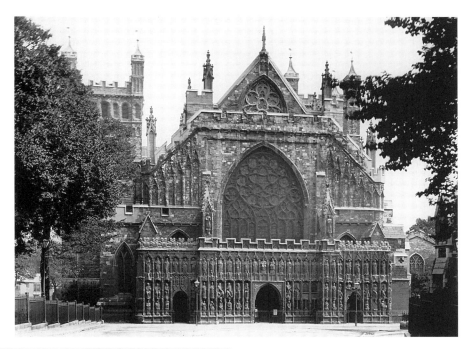

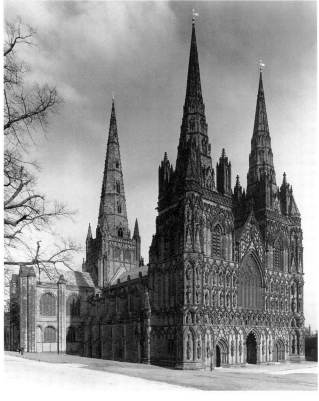

33 West front, Exeter Cathedral. CI.

34 West front, Lichfield Cathedral. CI.

locations have been suggested. Of the other figures, the Evangelists and Apostles commonly accompany Christ. Apostles were among the Romanesque sculpture reused in the 14th century at York, although unsystematically applied.[136] At Wells, they were added beneath the enthroned Christ in the great gable in the 15th century. A set of Evangelists and Apostles also flanks figures (probably) of Christ and God the Father in the 15th-century upper tier at Exeter.[137] The saints find their fullest expression on the façade at Wells.[138] At Exeter, the Four Latin Doctors occupy prominent positions on the lower buttresses (15th century).[139] As a group, these fronts deserve further study.

3. Style and Date

It has been argued that the surviving large-scale figure sculptures might all be of a single period, although the consoles of some are more closely associable than others. Stylistic analysis suggests a qualification, in that the deacon martyr on the north face of the north turret shows differences of treatment (no. 166), in the form of the figure (made from two stones, rather than one), in the handling of the sides and back (there is little attempt to suggest recession, although this occurs on even the thinnest of the west-facing figures), and in the drapery. The folds around the feet are bulkier than those on the other figures. These are minor differences, however, and the deacon martyr could well have been made at a similar date.

A second qualification is necessary for the lost figure of St James at the top of the lesser south buttress (no. 150a). The only detailed sources for this are drawings and general views of the front in early photographs, but these reveal that the figure was shorter and the console substantially taller than the others in this tier (figs. 32, 64). The forked beard and tall hat might suggest the fashions of the second half of the 14th century – the beard was worn in the reign of Richard II.[140] As we shall see, the other figures are probably earlier than this. This one was presumably intended to complete their symmetrical arrangement. As on other west fronts, additions continued to be made, such as the lost figure with its angel console to the right of the south-west door (no. 208). The proliferation of images in the later middle ages is demonstrated by other new figure sculpture in the Close, for the remains of a group, possibly a Crucifixion, with console block and sheltering gable, were identified recently on the west wall of the west walk of the cloister (see fig. 47).[141]

Writers since Prior and Gardner have recognised that the surviving large figures are all in the soft style initiated in the 1290s, notably on the Eleanor Crosses and on

---

[136] *Romanesque*, pp.12, 50–54, cat. nos. 23–35; Norton 1993/94, pp.527–28.
[137] Henry 1991, pp.139–41.
[138] Sampson 1998, pp.153–55, 158–59.
[139] Henry 1991, p.140.
[140] *Wilton Diptych*, pp.22, 24, fig. 6 on p.23.
[141] Ayers 1994.

35 Synagogue (restored), stone, Chapter Room doorway, Rochester Cathedral. CI.

36 St Mark, stone, chancel, Edington Priory, Wilts. CI.

tomb effigies in Westminster Abbey.[142] In this, play is made of contrasts between vertical falls, horizontal folds and swags with a sinuous hemline, all in a soft material. The figure itself might swing off the hip. The style prevailed in different forms until the 1340s and after, including the impressive stone figures of Ecclesia and Synagogue on the jambs of the Chapter Room doorway in Rochester Cathedral, *c.*1340 (fig. 35), and two splendid headless Evangelists (fig. 36) from a set around the choir at Edington Priory, Wilts. (begun 1351, consecrated 1361).[143]

[142] Prior and Gardner 1912, pp.342–46, figs. 387–88; Stone 1955, p.144; Blum 1996b, p.76.
[143] Hirschhorn 1977; *BoE Wilts.*, p.209.

37 Queen Eleanor, stone, Hardingstone Eleanor Cross, Northampton, *c*.1291–93. CI.

Where does the Salisbury sculpture fit into the stylistic sequence? The original comparison with the Eleanor figure on the Hardingstone Cross is good but not entirely convincing (fig. 37). As previous commentators have observed, the prelate with whom the Eleanor is compared by Prior and Gardner has been photographed from an angle that conceals the swing in the pose, a swing less prominent in her figure. The surviving Salisbury sculptures almost all display a high degree of sway, the counterpart perhaps to the Curvilinear Decorated style in English architecture. Their drapery is not of the relatively bulky material on the Eleanor figures either, but of a finer looking cloth, reminiscent of that shown at Rochester or Edington and, in painting, on the Musée de Cluny frontal, *c*.1330–40;[144] in the miniatures of the Majesty Master in the so-called De Lisle Psalter (BL, MS Arundel 83 II), before 1339;[145] and in the stained glass of the west window of York Minster, *c*.1339.[146]

The big pouchy folds, often swinging dramatically in opposite directions, may be a further indicator of date. They have been compared to those, in stone, on the Synagogue figure at Rochester;[147] but also to the wood Virgin from an Annunciation group in the Vicars' Hall at Wells Cathedral, perhaps *c*.1350 (fig. 39).[148] They can be found earlier but are common in sculpture of the 1330s and later, both in England[149] and on the Continent.[150] In Salisbury, they are evident on the mourning angels that wittily adorn the central arch of Bishop Martival's tomb (d.1330), as crockets (fig. 38).

[144] Norton, Park and Binski 1987, p.79, eg pls. 6, 7, 10, 11.
[145] Sandler 1983, pls. 20–24; Sandler 1986, cat. no. 38.
[146] CVMA, GB, III, 1, pp.4, 22–23, pl. 8.
[147] Hirschhorn 1977, pp.74–79, n. 282; Prior and Gardner 1912, figs. 33, 393.
[148] *Age of Chivalry*, cat. nos. 526–27. The hall was finished by 1348 (Colchester 1982, p.212).
[149] Tomb effigy of Bishop Droxford (d.1329), Wells Cathedral: F. H. Crossley, *English Church Monuments A.D. 1150–1550*, London, 1921, p.190. Percy Tomb, Beverley Minster, Humberside, 1340s: N. Dawton, 'The Percy Tomb at Beverley Minster: the Style of the Sculpture', in *Studies in Medieval Sculpture*, ed. F. H. Thompson, Society of Antiquaries, Occasional Paper (new series) III, 1983, pp.122–50; Prior and Gardner 1912, fig. 394.
[150] In the Rhineland and Low Countries: *Rhin–Meuse*, cat. nos. O7 (Mosan, *c*.1330–40), O8 (Mosan, 1344); also N5 (Cologne, *c*.1330), N13 (Liège, *c*.1330).

38 Tomb of Bishop Martival (d.1330), north side of the choir, Salisbury Cathedral. CI.

39 *(left)* Virgin of the Annunciation, wood, Vicars' Hall, Wells Cathedral. Victoria & Albert Museum, London.

40 *(above)* Second seal of Richard Bury, Bishop of Durham, 1334–35. CI.

The second seal of Richard Bury, Bishop of Durham, by a continental maker (1334–35), offers a general comparison in miniature for the prelate in the lowest zone at Salisbury (fig. 40).[151]

Another possibly diagnostic feature is the drapery of St John the Evangelist (no.129). His mannered pose is complemented by a strange arrangement across the hips, whereby the robe is tucked under the right elbow and then swung across the body to be supported under the other. The vertical pleats under the right elbow can be found in earlier English stone sculpture, including one of the weepers on the tomb chest of Aymer de Valence (d.1324) in Westminster Abbey. They are repeated on the wood Virgin of the Annunciation at Wells and in the stained glass of the great east window there, c.1340.[152] They tend to suggest a date in or after the second quarter of the 14th century, rather than the first.

One aspect of the iconography also points this way. Drawings by Carter and Cockerell reveal that the Baptist was wearing a camelskin with head and hooves attached: the back legs of the pelt were tied across the chest and the animal's head was hung between the saint's legs (fig. 32).[153] The earliest known example of a skin with a head on it is of the mid-14th century, in England, in a window of the parish church of St Denys Walmgate, York (fig. 41).[154] In the late 14th century

41 St John the Baptist, stained glass, north aisle, St Denys Walmgate, York. F.H. Crossley and M.H. Ridgway.

[151] *Age of Chivalry*, cat. no. 675.
[152] Ayers 1996, pp.292, 299–302.
[153] BL, Add. MS 29939, f.40 (no. 11); RIBA, British Architectural Library, Drawings Collection, H10.
[154] Rushforth 1936, p.235, n. 4.

it appears on the Wilton Diptych, which belonged to Richard II (c.1396–99),[155] and in stained glass made for William Wykeham, Bishop of Winchester, for his foundation of Winchester College (c.1393).[156] The Salisbury figure could be the earliest known instance of the motif, but at present it appears isolated.

The surviving consoles in the lowest zone are the only ones to offer positive evidence for dating. That beneath the standing prelate includes – the detail is nearly gone – distinctive trefoil leaves with voluted terminals (fig. 30a). These are common in the later 14th century and beyond, but relatively rare before the 1320s.[157] They occur among the roof bosses in the lower chapel, St Stephen's, Westminster Palace, as part of a campaign that Wilson argues was completed by 1297, when work was brought to a halt until the 1320s.[158] They occur again on the undated north porch of St Mary Redcliffe, Bristol (usually placed on stylistic grounds c.1320[159]), on wood misericords at Wells (from 1325) and, at Salisbury Cathedral, on the tomb of Bishop Martival (d.1330), on the north side of the choir, as crockets to the arches that flank the central opening (fig. 38).

If some features of the west front figure sculpture could date from the 1340s or later, the ballflower on these consoles points in the opposite direction (fig. 30c). It might date from as early as 1300, or shortly before, when the motif was first introduced into England, but it was falling out of fashion by the 1330s.[160] At Salisbury, it occurs on the central tower and on the tomb of Bishop Ghent (d.1315) on the south side of the choir.[161] Ballflower is one of the motifs that associates this tomb with the tower campaign.[162] On the west front, ballflower suggests that the consoles and the figures they supported were made in the first quarter of the 14th century or shortly thereafter. If the coherence of the surviving sculpture as a group can be accepted, then the ballflower and the other features, taken together, suggest a similar date.

The exact sculptural context of the west front figures remains elusive. Apart from the tombs of Bishops Ghent and Martival, which are rich in decorative carving but conspicuous in their lack of three-dimensional effigies or any large-scale figure sculpture, there is no work of comparable date either in the cathedral or city. In that similar decorative motifs are used, however, the voluted trefoil leaf and ballflower, the whole scheme should perhaps be associated with work on the central spire and the tombs of Bishops Ghent (d.1315) and Martival (d.1330). Completion of the formal western approach to the cathedral might, then, have been a natural corollary to the creation of the new landmark over the crossing. As Tatton-Brown has suggested, the

---

[155] *The Wilton Diptych*, pp.59–62, pls. 2, 6.
[156] *Age of Chivalry*, cat. no. 613.
[157] Tracy 1987, pp.27–28, pls. 84a, b, c, 85a, b.
[158] *Age of Chivalry*, cat. no. 324.
[159] *Age of Chivalry*, cat. no. 490.
[160] Morris 1985, esp. p.112.
[161] Morris 1996, pp.46–47.
[162] Tatton-Brown 1991b, p.95; Tatton-Brown 1995.

bishops themselves may have taken a particular role in promotion of the work, as the Deans were absentees.[163] Martival issued important statutes for the cathedral in 1319, including indulgences for the fabric, in which he refers to the achievements (including architectural) of his predecessors, placing himself in their succession.[164] The wider context for these additions, in new work around the cathedral Close will be considered in the next section.

Such a date would be consistent with the only known documentary evidence, the reference to an image of the Virgin in the west porch by 1341. It was argued above that this was once on the wall to the right of the great west door. If this had been inserted at the same time as the other statues that were added to the porch, which are probably contemporary in turn with those higher up on the façade, then the document would provide a *terminus ante quem* for all of them. In that the style of the surviving figures suggests the second quarter of the 14th century, it is conceivable that their addition had taken place not long before; and even that their creation had played a part in prompting the dispute between the Chapter and their Treasurer which generated the documentary record (see above).

THE PORTER'S LODGE

On the north side of the west front the access from the passageway of the north door into the northern stair-turret has at some date been adapted for use as a porter's lodge (fig. 11).[165] An inserted fireplace occupies the north-east corner of the ground-floor chamber, facing directly on to the base of the spiral stair. This has been regularly used, since the stonework of the back and sides at the level of the grate has been reddened by heat. The 13th-century vaulting has been breached in the north-eastern corner to allow the formation of a flue, which runs slightly eastwards above this point before turning sharply to the east; this must have discharged in the area of renewed stonework near the base of niche no. 163, the southernmost of the lowest zone of niches on the east face of the turret.[166]

It is possible that this chamber was panelled, at least in part, since there are numerous nail holes – some of which are clearly early and incorporate large round flat-headed nails. Within the chamber immediately inside the door, these tend to be concentrated at the top of the joint line of the springer blocks, and this line is also occupied by nail holes on the inner bay of the east wall and the newel and the stonework to the east of it. Numerous holes also existed in the jambs of the window at both this height and (on the southern jamb only) the course above.

---

[163] Tatton-Brown 1995.

[164] Wordsworth and Macleane 1915, pp.194–201.

[165] The plan in RCHME 1993b gives this as 15th to 16th century, but it could well be later. It has little in the way of dateable features.

[166] The chimney is shown in a drawing by J. Buckler: BL, Add. MS 36392, f.42.

The wood door is 15th-century in style, similar in construction to those that were added at the foot of other stair-turrets in the cathedral, of vertical planks on the front, horizontal planks on the back and nailed.[167] As on these other doors, a quatrefoil hole has been cut through, allowing a view on to the passage outside. There is a sliding cover for this spy-hole. Directly opposite, in the passage, there is a late medieval recess in the south wall, which may have had a shelf and seems to have been enlarged downwards at some point, having also an associated lead-set fixing. This may have been for an image and candle pricket.

Outside the north door of the façade, immediately to the south, in the sheltered corner formed by the north central buttress, a large area of burning on the plinth may be associated with the presence of a brazier. The pinkening of the stone starts too high up the plain ashlar for it to be the result of a bonfire, nor is it in a position that is likely to be associated with lead-working or other hot-work on the building. So close to the lodge, it may be associated with occasions when the porter was required to be on duty outside, to make his life more tolerable.[168] This accumulation of evidence may suggest that the north door was used for access from the late middle ages.

The masonry that blocks the northern end of the 'singer's gallery', effectively closing it off from the northern stair turret, should perhaps also be associated with the later middle ages (fig. 11). There are traces of a doorway (the pintles on the newel and lock-plate on the outer wall) on the stairs just below this level.

THE FRONT IN CONTEXT

As an institution, Salisbury Cathedral was served by a chapter of secular canons and the majority of surviving English screen façades designed for sculpture in the 13th and 14th centuries ornament buildings of this type (Wells, Lincoln, Salisbury, Lichfield, York).[169] It is perhaps not surprising that rich cathedral churches should explore the adaptation of the form for sculpture, as an external and public display. Yet, the ambition of these designs was not always fulfilled. Far from being executed at one time, immediately after the building, sculpture was often supplied piecemeal, over a long period and sometimes not at all. Of the other secular cathedrals, Wells and Exeter had relatively complete schemes by the end of the middle ages (figs. 5, 33), but the work is of several periods.[170] Lincoln and York Minster were less complete (fig. 42).[171]

---

[167] The authors are grateful to Tim Tatton-Brown for this analysis of the doors.

[168] What may have been a canopy for protecting such a sentry from the worst effects of the weather is shown in an equivalent position in Tom's engraving (c.1730) of the west front of Wells Cathedral.

[169] The Benedictine abbey of Peterborough has an early 13th-century screen façade (with some remaining sculpture), but of a different kind from Wells or Salisbury: Webb 1956, p.104.

[170] Sampson 1998, pp.182–89; Henry 1991.

[171] On York, see Romanesque, pp.50–58; Norton 1993/94, pp.524–28.

As shown, Salisbury, too, had an incomplete scheme, with sculpture of more than one date. If less spectacular than the Gothic façades of the High Gothic cathedrals of the Ile de France, such partial schemes are nevertheless revealing of contemporary priorities.

This section explores the importance of the Salisbury west front to its cathedral, as a symbol, and its place in the liturgy of the church, but also the extent to which it was directed or adapted to different audiences over time. The term 'west front' is not a medieval one. The chronicler Matthew Paris uses the word 'frons' to refer to the east end of the cathedral, the most sacred and liturgically important part of the building.[172] Looked at from the inside, the west end was the least important part of the church, the nave being the part most accessible to the general public. As an entity, the façade itself is not referred to at all in the liturgical sources, but only the 'ostium occidentale' or west door, through which processions passed. That does not mean that it was unimportant, however, for the elaborate design implies that it was conceived as the single most important feature of the exterior.

42   West front, Lincoln Cathedral. CI.

This is because it centred the cathedral's most important doorway, in a hierarchy defined by context, materials, design, sculpture and polychromy.[173] A comparison with the other doors reveals that it is more ornate than any of those around the cloister and slightly larger than that within the north porch or into the Chapter House (front cover, fig. 43). Like these, and like major doorways elsewhere, it has a double opening. By comparison, the triple-gabled porch and the wider context of niches across the front define its higher status. In relation to the front as a whole, the extent of the doorway's decoration is a further measure of its importance throughout the middle ages. It has been argued that the central porch was peopled with sculpture and painted

[172]   M. Paris, *Historia Anglorum*, III, ed. F. Madden, 1869, p.260; Blum 1991, p.14, n. 43. The term *frons* is used similarly at Worcester: *Annales Monastici*, IV, ed. H. R. Luard, London, 1869, p.415. The authors are grateful to Peter Draper for this reference.
[173]   For a discussion of the doors at Amiens, see Kimpel and Suckale 1985, pp.11–17.

in bright colour from the beginning, whereas the rest of the front was not. The priority of the great west doorway over the rest of the façade seems to have been observed to a greater or lesser extent in west fronts as far apart chronologically as Wells Cathedral in the 13th century and Bath Abbey in the early sixteenth.[174]

How was this entrance conceived? Blum suggested that the 14th-century sculpture represented the Apocalyptic Vision of the Heavenly Jerusalem (Revelation 21), as had been proposed by Brieger for the earlier and fuller scheme at Wells.[175] Every church was likened to this at its dedication.[176] At Salisbury, there was a prominent reminder of the dedication in the copper alloy crosses that were placed in the central gables of the two flanking portals in the 13th century. The three west doors and their triple gables fall in with the emphasis on gates in threes in the text (Revelation 21, 13), so that the idea may have been implicit from the beginning. The 14th-century sculpture can also be read in this way. The prominent eagle of St John in the gable probably associates the enthroned Christ with the description in Revelation (Revelation 4, 8). The Apostles are the foundations of the New Jerusalem (Revelation 21, 14) and the martyrs are those who rule with Christ for a thousand years (Revelation 20, 4). The addition of battlements may also have had this connotation (see below).

The Heavenly Jerusalem is not, however, sufficient explanation for the variety of English surviving and recorded west fronts. The dedication service in the Sarum liturgy suggests a range of allegorical interpretations for each church, reflecting exegetical techniques that would have been familiar to the educated clergy (the Church, the Gate of Heaven, the Body of Christ, the Bride of Christ, Noah's Ark, Jacob's Ladder).[177] Their application to doorways is apparent from inscriptions associated with Romanesque portals and in contemporary French portal sculpture, confirming the importance of the doorway as the place to convey such meanings.[178] Above the great west door at Wells, the Coronation of the Virgin and the associated types of Solomon and the Queen of Sheba must refer to the Virgin as the Church and the Bride of Christ.[179] At Salisbury, the Virgin may be present primarily as the dedication saint, but if she were shown originally with the Christ Child and framed by Old Testament ancestors, he might also be the son of David of the dedication service, the Christ Incarnate – and the church/Church his body.[180]

The decision to display sculpture across a whole façade posed a vast challenge, to expand upon the sacred significance of the church. Formally, there was inevitably a tension between the ancient significance of the entrance at ground level and the logical

[174] Sampson 1998, p.132.
[175] Blum 1996a, p.629; Brieger 1957, pp.41–42.
[176] Wickham Legg 1916, pp.202, 203 (lesson).
[177] Wickham Legg 1916, pp.202–203.
[178] Kendall 1998, Part 3. On the transept portals at Chartres, for example, see Katzenellenbogen 1959, Part 2.
[179] Sampson 1998, pp.154, 158.
[180] Wickham Legg 1916, p.202: 'Filius ille David qui nos sibi consociauit hac in matre domo et deus est et homo'.

Salisbury Cathedral
Principal Doorways

0   ft   10

0   m   3

a. North Doorway

b. Chapter House Doorway

c. Doorway to W. Cemetery

d. Doorway to S. Transept

e. Doorway to Canons' Cemetery

43 The cathedral's other doorways.

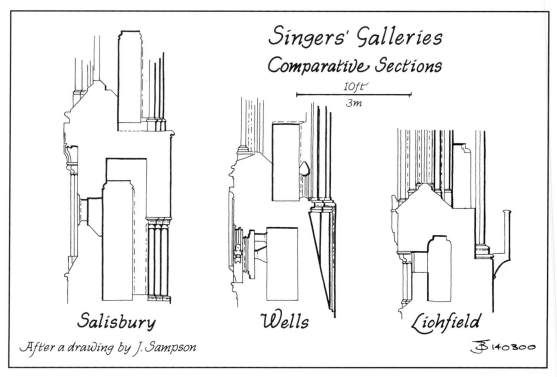

44 A comparison of the wall passages at Salisbury, Wells and Lichfield Cathedrals.

culmination to a visual hierarchy at the top of the composition. The unfinished 13th-century front, as now revealed at Salisbury, is a vivid demonstration of the continuing importance of the door. Where the screen was almost filled, at Wells, the answer to the compositional challenge that it posed was, in part, to place the church within a great history of salvation, from the Creation to the Last Trumpet.[181] The 14th-century additions on the central buttresses at Salisbury might also be read as a limited chronological ascent from the earlier Incarnation, proposed within the porch, to the end of time.

In so far as the screen front was intended to present an image of the Church in Heaven, it presented also a counterpart to the hierarchy of the Church on earth, which reforming popes and prelates of the first half of the 13th century were reinforcing in Lateran Councils and synods. The analogy would be particularly appropriate at Salisbury, where the architecture of the cathedral has been read in other ways as a manifestation of the ideas of reforming clergy.[182] Bishop Poore, present at the Fourth Lateran Council, was active in establishing much copied diocesan statutes

[181] Kowa 1990, p.134; Sampson 1998, pp.153, 159–61.
[182] Draper 1996; Jansen 1996.

(1219 x 1228).[183] Although most of the front's sculpture was never executed, the prominence of the consecration crosses is consistent with contemporary concerns to ensure that churches should be properly dedicated. This was the first item in the canons of the legatine council held in London by Cardinal Otho, in November 1237.[184] The inlaid Salisbury crosses would be copied in the diocese, at Uffington and Edington.[185] The importance of the dedication also helps to explain the presence of the Virgin in the tympanum, as the dedication saint. In the 14th-century additions, the prelates added at the top of the central buttresses may demonstrate in brief the particular status of this church as the seat of a bishop.

The Sarum liturgy ritually reinforced the layers of symbolic importance of the front as an image of the institution and of the great west door as a symbolic threshold. On Palm Sunday, the clergy left their cathedral church in procession before re-entering it to re-enact Christ's entry into Jerusalem, at the beginning of Holy Week.[186] It is presumed that the procession proceeded around the cloister and emerged from its west door, before taking up a second station before the west front, where a choir 'in eminenciori loco' sang the hymn 'Gloria, laus'. The procession then moved to the doors of the church ('ad ianuas ecclesie') and entered.[187] The architecture makes provision for the Palm Sunday liturgy. A gallery within the thickness of the wall and a series of perforated openings above the central porch were probably for a choir to sing out the 'Gloria, laus' (fig. 11). Such galleries have been identified in other 13th-century English cathedral façades at Wells and Lichfield, and elsewhere (fig. 44).[188]

The sculptures intended for the niches that fronted the passage at Salisbury were presumably conceived to be participating in the liturgy, just like the angel busts in the equivalent location at Wells, deliberately involving the heavenly church in the ritual of its earthly counterpart and implying again their relationship. In a similar way, the south transept portals of Chartres Cathedral arrange the saints according to the divisions of the litany.[189] The role of liturgical performance in shaping the architecture is revealing. The re-enactment of Christ's Passion and the celebration of the Resurrection in Holy Week were the central events of the liturgical year, but it came around only once. The place of the great west door at the beginning of this liturgical re-enactment and its physical manifestation in the architecture of the building underlines its place as the church's symbolic threshold, the point of entrance not only to this church, but also to Jerusalem and the Heavenly Jerusalem.

---

[183] Powicke and Cheney 1964, pp.57–96.

[184] *Ibid.*, pp.245–46.

[185] T. Tatton-Brown, 'The Salisbury Cathedral Consecration Crosses', *Transactions of the Monumental Brass Society*, xvi, 2, 1998, p.116.

[186] Blum 1986, pp.146, 148; Wickham Legg 1916, pp.92–98.

[187] Wickham Legg 1916, p.96.

[188] McAleer 1988, pp.147–49; Sampson 1998, pp.168–73; S. Barry, 'The Architecture of the Cathedral', in *A Worthy Foundation, The Cathedral Church of St Canice, Kilkenny*, Mountrath, 1985, pp.38–39.

[189] Katzenellenbogen 1959, ch. 3.

45   View from the north-west.

46 Figurative capital, doorway, north porch, Wells Cathedral. CI.

The great west doorway is recorded to have been used liturgically on only a few other great feasts, but they confirm this role. The 15th-century Processional records that processions passed through it on Ascension Day and in the preceding Rogation tide.[190] On Ash Wednesday and Maundy Thursday, at the beginning and end of Lent, penitents would be ritually and symbolically expelled and readmitted respectively, through the west doors, which represented therefore the entrance into not only this church, but also the Church in general.[191] Before his enthronement, each new bishop would also arrive barefoot here to take an oath to observe and defend the customs of the church, in a ritual abasement before the church and its traditions.[192] There may have been other unrecorded uses, but it is unlikely that the great west doors were often used for public access. The use of the two doors into the aisles is not recorded, although there were adaptations to both in the later middle ages, as we have seen, and that on the north accommodated a porter.

In relation to the rest of the cathedral, the formal relationship between the west doors and others, particularly the nave north porch, deserves further study (figs. 20, 45).[193] Such nave porches were already established in the west of England at Malmesbury Abbey and Wells Cathedral, both known to the designer of the Salisbury front, and it has been suggested that the south transept porch at Old Sarum inspired them all.[194] Their splendour might imply that they were formal entrances. In fact, the north porch appears barely at all in the liturgical sources for Salisbury. There is no sign here of the penitential function proposed for the Romanesque north door at

[190] Wordsworth 1901, pp.91, 94.
[191] Wordsworth 1901, pp.63 n.1, 68–69, 70 n.3. The Consuetudinary had specified the south door, at Old Sarum: Frere 1898, pp.138, 143–44. The Sarum Missal in use at Salisbury in the 13th century specifies 'ad ianuas ecclesie', which is presumably the west doors: Wickham Legg 1916, pp.51, 102.
[192] Wordsworth 1901, pp.104–105, 126. For the formal reception of bishops here, see also Wordsworth and Macleane 1915, pp.300–301.
[193] Webb 1956, p.104; Draper 1996, p.24.
[194] Stalley 1971, p.75.

Saint-Lazare, Autun.[195] As shown, the readmission of penitents at the end of Lent was here through the west doors. Elsewhere, porches were used in a variety of other ways, including for legal purposes in the pre-Conquest nave south porch at Canterbury Cathedral, as recorded by Eadmer.[196]

At Wells, it is possible to be more precise, for the porch is referred to as the 'magna porta canonicorum', or 'great gate of the canons'.[197] This suggests that it was used by the resident canons themselves, whose houses stood nearby. The sculpture invites a wider interpretation, however, for the inner doorway includes figures representing the authority of the church, with an exhortatory inscription (fig. 46). The right capital shows a bishop, and the left a cleric with a scroll inscribed in Latin 'INT[RA] : IN GAVD[IUM DOMIN]I: TUI', or 'Enter thou into the joy of thy lord' (Matthew 25, 21).[198] The clergyman and the text that he presents therefore address the 'good and faithful servants' of Christ's parable in Matthew's Gospel. Such inscriptions are uncommon in English sculpture and this one, albeit in Latin, may be a visual acknowledgement that the north porch was envisaged by the cathedral authorities to be used not only by the clergy, but also for more general access by the faithful. Text and image are here enlisted to engage with an audience, in a way more familiar from Romanesque sculpture on the continent.[199] The doorway is the point of entry to the church, but also allegorically to the Church of the faithful and the joys of heaven.

This raises the question of the wider setting of the cathedral complex and the town. They were planned together in the early 13th century, but like many others in England the church was physically isolated within a close (fig. 47).[200] By contrast, the façades of some continental cathedrals overlooked squares, and their porches might serve a variety of public purposes.[201] Around those at Wells and Salisbury there lay a cemetery, enclosed until the mid-14th century at Salisbury by a substantial wall.[202] The area is referred to in the liturgical sources as the 'atrium', demonstrating the conception of such consecrated burial places as liminal to the church.[203] Directly to the west of the front stood a churchyard cross in the later middle ages and a sculpture, probably a Crucifixion, was inserted against the west wall of the cloister, perhaps c.1400.[204] The Heavenly Jerusalem presented in stone on the west fronts at Wells or

---

[195] Werckmeister 1972, pp.17–23.
[196] Willis 1845, pp.11–12. We are indebted to Dr Richard Plant for this reference.
[197] HMC, I, p.18 (1207).
[198] Tudor-Craig 1982, p.107; Colchester 1987, p.61.
[199] Kendall 1998.
[200] RCHME 1993a, pp.38–40; Erlande-Brandenburg 1994, pp.166–74, 204–17.
[201] Erlande-Brandenburg 1994, pp.201–204; W. W. Clark and R. King, *Laon Cathedral, Architecture,* 1, Courtauld Institute Illustration Archives, *Companion Text,* 1, London, 1983, pp.23–24; Williamson 1995, p.4.
[202] HMC, I, p.74 (1243); RCHME 1993a, pp.44–45.
[203] Wordsworth 1901, pp.68 (Maundy Thursday), 94 (Ascension Day); Wickham Legg 1916, p.102 (Maundy Thursday). See also Binski 1996, p.74.
[204] Ayers 1994.

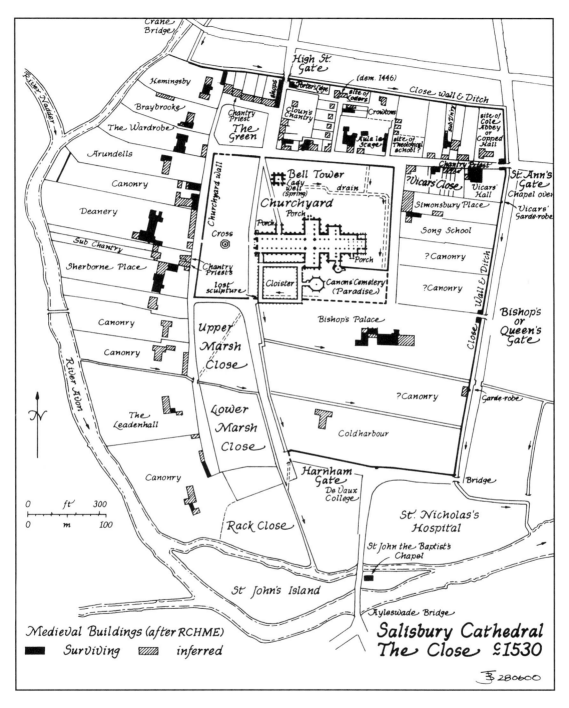

47 Plan of the Close.

Salisbury is a physical evocation of the Heavenly Jerusalem, before which the dead await the end of time. It is appropriate then that the Wells front should culminate in an extended frieze of the dead rising from their graves.[205]

Tombs of minor cathedral clergy are recorded to have been located before the west doorway within the central west porch in the 15th century. These were for Robert Cothe (d.1468), vicar choral and chaplain, and John Cooke, vicar and subtreasurer (d.1469).[206] The cemetery of the canons lay to the south-east of the church, but the porch may have offered some particular attractions.[207] The burials might be seen in the tradition of higher status monuments, like those in the west porch at Chichester Cathedral or the chantry of Bishop Grandisson (d.1369), built within the thickness of the west front at Exeter.[208] Symbolically, the tombs were even closer to the threshold than the burials in the churchyard. More specifically, Cothe's will explicitly refers to burial before an image of the Virgin, the great intercessor, whose presence here has already been mentioned.

Facing the wider world, such images might engage a public beyond their own communities. A porch statue is among the early recorded miracle-working images to interact with their audience.[209] When people of the town took shelter from attacking troops at the north door of the Benedictine abbey church at Déols (Indre), in 1187, a statue of the Virgin and Child was damaged by a stone, thrown by an insurgent.[210] It bled and the Virgin was subsequently seen to expose her breast. In the face of this divine intervention, hostilities were suspended. Closer in time and place, devotion to an image of the Virgin in the early 13th-century north porch of the parish church of St Mary Redcliffe, Bristol, may have inspired the hexagonal extension to this around 1320.[211] By this date, three-dimensional images of the Virgin and the saints were proliferating as objects of devotion, just as the images in the Salisbury porch were multiplying. There is no evidence that the Salisbury Virgin worked miracles, but the relative accessibility of such images might help to explain the recorded devotional activity, although the town lay on the other side of the cemetery. The cathedral community was closer. Indeed, the Deanery, the largest of the 13th-century close houses, was directly opposite.[212]

Other building in this period presented the cathedral in a new way. After the completion of a mighty new landmark in the central tower and spire, there was renewed interest in constructing a close wall (fig. 47).[213] As elsewhere, this was no doubt

---

[205] Sampson 1998, p.181.
[206] Malden 1904, pp.29, 30; Salisbury, Cathedral Archives, Machon's Register, pp.237, 238.
[207] RCHME 1993b, p.8 n. 7.
[208] Cook 1947/1968, pp.127–28.
[209] Vauchez 1999, pp.85–86.
[210] J. Hubert, 'Le miracle de Déols et la trêve conclue en 1187 entre les rois de France et d'Angleterre', *Bibliothèque de l'Ecole des chartes*, 96, 1935, pp.298–300.
[211] *Age of Chivalry*, cat. no. 490; Brakspear 1922, pp.274, 290–91.
[212] RCHME 1993a, p.201.
[213] RCHME 1993a, pp.38–53.

answering security needs,[214] in response to conflict between Bishop Ghent and the increasingly thriving town, but enclosure was also a visual manifestation of lordship.[215] At Chichester and Wells it was at or near one of the gates into the close, rather than at the west front, that the bishop took his oath to obey and uphold the cathedral customs.[216] At Salisbury, building may have commenced in December 1276, when the king granted the right to reuse stones from Old Sarum for the precinct wall.[217] Licence to crenellate was then granted in August 1327, although construction would continue for many years.[218] Bishop Wyvil was granted permission to crenellate his palace and other manors in August 1337.[219] The crenellation of the front itself, at some unknown date, is now recorded only in prints and drawings (fig. 48), but may be read in this wider context. Within the new enclosure, this defined a higher lordship and the heavenly city. At Exeter, angels may have manned the battlements of the west front screen.[220]

As a direct consequence of the building of the new close wall, another change took place within the precinct, opening up the space internally (fig. 47). Following a chapter decision of 8 May 1342, the wall surrounding the cemetery that lay about the cathedral itself, some nine feet high at its junction with the west wall of the cloister, was dismantled to provide building materials, removing a substantial barrier between the canons' houses around the perimeter and the church.[221] The addition of sculpture to the west front could have been a part of this adjustment in the visual and symbolic presentation of the cathedral, which created a more coherent internal space, while redefining the outer boundary. If the new close wall was to keep the public and town within more clearly defined limits, the sculpture might be read as another visual manifestation of this assertiveness.

The later medieval sculptures seem rhetorically to reach out to a wider audience, in location, pose and gesture.[222] The survey has shown that three figures were added in the 14th century to the north side of the north turret (nos. 166–69), the side of public access, the approach to the north porch and the town (fig. 45, pl. I). By contrast, the south turret had only one sculpture, on its west face, even though it overlooked the canons' processional door to and from the west cloister. On this west face, some

[214] Lepine 1995, pp.114–15.

[215] Coulson 1982, esp. pp.71–75.

[216] Walcott 1877, p.81; Reynolds 1881, p.91.

[217] R. L. Poole ed., 'Dean and Chapter of Salisbury', in Historical Manuscripts Commission, *Report on Manuscripts in Various Collections*, I, London, 1901, p.362. The authors are grateful to Tim Tatton-Brown for a copy of a forthcoming article on the close walls.

[218] *Calendar of the Patent Rolls, Edward III. 1327–1330*, HMSO, 1891, p.159.

[219] *Calendar of the Patent Rolls, Edward III. 1334–1338*, HMSO, 1895, p.498.

[220] Henry 1991, p.141. For the secular origins of the crenellated cornice in 14th-century English architecture, see Bony 1979, pp.21–22.

[221] Chew 1963, no. 171; RCHME 1993a, pp.44–45. It is not certain, however, that the wall was of the same height all the way round.

[222] For a discussion of the development of the façade in relation to towns, see Erlande-Brandenburg 1994, pp.204–14.

figures are also turned unexpectedly towards the north, as if to address viewers approaching from this side and at least two had their hands raised, probably in blessing (nos. 124, 169). Similarly, at York, in the first half of the 14th century, 12th-century figures were chosen to decorate aedicules on the buttresses along the south side of the nave, the town side, whereas the north was left undecorated.[223]

The Salisbury west front is splendid but unfinished, and it remains to be asked why this might be. There is now no record of how its decoration was to be funded, unfortunately. In general terms, however, Salisbury is not unusual in failing to complete such a vast undertaking and the building chronology suggests some wider priorities for the cathedral community. It has been argued that the front was probably structurally complete in time for the 1258 consecration (see p.6). If completion of the Chapter House can be placed in the 1250s or 1260s, this would no doubt have drawn corporate funds in that direction.[224] The west front offered an institutional face to the world, but the meeting place of the community was also a symbol of institutional pride.[225] Such buildings inspired rivalry in the 13th century, exercising the ingenuity of master masons and the resources of Chapters. At Salisbury, the resident canons, their representatives and visitors could view sculpture of a different kind, indulging the contemporary interest in Old Testament narrative in the spandrels of the wall arcade.[226]

[223] Norton 1993/94, p.527.

[224] The date is controversial: Blum 1991, pp.32, 35–36; RCHME 1993b, pp.8, 10; for the date of the glass, Marks 1993, pp.141–43; for the tiles, C. Norton, 'The Decorative Pavements of Salisbury Cathedral and Old Sarum', in *BAA Salisbury*, p.98. Most recently, see RCHME 1999, pp.28–31.

[225] For chapter meetings, see Edwards 1949 (1967 edn), pp.67–68; Lepine 1995, p.181.

[226] Blum 1969; Morgan 1992, esp. pp.168–69; Blum 1996b.

From the Reformation to the Twentieth Century

JERRY SAMPSON, EMMA HARDY AND TIM AYERS

Less damage was inflicted on the west front in the 16th and 17th centuries than at some other English cathedrals, and Wyatt's restoration of 1789–93 did not cause as much destruction as elsewhere in the church. Scott's restoration of 1866–69 appears to have been a model of conservation for the Victorian period, in many ways more conservative than some modern programmes of work. The main reason for the criticism that Scott received at the time was the repopulation of many of the empty niches with new sculptures carved by James Redfern. Since Scott's repair there has been only one further major campaign prior to the experimental conservation of the north central buttress sculptures in 1982, in the underpinning of the southern stair turret carried out under the direction of Charles Ponting in 1909.

The stonework of the west front, although badly decayed, is also in many respects much better preserved than that of comparable buildings. At Wells[1] and Exeter Cathedrals,[2] and at Bath Abbey,[3] the proportion of renewed stone is considerably higher and, in Salisbury itself, the fabric of the Poultry Cross has suffered more than fifty per cent replacement since it was built around 1500.[4] Part of the reason appears to be that the prevailing winds blow across the water meadows to the south-west, carrying none of the pollutants to which the city centre was exposed. The Poultry Cross, built of the same Chilmark/Tisbury stone, lies at the heart of the town. There can be little doubt that the 13th-century masons also had access to better beds of stone than their successors.

The Sixteenth and Seventeenth Centuries

The incidence of deliberate damage to this part of the building in the religious upheavals of the 16th and 17th centuries seems to have been fairly slight and may have been carefully targeted. The discussion of the medieval sculptural campaigns has shown that the west porch was the focus of the earliest decoration, which was added to and repainted several times in the later middle ages. It is probably not a coincidence, therefore, that this is the area of the greatest losses. It is unlikely that the

[1] Wells Cathedral, west front archive, record drawings from the condition survey made by Jerry Sampson, 1980–86.
[2] Allan and Blaylock 1991, pls. A and B.
[3] Sampson 1992, col. pls. 1–3.
[4] Sampson 1999, col. pls.

prominent image on the wall to the south of the central west door survived much beyond the middle of the 16th century. It may have been taken down with official sanction, since the wall was carefully infilled with mortared ashlar, so that all trace of its presence was erased (fig. 31).

That the reformers were active within the central porch is also evident from the condition of the west doorway, which is recorded to have displayed an image of the Virgin Mary. The middle order of the arch was renewed by Scott in 1866–69, but photographs taken by Fenton in about 1858 show that almost none of the original deeply undercut band had survived, suggesting systematic destruction (fig. 16). The sculptures in the tympanum, including Mary, would almost certainly have been taken down or defaced at the same time and the photograph shows that the support in the central niche had been cut away. A roughly cut hole in the gable of the central niche canopy may represent the fairly brutal removal of some metal decoration.

Even here, however, some of the accessible sculptures in the lowest register may have survived for a while. The southern blind arcade of the central porch, like the northern, contained medieval statuary – as the presence of a surviving fixing hook demonstrates. Both the central and the southern niche on this side also received subsidiary metal fixings, which probably represent the remains of much later stays to retain the sculptures, inserted in the 16th or 17th centuries. The holdfasts are unlikely to be medieval – since horizontal hoops at chest level would have been obtrusive – and the sculptures were gone by the 18th century.[5] In line with the other surviving figures in this lowest tier, they may have been beheaded, as a less drastic but still definitive denial of their authority.

Both the figures of the deacon martyr and the prelate in the lowest tier have lacked heads since the earliest reliable records of their detailed appearance, in Carter's drawings of 1802 (nos. 166, 169). Higher up, however, at least three medieval figures kept their heads through the Reformation; St Paul's is still visible in Fenton's photograph of c.1858 (fig. 64) (no. 95; he still retains the back of it). The figures in niches 124 and 150 are both recorded with heads but are now lost. It is difficult, therefore, to guess when the other lost figures for which there is evidence were removed from the front, and why. The lowest tier was obviously especially vulnerable, as the pattern of losses at Wells corroborates. Those flanking the central porch, on the exterior, might have experienced the same fate as those on the tympanum, at the same time – or perhaps they survived, like the prelate and the deacon martyr, falling victim to more natural causes or casual vandalism. There may have been metal restraints to support the remains of the figure in niche no. 187. Several of the Salisbury figures are spectacularly thin, because their niches have flat rather than concave backs, making them especially vulnerable to decay.

---

[5] They are not shown in Spratt's 1737 drawing (fig. 49), nor in any of the later 18th- or early 19th-century illustrations.

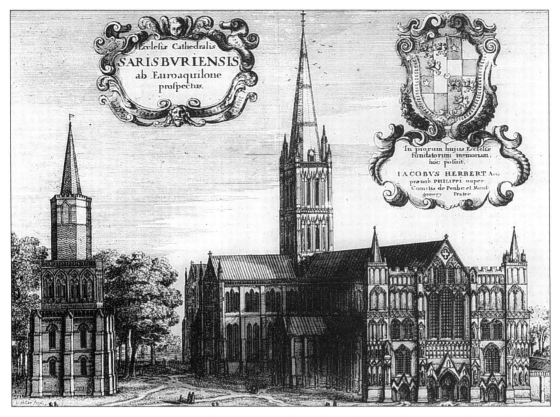

48   The west front, drawn and engraved by W. Hollar, published in W. Dugdale, *Monasticon Anglicanum*, III, 1673, following p.374. Salisbury and South Wiltshire Museum.

The precise dates of the suggested deliberate removals and possible repairs remain obscure. The evidence for the destruction of images in the cathedral, both before and after the Marian reaction, has recently been reviewed.[6] An early date should perhaps be preferred for the removal of the proposed prominent images of the Virgin, although, in the cathedral treasury, a statue survived until 1644. In the 1620s repair work at high level seems to have been undertaken in the cathedral, extending to the west end of the nave, since the date '1620' is carved in the spandrel above the central and northern of the west windows. Parliamentarian troops occupied the Close in the Civil War, but it is impossible now to say now whether this affected the west front sculpture.[7] The spandrel figures in the Chapter House are reported to have been damaged at this time.[8]

[6]   RCHME 1999, pp.32–40.
[7]   For a partisan view, see Waylen 1857.
[8]   RCHME 1999, p.181.

It is only after the Civil War that visual records allow any assessment of the front. The earliest known relatively detailed representation is in a view of the cathedral from the north-west, a print, drawn and engraved by Wenceslaus Hollar (d.1677), published 1673, in Dugdale's *Monasticon Anglicanum* (fig. 48).[9] The present survey suggests that it was based on careful observation in various respects, such as the omission of sculpture in Zone B of the central buttresses and in the 11 niches over the central porch. This is also the first record of the crenellations that had been added in the later middle ages. He is not entirely reliable, however. His north view of the cathedral, dated 1672, incorrectly includes two complete tiers of sculpture on the north turret,[10] whereas the survey found evidence only for the lower of these. A south-west prospect was made in the same year as Dugdale's publication by Robert Thacker 'Designer to the King'.[11] A related drawing shows many sculptures clustered around the buttresses, but excludes some that must have been in their present positions and invents others.[12] If Hollar exaggerated the horizontal effect of the survivals, Thacker elaborated upon the vertical.

The Eighteenth Century

The condition of the front becomes clearer in the visual record through the 18th and early 19th centuries. By 1737, it is almost certain that there was the same number of full-length figures or subjects as remained until the 1860s. This is revealed in a dated view by Thomas Spratt, in pen and ink and wash, now in the Society of Antiquaries (fig. 49).[13] The figures are shown indistinctly in pencil, but in all the positions known from later sources. It is not known under what circumstances this drawing was made, but its accuracy is evident in the inclusion of the bird over the mandorla in the great gable (no. 23) and of the little bracket for a lost sculpture to the right of the south-west door (no. 208), a relatively inconspicuous detail. Like Thacker, he shows a low wood barrier, with gaps, set some distance in front of the porches. These would be replaced by tall iron railings, across the buttresses, in the early 19th century.

The extent to which the ancient fabric was repaired is harder to assess. The freshness of newly tooled stone is rapidly reduced by weathering, and the longer the weathering

[9] W. Dugdale, *Monasticon Anglicanum*, III, 1673, following p.374; NMR, Cobb Collection, 'Salisbury & Malmesbury' album, f.13 (with the dedication, 'In piorum hujus Ecclesiae fundatorum memoriam hoc posuit, IACOBUS HERBERT, Arm. praenob. Philippi nuper Comitis de Penbr. et Montgomery frater'; Salisbury, Salisbury and South Wiltshire Museum, PD 70). Hollar was in England 1636–44, 1652–77. Byrne engraved a version for the monumental re-edition, W. Dugdale, *Monasticon Anglicanum*, ed. J. Caley et al., VI, pt iii, London, 1830, following p.1292.

[10] W. Dugdale, *Monasticon Anglicanum*, III, 1673, following p.374; Salisbury and South Wiltshire Museum, PD 69; NMR, Cobb Collection, 'Salisbury & Malmesbury' album, f.12 (with the dedication, 'Pristinae Pietatis memoriae, hoc posuit, Rev. in Christo Pater Seth Saresbur's Episcopus, Ao 1672'). Dugdale's northern view may have influenced the undated 'North West Prospect of the Cathedrall Church of St. Mary Salisbury', engraved by Collins (London, Society of Antiquaries, Coleraine Collection, VII, f.13), which again shows figures in the two lower tiers.

[11] Bodl., Gough Maps 41K, f.8.

[12] RCHME 1999, fig. 142.

[13] London, Society of Antiquaries, Coleraine Collection, VII, f.14.

has been taking place the more nearly the newer stone resembles the original. Furthermore, in the period up to the later 18th century, prior to the introduction of cements, the lime mortar mixes tended to consist of the same basic ingredients: one part of lime putty to two or three parts of a local and easily obtained aggregate – more often than not the stonedust produced from working the new block, itself usually of the same geological origin as the primary fabric. A lime/Chilmark stonedust mortar mix made in 1300 and one made in 1600, 1700, 1800 – or even 2000 – will not be substantially different. The mortars fixing two later medieval insertions, the corbel of the niche in the south side of the central porch and the corbel to the south of the south door, are both very similar to the standard mix from the primary fabric. For these reasons, it is possible that periodic repairs have remained unremarked during the current survey of the façade.

The difficulty of identifying such early interventions may be exemplified on the northern spirelet. Here there is an area of masonry bonded with a white lime mortar which is apparently identical with that of the 13th-century fabric, but where oyster-shell gallets, which are absent elsewhere, appear in almost every joint. This represents a discrete patch surrounded by the more normal jointing. It is tempting to suggest that it represents merely the temporary availability of oyster shells during the original construction, or perhaps a group of new fixer masons using an 'outside' technique; but the joints themselves are unusually wide and it seems more likely that this is an area of repair or refixing. It is known that the great spire over the central tower has been struck and damaged by lightning several times (in 1431, 1641 and 1741 at least); perhaps the north spirelet was similarly damaged and this rebuilding represents the subsequent repair.

49 'The West Front of Salisbury Cathedral', drawing by Thomas Spratt, dated 1737. Society of Antiquaries, London, Coleraine Collection, VII, f.14.

The earliest repairs that can be identified on the basis of differences in the bonding mortar fall into three groups: an orange mix found only in the blocking of the niche in the south elevation of the central porch (see above); a white lime and coloured sand mix, similar to that associated with repairs to the cloister buttresses specified by Sir Christopher Wren following his 1669-89 surveys, but probably not executed until the 18th century; and a pinkish lime mortar mix containing crushed brick or tile in its aggregate (fig. 50).

The second of these is found only bonding putlog hole filler-blocks in Zone A on the southern link wall between nave and stair turret, suggesting that an inspection scaffold was erected here in the 17th or early 18th centuries, but that little structural work was done. The red aggregate mix is the most widespread and has also been found as a pointing medium on the south nave clerestory.[14] On the façade it is generally associated with repairs and repointing to the heads of the buttress niches on Zones C and D, where the canopies project outwards from the buttress face. It is likely that a fall of stone (perhaps a finial) from one of these positions led to a brief scaffolding and inspection of the other positions to ensure that the canopies and the medieval sculptures beneath them were secure. The gable stone containing a head in a quatrefoil over niche no. 87 was renewed as part of this campaign, and the renewal is a passable imitation of the medieval work. It is probably best dated to the second half of the 18th century.

The style of a number of the finials on pinnacles around the cathedral, including that on the apex of the southern spirelet, is distinctly 18th-century in character. Those on the west front were refixed by Scott in the 19th century, so that the original mortar is not available for comparison. It is, however, evident from these survivals that repair work at high level must have been undertaken on a regular basis to minimise the danger of falling stonework.

Repair work to the medieval central west doors may well have taken place in 1722 (and perhaps again in 1744). The engraved brass lock-case on the interior of the northern leaf is inscribed 'Taylor fecit 1722', and on the exterior the earliest graffito is 'I.K. 1722', perhaps the initials of one of the workmen. Two further graffiti – 'I. Thring 1744' and 'CC 1744' – cut into the same plank on the exterior of the north leaf could relate to a second episode of repair. Red paint fills these 18th-century graffiti, indicating that a painting of the doors in this colour took place after this time.

James Wyatt's Restoration

The façade suffered much less at the hand of James Wyatt than the interior of the cathedral. His main alterations were to the glazing, but it is likely that he was also responsible for the renewal of the gable cross (fig. 50). The existing cross is carved from a fine-grained Bath stone, and may have been a Latin cross with foliate terminals

---

[14] Jones 1995, record drawings.

before Scott's restoration, when the four curved stones forming the wheel were renewed or inserted.[15]

Between 1788 and 1792 Wyatt oversaw the destruction of much medieval glass in the cathedral and its replacement with plain glazing.[16] Francis Eginton's Birmingham workshop was responsible for the new glazing of the Trinity Chapel, with diamond panes in reddish-brown bearing roses, and it seems likely that the geometrically patterned west windows were also made by this workshop; their general form is shown in Le Keux's engraving of the front (endpaper). In inserting the new glass Wyatt appears to have followed the medieval system of enclosing the glass within a wooden frame, which was then fitted into rebates in the external faces of the jambs and retained on internal ferramenta.[17] On the exterior, iron holdfasts were hammered into each of the bed-joints of the jambs and nailed on to the face of the wooden frame; many of these have survived, being flattened and bent back during later repairs. The new frames were painted red and it is possible that the red paint on the exterior of the west doors is also of this period.

The Wyatt windows survived for only about thirty years before they were replaced, between 1819 and 1824, with ancient glass assembled by the local glazier John Beare, as reported in the *Salisbury Journal*.[18] It is to this period that most of the dated graffiti on the stones of the window heads belong.[19] In 1880 William Osmond, mason to the cathedral, wrote a memorandum which recorded all the work that the family firm had undertaken there since 1818 and noted that his father was employed in 'June 1824 Cutting holes and fixing bars to the 2 side compartments of the West window'.[20] This, taken with the incised dates on the central west window, suggests that the centre light was prepared and fixed first (the old glass being taken down perhaps in 1822

[15] Nash's drawing for Dodsworth 1814 (opp. p.128) is generally the most accurate of the engravings for this period and shows a Latin cross; Mackenzie's drawing for Britton 1836, pl. V (also c.1814) shows a wheel cross, but omits the eagle from the gable beneath, casting some doubt on its accuracy. The cross was repaired in or slightly before 1866 under a different contract to the main restoration and, therefore, does not appear in Scott's detailed specification for the first phase of his repair. Infuriatingly the pre-1866 photographs do not show the cross, or show insufficient detail to establish the original form.

[16] The glass is not dealt with here, only the fixings of the glazing as they affect the masonry of the façade. For Wyatt's work, see Dodsworth 1814, pp.177–84; Cobb 1980, pp.111–14. For the glass, see Spring 1979, pp.5–7; RCHME 1999, pp.97, 99.

[17] The frames and ferramenta of the west windows were probably subject to numerous minor repairs in the five hundred years prior to Wyatt's reglazing, but little physical evidence of them has been found on the jambs beyond occasional (and apparently piecemeal and random) slots, probably for the insertion of iron reinforcements.

[18] In June 1824 the Salisbury Journal reported: 'The great window of our church is now compleated. It is composed of various portions of stained glass, some taken from different parts of the Cathedral, and other parts were purchased in London, having been collected on the Continent. The whole has been extremely well arranged by Mr. Beare of this city. It is very appropriate to the elegant edifice in which it is placed, and the brilliancy of the effect cannot fail to satisfy the lover of ancient glass.' Quoted in Spring 1997, p.2.

[19] All three window heads bear the name or initials of J. G. Bodenham, while the central light has 'H. R.', 'I. Burgess' and 'W. Rand[ell]', with the dates 1822 and 1823 – these almost certainly being amongst the workmen who removed and refixed the glazing at these dates. On the interior of the south window head is the pencilled legend: 'J Coles, window scaffolded to this height June 1879', from an otherwise unrecorded intervention.

[20] Osmond 1880.

and the new window inserted in 1823), before the two side lights were fixed in the summer of 1824.

The Osmond Family Workshop

The Osmonds were engaged upon various projects in and around the cathedral for over sixty years, from 1818 into the 1880s. William Osmond (1791-1875), a friend of A. W. N. Pugin from the 1830s (who is supposed to have persuaded him of the virtues of the Gothic style),[21] was the head of a family firm of masons working from a yard at 13 St John Street, opposite St Ann's Gate into the Cathedral Close. Much of the frontage (complete with Neoclassical porch and Doric columns) and the monumental inscription still survive. Both William and his son William Jnr (1821-1890) were capable sculptors, responsible for a considerable output of high-quality sepulchral monuments, at least thirty-five of which were produced between 1820 and 1862.[22] The lack of dated examples after 1862 may indicate that they were the speciality of William Snr, and that their production lapsed in his old age. As well as undertaking maintenance works at the Bishop's Palace, the family executed the repairs to the Poultry Cross that recreated its superstructure in 1852-54.

In August 1820, Osmond blocked the quatrefoils in the singers' gallery and undertook a campaign of repointing on the west front. It is likely that this was done in either Roman cement or ashes and lime mortar. Both are found in restricted areas on the stonework and in the cracking systems associated with the settlement of the south turret. The upper surfaces of the medieval string-courses had been severely eroded by drip-action and the cavities created in this way were filled with Roman cement either at this time or in 1866-69. Two years later, in 1822, while the west windows were under repair, Osmond was engaged in fixing iron railings outside the west doors, as the 'Memorandum' records. Earlier engravings show low barriers at the west doors, but photographs by Fenton, c.1858 (figs. 16, 64), show railings across all three.

The Osmonds' main (albeit temporary) contribution to the west front was the renewal of the decayed Purbeck shafts, capitals and bases around the west windows, in Chilmark stone, in 1856.[23] This work was executed using a brown 'Roman' cement,[24] traces of which remain. Similar partial replacements had taken place at Wells in the

---

[21] Osmond was producing Gothic monuments from at least 1828 (Bishop Fisher, Salisbury Cathedral), however, when Pugin was only 16 years old. According to Edward Pugin, A. W. N. Pugin lived at Osmond's house before moving into St Marie's Grange, just outside Salisbury, which he had built in 1835. See Atterbury and Wainwright 1994, p.293 and p.43.

[22] Inventory of works based on those listed in Gunnis, RCHME Dorset, RCHME 1987 and the Buildings of England series.

[23] The 'Memorandum' states, in 1856, 'West Window of Nave repaired with new Chilmark stone. Columns – Bases and Caps. (External).'

[24] According to the 'Memorandum', this cement was used by the Osmonds on the Poultry Cross in 1852–54 and for pointing on the cathedral up to 1848, when Portland cement was adopted for the pointing of the spire.

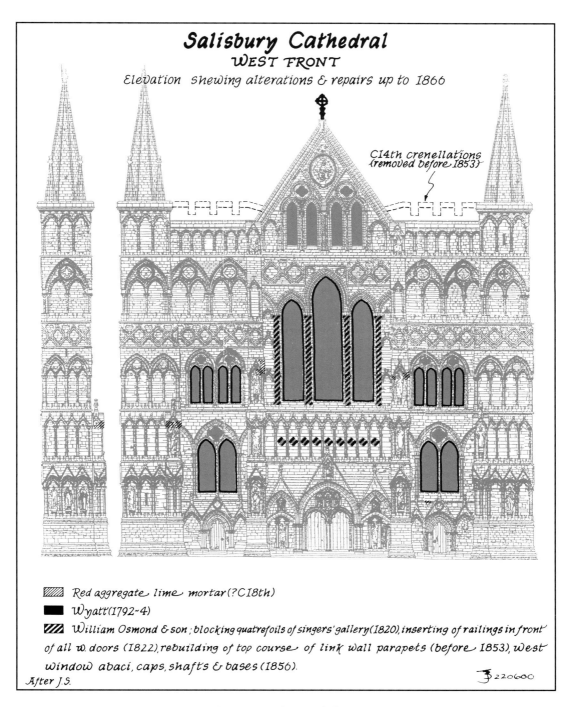

Salisbury Cathedral
WEST FRONT
Elevation shewing alterations & repairs up to 1866

C14th crenellations
(removed before 1853)

▨ Red aggregate lime mortar (?C18th)
■ Wyatt (1792-4)
▨ William Osmond & son; blocking quatrefoils of singers' gallery (1820), inserting of railings in front of all w. doors (1822), rebuilding of top course of link wall parapets (before 1853), west window abaci, caps, shafts & bases (1856).
After J.S.   220600

50 Alterations and repairs before 1866.

51 J. M. W. Turner, *West Front, Salisbury Cathedral*, watercolour on paper. Harris Museum and Art Gallery, Preston, Lancs., P1257.

1830s to 1850s, when the lost blue lias shafts were renewed in pale yellow Doulting stone. Both Scott at Salisbury and Benjamin Ferrey at Wells reversed these restorations completely, however, in order to maintain or reinstate the colour contrast intended by the medieval masons, despite the complaints of the cost-conscious Wells Chapter Clerk that the work had only recently been done. At Salisbury, Scott also reversed the Osmonds' other contribution to the west end, since in his 1866 specification he simply states, 'Take down and remove the iron railing'.

One other piece of work may have been undertaken by the Osmonds, though it is not mentioned in the 'Memorandum', namely the removal of the crenellated parapet that crowned the link-walls well into the 19th century. Shown in early 19th-century engravings, drawings and watercolours (endpaper, fig. 51), they were gone by March 1853, when William Russell Sedgfield took a dated photograph (fig. 60).

New Images of the Front

By this time, there was a far greater interest in the representation of the front, in paintings, prints and drawings. The concern was not necessarily with accuracy, but often rather with effect and the picturesque.[25] There are fine sketches and views by John Constable and J. M. W. Turner (fig. 51).[26] Other visitors were more antiquarian in intent, including Wyatt's implacable critic John Carter. In 1802, Carter made pencil sketches, which include detailed views of the sculptures then surviving (fig. 32).[27] Some of his work was published in the series 'Ancient Architecture of England' (pls. LXXIV, LXXV)[28] and a full view of the front was published on 1 June 1805.[29] Another distinguished antiquarian draughtsman J. Buckler made pencil sketches of both the north and west faces (Catalogue fig. 4).[30] More finished views are in the collection of the Wiltshire Archaeological and Natural History Society, Devizes.[31] From these, he produced prints: a view from the north-west, published May 1803,[32] and a view from the south-west, published March 1813.[33]

As interest in the medieval past gathered momentum, views of the front were produced and appeared in two volumes, one in a local context and the other as part of a wider survey. Dodsworth's *Historical Account of the Episcopal See, and Cathedral Church, of Sarum, or Salisbury*, 1814, includes views of both the west front and the north porch (with the front's north turret) drawn by F. Nash.[34] The relevant engravings in Britton's study of the cathedral (published 1836) are less accurate.[35] Cockerell's book on the *Iconography of the West Front of Wells Cathedral*, published in 1851, includes an appendix 'on the sculptures of other medieval churches in England', in which he describes the Salisbury figures.[36] He also made drawings, which are now in the drawings

[25] An engraving in the Cobb Collection, album for 'Salisbury & Malmesbury', NMR, Swindon, shows no sculpture at all: a NE view, by G. B. Jackson, publ. 8 August 1761 (f.16). Nor do a pen sketch of the west front, dated 21 August 1769 (Bodl., Gough Maps 32, f.46v); and a pen and wash study of about 1800 in the Victoria & Albert Museum (Department of Prints, Drawings and Paintings, E638-1920). S. H. Grimm had painted the west front from the SW a number of times. The most detailed version is a grisaille in pen and wash, in Oxford, dated 'September 1777', but there is another image in colour in Oxford and a second in the Salisbury and South Wiltshire Museum, Salisbury (Bodl., Gough Maps 32, ff.44v (grisaille), 45r (colour)); Salisbury and South Wiltshire Museum, PD 112, dated 'c.1775'. According to a note on the back of a photograph in the Conway Library, Courtauld Institute, the colour version was exhibited at the Royal Academy, 1778. From his work, an aquatint was made by V. Green and F. Jukes, 1779 (Bodl., Gough Maps 32, f.45v).

[26] Preston, Harris Museum and Art Gallery, P1257, Turner's view from the SW. His watercolour of the north porch, 1796, includes the east and north faces of the north turret (Salisbury and South Wiltshire Museum, Salisbury). Constable's many sketches of the cathedral include several views of the front (G. Reynolds, Victoria and Albert Museum, *Catalogue of the Constable Collection*, London, 1960, e.g. cat. nos. 187, 195, pls. 147, 150).

[27] BL, Add. MS 29939, ff.32–43.

[28] London, Victoria & Albert Museum, Department of Prints, Drawings and Paintings, 29481-33 (west front and plan, 'J.C. dt 1802', published 1 June 1805), 29481-34 (details).

[29] Illustrated in Cochrane 1971, p.8.

[30] BL, Add. MS 36392, ff.21v–22 (August 1802), 35, 39, 40 (1811), 42 ('Augt. 1813 & 14'), 47 (1811), 55v (1811), 78, 85 (1813), 87 (1811), 89 (1811).

[31] John Buckler Collection, IX, pp.35–37. Illustrated in RCHME 1993b, pl. 52.

[32] Bodl., Gough Maps 41K, f.10.

[33] Bodl., MS Dep. a 23, f.33.

[34] Dodsworth 1814, pls. opposite pp.128, 182. They were published independently in 1813 and 1814, respectively.

[35] Britton 1836, pls. IV ('North Porch', drawn by F. Mackenzie), pl. V ('West Front', Mackenzie), XVIII ('West End ...', drawn by R. Cattermole). These had been published independently in 1815 and 1814, respectively.

[36] Cockerell 1851, pp.95–98. His preliminary notes are in the library of the RIBA: Cockerell Papers, Box 6, CoC.1/83, 'Notes for *The Iconography* ...', [pp. ii–iii].

collection of the Royal Institute of British Architects (Catalogue, fig. 3).[37] Such publications contributed to a growing respect for and greater understanding of the medieval fabric.

By the time that G.G. Scott's restoration was underway, a new medium had been developed and the cathedral proved as attractive to photographers as it had to the watercolourists, painters and engravers that the new medium challenged. This interest and its uses are examined elsewhere in the present volume by Anthony Hamber.

G.G. Scott's Restoration, 1866–69

Scott's restoration, as revealed by the current recording programme, has proved to be remarkably conservative in extent and nature, even by modern standards of architectural conservation. His reputation as a heavy-handed restorer derives probably from his debates with Petit in the 1840s, Ruskin in the 1850s and Morris in the 1870s, all of whom represented the anti-restoration movement. In regard to his work at Salisbury, it seems entirely undeserved.

An inveterate writer of papers on the aims and ethics of restoration, Scott described his approach to the repair of ancient church fabric on numerous occasions. He himself was wont to quote from a paper entitled 'A Plea for the Faithful Restoration of Ancient Churches':

> Restorers, even when disposed to be conservative, often mistake the true meaning and object of restoration, which is not to make a building look as if it were new, but (so far as concerns the fabric) to put it in seemly repair; to replace features which have been actually destroyed by modern imitations, *where they can be indisputably traced*; to clear the ancient surface from modern over-laying, and to check the progress of decay and dilapidation. The more of the ancient material *and the ancient surface* remain, and the less new introduced, the more successful the restoration. If more cannot be saved, even one or two old bemossed stones, in a window or a cornice, give value and truthfulness to the work; but when it is possible, *all* or the *great majority* of the old stones should retain their *untouched and unsmartened surface* ...[38]

In the same source he has this to say concerning the replacement of carved detail:

> An original detail (especially in carving), though partially decayed or mutilated, is infinitely more valuable than the most skilful attempt at its restoration. A decayed or broken capital, or bas-relief, retains a beauty and an interest which can never attach to a perfected copy; and it is much better, as a general rule, to leave such fragments of art

---

[37] RIBA, British Architectural Library, Drawings Collection, H10, unnumbered pencil drawings. Brief notes for his section on Salisbury are in the RIBA Library: Cockerell Papers, Box 6, CoC.1/83, folded sheet.

[38] From a letter dated 1 July 1859 to the Dean of Lincoln, quoted in J. C. Buckler, *Lincoln Minster*, Oxford, 1866, p.10. The italics are Scott's own.

to tell their own story, which they will do with immeasurably greater truthfulness without our aid.[39]

An insight into the day-to-day practice on a site under Scott's direction was given by his devoted clerk of works James Irvine, recording a conversation which took place in 1870:

> On going over the scaffolding of the west front of Wells Cathedral with Mr. B. Ferrey R.I.B.A. before any cutting-out had taken place and when he officially put me in charge as his Clerk of Works, he asked me what orders Mr. G. G. Scott had given me as to the repairs of the West Front of the Bath Abbey. I told him Mr. Scott's orders were 'Not to remove one inch of old work that could be preserved', and that if we had any doubt about the necessity of removing any part, however small, to leave it untouched until he himself should see it, and decide in person, and to always err on the side of leaving work uncutaway.[40]

In referring to the general repair of the exterior of Salisbury Cathedral, Scott himself says:

> The stone, though generally in fair preservation, was partially decayed, and the whole building was gone through carefully and conservatively, replacing only such stones as were irrecoverably perished.[41]

The extent and nature of the replacements tend to confirm that Scott's practice matched his theory (fig. 52). The bulk of the renewed stonework consists of the addition or replacement of consoles for figure sculpture, capitals and shafts, together with restricted repairs to string-courses and arches.

Scott's 1866 Specification

Scott's original 16-page specification for the central section of the façade, representing the first phase of the work, survives in the cathedral archive.[42] The general instructions serve to underline its careful and conservative nature, and could be beneficially inserted into some modern specifications:

> The dimensions of the various works required to be executed are to be ascertained by the contractor with the assistance of the Clerk of the Works from careful admeasurements of the ancient portions of the building with which the new must correspond both as regards details and dimensions.

---

[39] *Ibid.*
[40] Wells Cathedral Archive, CBD Bundle 32.
[41] Scott 1879, p.300.
[42] Dean and Chapter Archives, Salisbury Cathedral.

To ensure a close match between the old and new work:

> All stones to be dressed in precisely the same manner as the ancient stones of similar work.

Close and careful control of the cutting out of old work was being exercised in the same way that James Irvine outlined to Benjamin Ferrey, so that,

> ... no old work is to be cut out without special instructions from the architect or clerk of the works.

Where such work as had to be removed was of interest, it was to be preserved for future study:

> All unusual fragments of carved work sculptured works and stones, all coins, antiquities, and other objects of interest are to be reserved, carefully preserved and deposited in such place as will be directed.

With regard to the specific schedule of replacement, this is considerably more extensive than the work which was actually carried out. As with many modern specifications, it may be more an assessment for the purposes of pricing the work than an accurate record of what was intended to be done. It certainly serves as a warning against evaluating Scott's work on a building from his specification alone.

At least one aspect of the specification was reversed subsequent to closer examination of the fabric. There are several references to the cleaning of the stonework within the central west porch,[43] but this was not carried out, presumably because the wealth of medieval paint became apparent. Scott was also repairing original stonework with small dark mortar patches, presumably colour matched to the discoloured stonework, so that the damaged blocks could be retained – in all 178 such repairs were specified within the porch.

Scott's Work as Executed

The repairs specified by Scott were carried out by G. P. White of Pimlico, who had already been employed at Salisbury, as the reference that the Dean of Salisbury supplied to Dean Johnson of Wells in 1870 makes clear:

> ... I have the greatest pleasure in answering your inquiries respecting Mr White. He was recommended to us originally by Mr Clutton, the Architect, under whose direction our Chapter House was restored. That work was executed by Mr White in a manner so entirely to our satisfaction, that when we entered upon the more arduous undertaking of restoring the Cathedral itself, it was committed to him by Mr Scott, in consequence of the high character we were able to give him.

[43] For example: '... cleanse and point the stone ribs and groining', and 'cleanse and point all the old stonework' in the blind arcades.

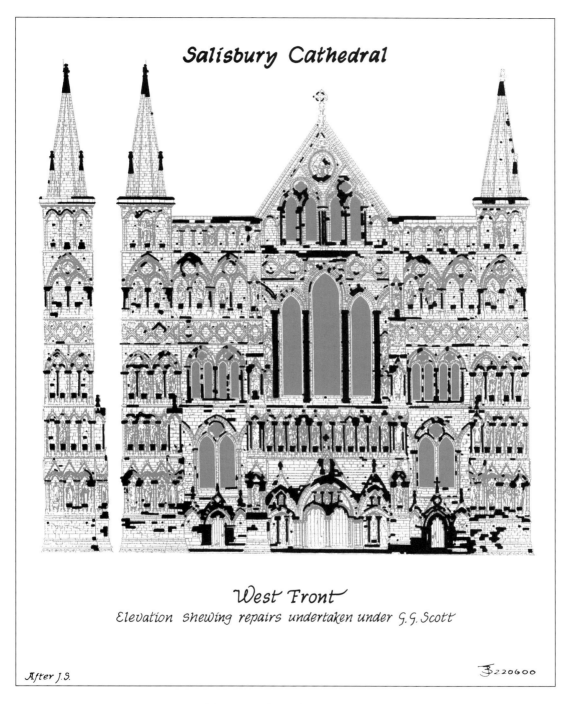

Salisbury Cathedral

West Front

Elevation shewing repairs undertaken under G.G. Scott

After J.S.

220600

52   The extent of G.G. Scott's restorations.

During the five years that he has been thus engaged, he has continued to deserve our unabated confidence – in proof of which I may mention that having now completed the Exterior we have intrusted him with the restoration of the Interior, which we have just commenced.

From what I have stated you will understand that I have no hesitation in saying that, as far as I have had an opportunity of judging, you could not employ a more efficient and trustworthy man than Mr White.[44]

The work on the façade was to be undertaken on the basis of two successive contracts:[45] the first, which began immediately upon the signing on 10 August 1866, comprised the central screen and the central pair of buttresses which frame it. The second comprised the repair of the stonework of the west elevations of the aisles and the stair turrets. At that time the estimated cost of the two contracts was given as £2,272 and £1,991 respectively, probably reflecting the degree of complexity in the repair of the central porch.

Scaffolding had been erected on at least part of the west front by early April 1866,[46] and in his specification, signed in August, Scott notes that 'the Cost of the Scaffolding which has been already erected is included in the amount of this contract'. It may well be that the whole of the centre screen was entirely scaffolded, since the cross at the apex of the gable is referred to in the specification as being in 'the former Contract', and is not itemised for repair.

The stone which Scott drew for his renewals is paler and generally coarser than that of the 13th-century fabric, he recorded that:

> I made a very careful survey of the Chilmark and Tisbury quarries, and selected nearly all the stone to be used from what is called the 'trough bed' at Chilmark, which is a bed but little used in the old work, though superior in strength and durability to any of the others. It is almost a pure limestone, very shelly and hard, and was left unused by the old masons simply because the quarries were subterraneous, and this bed formed their ceiling. There is a corresponding bed in one of the quarries at Tisbury (that nearest to the village), but it is not so hard or good as that one bed at Chilmark. The quarries at Teffont I do not know, but I believe that they also contain this bed.[47]

Scott's stone is quite variable. On the body of the west front, particularly on the west face, the pale, very shelly variety of this bed predominates. On the south turret's

---

44 Wells Cathedral Archive, DC/ Add. 2012/97: letter dated 22 February 1870, the Dean (H. P. Hamilton) of Salisbury's reference for George Peter White of (39 (later 152) Vauxhall Bridge Road) Pimlico.

45 Neither contract survives, but a copy of the first is preserved at Wells, where it was used as a model for the contracts (also let to G. P. White) for the restoration of the west front between 1870 and 1874: Wells Cathedral Archive, DC/ Add. 2013/1–4.

46 *The Times*, 3 April 1866, p.5.

47 Scott 1879, pp.300–301. The new stone is fixed using Roman cement, but is pointed with the harder Portland cement. Scott used Roman cement to fix the new tracery of the west window of Bath Abbey in c.1870–74.

south and east faces the stone, while pale, is generally less shelly; while on the rest of the turret the greyer bed seems to have been used for the few stones which were renewed. The very earliest figure sculptures by Redfern, the Christ in Majesty and the Angels from Zone A, are also carved in stone from the trough bed, but all of the remainder are carved from a bed of the softer, more consistent building stone – presumably the shelly inclusions made the block too unpredictable for figure sculpture.

Outside the central west porch Scott renewed lost or irreparably damaged Purbeck marble with a blue-grey fossiliferous Devonshire marble veined in red. The colour is not a particularly good match for the iron-rich bed of Purbeck, which weathers to a dark brown, and this was particularly obvious in the west porch, where the two stones were placed side by side at ground level. A colour treatment had to be applied to the new stone in order to tone it in with the original.[48]

Within the porch Scott retained the 13th-century Purbeck capitals and repaired them with newly carved Purbeck, set in a hard brown mastic or glue which has turned grey over time. The central shaft between the doors was also renewed in Purbeck marble.[49] Scott was careful to preserve at least one stone of the original Purbeck cusping in the inner order on each of the three doors, to ensure that the evidence on which his Devonshire marble restorations were based still remained. The openwork middle order of the central west doors had been smashed, leaving only fragments adhering to the parent block at the extreme edges (fig. 16). Scott kept these, reconstructing a richly complex foliate latticework around them.

Faithful copies of carved work were made elsewhere on the façade, perhaps the most important of these from an archaeological perspective being the renewed consoles for the new figure sculptures. In the upper tiers Scott's carvers adapted the surviving 13th-century console in niche no. 95, but in the lowest tier he used the 14th-century foliate and ballflower forms which survived on the consoles in niche no. 169 and nos. 178 and 187 respectively. However, by far the most important and controversial item in Scott's restoration was the repair of the medieval figure sculptures and the creation of new figures for the majority of the empty niches on the west elevation of the façade.

J. F. Redfern's Figure Sculpture

The Revd H. T. Armfield, a minor canon of Salisbury Cathedral, was Scott's principal adviser on the iconography of the sculpture of the west front. His scheme was based

[48] It is possible that this problem finally deterred Benjamin Ferrey from using this stone at Wells, to replace the lost blue lias elements. His initial proposals of September 1868 had specified Devonshire marble, but the work was executed in Kilkenny marble.

[49] In June 1869 John Haysom wrote to the Wells Cathedral Restoration Committee, 'I beg to inform you that I have a good stock of Purbeck Marble, and should you in your restoration require any I shall be most happy to serve you. I have just sent some to Salisbury Cathedral. The Clerk of Works came down to the Quarry and took out the sizes they required and he expressed himself quite satisfied with the quality.' Wells Cathedral Archive, DC/Add. 2012/45.

53 'St Christopher', in Mrs Jameson, *Sacred and Legendary Art*, revised edition, London, 1891, p. 446.

upon C.R. Cockerell's interpretation of the remains of the medieval scheme.[50] A writer in *The Builder* observed, quoting from the Dean and Chapter's report on the restoration programme of 1869:

> The Late Professor Cockerell has stated that there were originally on the exterior of the Cathedral 160 figures of which 123 stood on the West Front. From a minute examination of them it was inferred that the whole series of the West Front formed a *Te Deum* or theological scheme.[51]

Armfield devised a 'meaning-grid' illustrating the relationships between the various saints, prophets and angels based upon the *Te Deum Laudamus*. Below the Christ in Majesty were ranged:

> … a tier of angels; a tier of Old Testament patriarchs and prophets; a tier of apostles; a tier of doctors, virgins and martyrs, and beneath them all, a tier of worthies eminent specially in the English Church, and some of them particularly connected with the diocese of Salisbury, comprising founders, bishops, martyrs and princes.[52]

Armfield published two works describing the scheme: *The Legend of Christian Art illustrated in the Statues of Salisbury Cathedral* (1869) and *Guide to the Statues in the West Front of Salisbury Cathedral, being a chapter from the Legend of Christian Art* (1869).

His main source for the details was Anna Jameson's book, *Sacred and Legendary Art*, as he explained.[53] The placing of the Apostles and the Evangelists below the Prophets and Patriarchs he states to have been influenced by this. The grouping of the Patron Saints of Christendom, 'those saints who had not a scriptural or apostolic sanction, yet were invested by the popular and universal faith with paramount authority' (St

---

[50] Cockerell 1851, pp.95–98.
[51] *The Builder*, 15 May 1869, p.384.
[52] Armfield 1869b, p.5.
[53] Armfield 1869a, pp.12–13: 'Of modern books in English I have had constantly before me Mrs Jameson's *Sacred and Legendary Art* – a book which is full of noble sentiment, as it is accurate in fact and elegant in diction. Its accomplished author has, I observe, relied in great part upon the *Legenda Aurea*, a fountain which has also been open to me.'

George, St Sebastian, St Roch, SS Cosmas and Damian, St Christopher and St Nicholas, nos. 134-40),[54] together with the four Virgin Martyrs (St Barbara, St Katherine, St Margaret and St Ursula, nos. 132-33, 141-42), also appears to be derived from it. So too were the Four Latin Fathers (nos. 119-22) and Four Great Virgins of the Latin Church (nos. 152-55).[55]

The iconography of some individual statues was, to varying degrees, derived from the text and engravings of the third edition, published in 1857.[56] The St Christopher (no. 137), for example, appears to be based upon the engraving of Paolo Farinato's drawing, dated to 1560 by Mrs Jameson (fig. 53). Although the figure has been elongated to fit the shape of the niche, the pose, drapery and attributes are all similar. The statue is also very much in the spirit of the text:

> The allegory, in whatever sense we interpret it is surely very beautiful: to my fancy there is something quite pathetic in these old pictures of St Christopher, where the great simple-hearted, good-natured giant, tottering under his incomprehensible burden, looks up with a face of wonder at the glorious child, who smiles encouragement and gives his benediction from above.[57]

The figures of Roch, Cosmas and Damian (nos. 134, 139, 140) are again influenced by both the text and the illustrations, but are rather more freely adapted (fig. 54). Some figures, such as the virgin patronesses, however, may have been derived from other as yet unidentified sources, as they do not seem to be related to Mrs Jameson's illustrations or text at all.

It appears that the scheme was revised at least once as work on the west front progressed. An undated drawing showing Armfield's scheme in the cathedral archives

[54] Jameson 1857, p.v.

[55] An early draft for the iconography, in the cathedral archives, also included Jameson's group of Deacon Martyrs.

[56] In his youth, the sculptor Redfern is reported to have worked from woodcuts: *Dictionary of National Biography*, ed. L. Stephen and S. Lee, XVI, London, 1921–22 edn, p.819.

[57] Jameson 1857, p.445.

includes names for intended figures in virtually all of the niches (fig. 55), whereas the list of statues yet to be provided in Armfield's 1869 pamphlet includes only those for the empty niches on the west elevation and the returns of the west-facing buttresses. Some of the Redfern statues that were eventually installed also deviate from Armfield's original plan. The censing angels intended for the niches flanking the central nave windows, for instance, were abandoned in favour of a set of the Evangelists (nos. 89-92).

The sculptor selected by Scott to execute the statues was James F. Redfern, who was described at the time as 'a sculptor of rising reputation'.[58] The *Building News* described the sculptor's background and early career at some length in an obituary which appeared in June 1876:

> Mr Redfern was born at Hartington, in the Dove Valley, near the Peak. Almost as soon as he could walk his taste for art was apparent, and he made attempts to draw figures on the flagstones of his father's cottage floor with a chalky material abounding in the neighbourhood known as 'idlestone'. In the same substance and with the aid of a pocket-knife he made his first essay in carving; under the direction of his father, who possessed some artistic skill, he had made wonderful progress 'ere he reached the age of six, when his father died. By the time he was sixteen his talents attracted the attention of the late Rev. Mr Winger of Hartington, at whose instigation the young sculptor carved, still with his favourite pocket-knife, but in alabaster instead of common 'idlestone', a group of a warrior and a dead horse. This piece coming into the possession of Mr Beresford-Hope, proved the turning point in the young artist's career. Mr Hope sent Redfern to a school where he had an opportunity of developing his still latent genius, and afterwards provided means for the completion of his studies under Continental masters.[59]

With Beresford-Hope's support Redfern was able to study under J. R. Clayton,[60] the well-known stained glass artist, who had begun his career as a sculptor, but also later in several continental ateliers, including that of Charles Gleyre, in Paris, where Monet and Renoir also studied.[61] By 1859 Redfern had settled in London. He exhibited at the Royal Academy between 1859 and 1876, mainly religious works designed for use as church decoration, the earliest being *Cain and Abel* in 1859 and a *Holy Family* in 1861.[62]

Redfern worked for Scott on a number of occasions, most famously producing eight figures of the Virtues for the Albert Memorial in London. The west front at Salisbury was his largest single commission, but he also provided sculpture for other

[58] *The Builder*, 15 May 1869, p.384.
[59] *Building News*, 23 June 1876, p.620.
[60] S. Redgrave, *A Dictionary of Artists of the British School*, London, 1878 (1970 facsimile), p.350.
[61] *Architects, Engineers and Building Trades Directory*, 1868.
[62] A. Graves, *The Royal Academy of Arts: a complete dictionary of exhibitors*, London, 1905, VI, p.246.

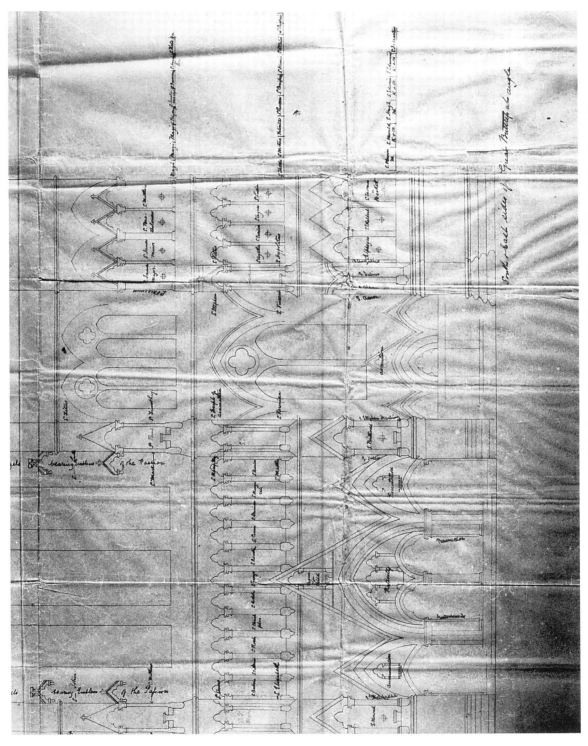

55 Part of a drawing for the iconographical scheme of the west front. Dean and Chapter Archives, Salisbury Cathedral.

56 *(above)* J.F. Redfern's sculptures for the south porch of Gloucester Cathedral, commissioned 1870. J. Sampson.

57 *(right)* St John the Evangelist, from the west front (no. 92).

restorations, including Lichfield and Ely Cathedrals, and Westminster Abbey. For the niches of the south porch of Gloucester Cathedral, statues of St Peter, St Paul, the Four Evangelists, King Osric, Abbot Serlo, St Jerome, St Augustine and St Gregory were commissioned in 1870, shortly after the main programme of work on the west front of Salisbury Cathedral had been completed. A number of these (St Mark, St Luke, St John the Evangelist, St Jerome and St Gregory) are strikingly similar to their counterparts on the west front (figs. 56, 57), in their facial characteristics and the forms of their drapery (nos. 89, 91, 92, 120, 121). The west front statue of St Mark is technically quite different from the other Redfern statues, however, and may have been executed from Redfern's designs by another workshop.

Scott regarded sculpture as an integral part of his architecture. A number of buildings feature elaborate schemes of sculptural decoration, such as the Foreign and India Offices (1863-68) and the Home and Colonial Offices (1870-74) in Whitehall, London, which are decorated in an Italian Renaissance style. Even if a lot of sculpture was not included in the original scheme, Scott sometimes made provision for adding it at a later date, as at the Gothic Midland Grand Hotel (1866-76) at St Pancras Station, London, where there are numerous empty niches.[63] However, it was quite unusual for such an extensive sculptural scheme to form part of a cathedral restoration.

The architect tended to exercise considerable control over the sculptural decoration of his buildings and he employed high calibre artists for figure sculpture, whenever this was feasible. He relied upon a handful of tried and tested sculptors and firms to provide architectural ornament. Typically he employed a number of artists to execute a wide range of different types of work: for example, John Birnie Philip, who worked for Scott primarily as a figure sculptor but sometimes provided decorative carving too. However, unlike Birnie Philip, Redfern produced only figurative sculpture. This may reflect the two sculptors' differing backgrounds. Redfern was, as we have seen, trained as a fine artist, whereas Birnie Philip began his career as a carver of decorative ornament.[64]

Initially, 30 statues were commissioned by the Restoration Committee from Redfern. They were to be paid for from funds raised by subscriptions, parochial collections and events such as a Choral Festival at Pewsey.[65] An annotated sketch of the front in the cathedral archives records this and several donations, as well as the cost of filling the empty niches with figures, assessed according to height (fig. 58).[66] The Revd C.B. Bicknell, rector of Stourton, had made a very large donation, by April 1868,[67] which was used to pay for the 11 Patron Saints of Christendom (nos. 132-42) beneath the great west window.[68] By May, Mr W.H. Poynder, of Rowhill, near Chippenham, had given money for two statues to fill the niches on either side of the west doors, St Osmund (no. 178b) and Bishop Brithwold (no. 187b).[69]

Developments on the west front of the cathedral were occasionally reported in the local, national and architectural press. Redfern was already preparing designs and models by January 1867, as a report in the *Building News* states:

> We have seen a model for one of the principal [figures] and are assured that the work
> is in good hands.[70]

[63] Read 1982, p.265.
[64] Read 1982, p.266.
[65] *The Builder*, 10 March 1866, p.173; *Salisbury and Winchester Journal*, 12 January 1867, p.5.
[66] Figures of 6ft. 6in., £53 each; 7ft., £65 each; 4ft. 9in., £30 each.
[67] *Salisbury and Winchester Journal*, 11 April 1868, p.5.
[68] *Salisbury and Winchester Journal*, 19 December 1868, p.6.
[69] *Salisbury and Winchester Journal*, 10 May 1868, p.5.
[70] *Building News*, 4 January 1867, p.3.

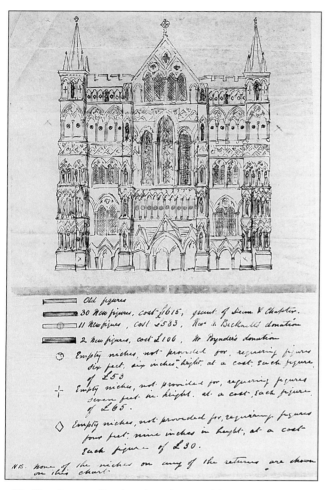

58 Drawing recording donations, the cost of future sculptures and the progress of work. Dean and Chapter Archives, Salisbury Cathedral.

This might well have been the model for the Christ in Majesty at the apex of the gable, as this was the first statue to be fixed in place around the beginning of October 1867.[71] It is carved from 'trough bed' Chilmark stone, the material preferred by Scott for his renewed stonework in the general repair programme. Four more sculptures (nos. 8, 14, 31, 37, all in the upper tier) are also carved from this bed, but the remainder derive from finer grained and more consistent beds. This suggests that Redfern was initially supplied with the coarse stone, but that, finding it intractable for producing fine detail, persuaded Scott to provide better carving block. This would place these five sculptures at the very start of the work and suggests that it progressed from the top downwards – the logical sequence, allowing the scaffolding to be struck as it continued.

The work progressed at a remarkably steady rate. Between about July 1867 and January 1870 55 statues were carved, that is seven to eight every four months. In December 1867 the *Sarum Almanac and Diocesan Kalendar* reported that seven of the smaller figures had been completed and put in place.[72] Fourteen statues, in addition to the Christ in Majesty, were in place by April 1868[73] and a report of December 1868 stated that 22 statues had been added during the year.[74] This rate of production is about two or three times that of a single copy carver, so it would appear that Redfern must have employed at least two or three carvers as workshop assistants.

[71] *Building News*, 4 October 1867, p.694. It seems likely that Redfern began his work at Salisbury by restoring the medieval sculpture.

[72] Quoted in *Salisbury and Winchester Journal*, 21 December 1867, p.7.

[73] *Salisbury and Winchester Journal*, 11 April 1868, p.7.

[74] *Salisbury and Winchester Journal*, 19 December 1868, p.6. The article refers to an account in *The Sarum Almanac and Diocesan Kalendar* for 1869.

It is likely that the sequence in which the statues were carved generally followed the pattern of the main restoration scheme, as the scaffolding could then be used to erect the statues once the rest of the repairs to the stonework and niches had been completed. The drawing in the cathedral archive, produced some time after May 1868, shows that the prophets tier (Zone B) was left uninhabited until well into the programme. Soon after the angels and Majesty had been fixed, the repair scaffold was probably struck, to near the base of Zone C, causing Redfern to concentrate on the sculptures for the lower parts of the elevation.

The donations of money towards the Patron Saints of Christendom and the figures flanking the central porch, recorded in April and May 1868, suggest that this area was being populated in mid-1868.[75] This probably represents the height of production in Zone D, which may have lasted throughout the year, to be followed by the Zone E figures and at least four of the prophets in Zone B, in 1869. Among the last sculptures of the main campaign were those of the central porch, installed in January 1870, and two of the prophets on the north link-wall.[76] Subsequent to 1869, Redfern carved two sculptures on the north elevation (nos. 116, 167), at least two of the Evangelists (certainly nos. 91-92; nos. 89-90 could be by another hand) and probably St Remigius (no. 125), which was fixed in 1873, with one other sculpture.[77]

Scott and Redfern's restored west front prompted a somewhat mixed response from critics in the later 19th and early 20th centuries. As early as 1870 a writer in *The Builder* expressed doubts about the archaeological accuracy of Scott's scheme and argued that modern 'decorative' sculptures were necessarily of far less importance than original medieval works, such as those at Wells.[78] Some writers at the turn of the 20th century were dismissive of the west front as a whole, regarding it as a 'sham' because it hid, rather than emphasised, the structure of the building. Ella Noyes wrote, in 1913:

> The West Front is the least interesting part of the church. The design is very much cut up and too elaborate, resulting in an effect of smallness; one resents its purely ornamental intention. It does not follow the architectural lines of the building, but is a mask designed, no doubt, chiefly for the display of sculpted figures in niches. These statues must once have been of great beauty, but now the lost or mutilated originals have all been replaced with bad modern substitutes ... Here and there a survivor of the old population still fills its place, supplied, alas! with a new head set on at a simpering angle.[79]

---

[75] *Salisbury and Winchester Journal*, 11 April, p.5; 10 May, p.5.
[76] *Salisbury Standard*, 8 January 1870, p.4.
[77] *The Times*, 22 September 1873.
[78] *The Builder*, 4 June 1870, p.437.
[79] Noyes 1913, p.85.

However, several popular guides to the cathedral presented more favourable reactions. *Brown's Strangers' Handbook and Illustrated Guide to Salisbury Cathedral* and *Ward & Lock's Historical Handbook and Guide to Salisbury Cathedral* both noted that the restoration had dramatically improved the appearance of the previously decaying front.[80] A short guide by Canon Fletcher, entitled *The Statues on the West Front of Salisbury Cathedral*, was first published in 1927 because, as he wrote in his introduction:

> So much interest is taken by visitors to Salisbury in the statues on the West Front of the Cathedral, and so frequently questions are asked as to whom they represent, that it has been thought a few notes on the subject might be helpful.[81]

Fletcher also drew his readers' attention to the remaining empty niches and informed them that further donations of statues would be welcomed. Shortly after, Allan Wyon carved the figure of Bishop Ken (no. 177), in 1930-31. Several other sculptures had been added to the west front subsequent to the main campaign and as many as four sculptors may be represented, although none has been identified by name. Before 1889 a figure of Job was carved (no. 61), and somewhere around 1900 Daniel was installed next to him (no. 62) – both figures were designated in Armfield's original scheme, although not for these niches. Three new figures in the lowest tier, however, had no place in it. The carving of King Henry VI (no. 168), on the north turret, and that of St Edmund of Canterbury (no. 172), nearby, probably date from the early years of the 20th century.[82] Bishop Ken is also an innovation.

Subsidence of the Southern Turret

One aspect of Scott's repairs has been examined only in the documentary sources, rather than from the building itself, namely the work that he undertook on the drainage system around the west front. In his autobiography he noted:

> The foundations were extensively examined all round the church, and underpinned or repaired where found necessary. They have been thoroughly defended by a mass of concrete surrounding them, with a channel formed above it.[83]

The nature of the channel and its associated drains on the west end was described in the 1866 specification, which was intended to be 'as has been already executed for the other parts of the Cathedral'.

There is no mention of underpinning on the façade at this time, although it is evident that movement had already occurred in several places. Around the head of the central west window there are signs of old settlement. It is possible that the course

---

[80] *Brown's Strangers' Handbook*, 1873 edn, pp.10–13, 33–35; *Ward & Lock's Historical Handbook*, 1889, pp.27–28.
[81] Fletcher 1927 (1928 edn), p.3.
[82] They are not shown in a photograph that shows Daniel *in situ*.
[83] Scott 1879, p.301.

of stonework which was replaced *c.*1866-69 above the west windows covers an inserted beam to spread the load away from the unstable area. However, the main cracking system is that on the south link-wall, where the instability was active from before the second quarter of the 19th century, as can be shown from the variety of mortars used to repoint it – ashes and lime mortar, Roman and Portland cements all being present. There are two successive applications of Portland cement associated with this cracking system and it is probable that the second can be dated to the period when Charles Ponting, the cathedral architect, had the southern stair turret underpinned in 1909.[84]

In that year, upon opening up the ground in this area, it was found that a layer of loamy clay existed between the base of the footings and the top of the gravel subsoil, and that the poor state of the drains had allowed this to wash out. Since this work provides our only insight into the form of the medieval foundations of the façade it is worth quoting part of the correspondence between Ponting and Canon Bernard:

> The foundations are of rubble masonry, with little or no mortar, and their projection beyond the walls is very insufficient, as measured by modern ideas. This is a common weakness in old work.
>
> It is of vital importance that this loam should be removed right through under the walls which form the shell of the turret … I advise therefore that a bed of cement concrete should be inserted under the foundations fully 2½ feet in depth and carried through the full thickness of the walls – about 5 feet, and left projecting 2 feet beyond the present footings. This can be done, with absolute safety, in small sections of about 2 ft to 2½ ft. in width, and it will entirely secure the masonry from any further settlement.
>
> … It would be of value in protecting the foundations from moisture, and lateral thrust, to fill up the trench with concrete to within a foot of the surface.[85]

Of interventions to the architectural fabric between Ponting's work and that undertaken in the 1960s, there is little sign. In the 20th century, increasing pollution levels and attack from acid rain accelerated the decay of the complex stonework, so that its condition by the 1990s was considerably worse than it had been before Scott's intervention. Many of the Redfern sculptures, only a century and a quarter old, were already in a state of advanced decay. The measures taken to conserve the front are discussed in a later chapter.

[84] The cracking is indicative of very slight rotation of the turret to the south: Andrew Waring, Report to the Dean and Chapter, Document 656/WF.
[85] Salisbury Cathedral Archive, letter from C. E. Ponting to Revd Chancellor Bernard, 2 February 1909.

Salisbury Cathedral

Niche 22

Niche 95
(St Paul)

Pierced quatrefoils retain
evidence of preparatory
treatment but no additional
layers

location of analysed white
deposit (?remains of ground)

Niche
178

Niche
195

Niches
166~8

Niche
169

Central Porch
interior & exterior

Angel
corbel

West Front
Elevation shewing medieval polychromy

After E.S.

₱ 220600

59 Distribution of paint traces across the west front.

The Polychromy

EDDIE SINCLAIR

The conservation of the west front was preceded by a survey of the entire façade for evidence of paint.[1] For such a survey to be commissioned ahead of a major conservation campaign marks a growing recognition, after centuries of neglect, of the important role of colour in architecture. Although there has been a growing realisation of the significance of colour within historic buildings, it has taken longer for that awareness to extend to exteriors.[2] At Salisbury, the surviving traces of paint are precious as they add to our fragmented knowledge of medieval exterior polychromy in general, but they also provide vital archaeological evidence that enhances our knowledge of this west front in particular.

In ecclesiastical architecture the painted decoration was more than an embellishment; it enhanced the dramatic impact of the liturgy. The intention was to decorate the most important liturgical elements with the richest of effects. It is not surprising, therefore, that at Salisbury the greatest concentration of surviving paint has been found within and around the central porch, with only fragmentary traces elsewhere. This area housed a statue of the Virgin Mary to whom the cathedral is dedicated. It was also the ceremonial entry for a great procession into the cathedral on Palm Sunday, when the central porch would provide a theatrical backdrop of colour and gilt, whilst the choir sang through the pierced quatrefoils above.[3]

Paint Survival

Whilst some paint will not have withstood the test of time, enough remains for it to be clear that the colour was not applied extensively. The deposits vary in scale from pin-head sized fragments, to stretches that span several centimetres; at times all that remains is a stain on the stone. They were found in just eight locations, with a ninth location apparently destined to receive paint (fig. 59). These are the central porch and the great west arch that frames it, with niches nos. 180 and 182 on the two porch gables, the gable niche of the Majestas (no. 22), St Paul in niche no. 95, niches nos.

---

[1] Reports, Phases 1 to 5.

[2] In 1991 the results of the polychrome survey of Exeter Cathedral west front, carried out 1979–83, were published (Sinclair 1991). This was the first time that such a survey had been undertaken on an English cathedral exterior.

[3] Sampson 1998, pp.170–71.

178 and 195, an angel corbel adjacent to the south-west doorway, the north face of the north turret (niche nos. 166-68) and niche no. 169. Inevitably, since only fragments of eight full-size medieval figures survive on the façade, most paint traces have been found on architectural elements. Of the original figures, just two retain evidence of paint: the deacon in niche no. 166 (see below) and St Paul in niche no. 95.

Of nearly two hundred niches, most polychromy survives on the lowest tier of figures. Here, six full-size niches (nos. 166-68, 169, 178, 195) and one full-size figure (the deacon in niche no. 166) retain colour, as do the niches of the central porch gables and the angel corbel to the south of the south-west door, though this is of later date. Higher up, paint survives in niche no. 22, around the iconographically central image of Christ in the gable, and on the head of St Paul in niche no. 95 on the south central buttress. Of particular interest is the ninth location, the pierced quatrefoils now hidden behind Redfern's sculptures over the central porch. These retain a preparation layer containing white lead and, although further layers of paint were not positively identified, this would suggest the intention to decorate these features, indicating that their framing niches were not intended for sculptures at the time when they were painted.

Picked out with colour the quatrefoils would, with the exterior of the porch and the two lower buttress figures, delineate an almost perfect square of polychromy at the centre of the façade (fig. 59, pl. I). This appears to have reached some degree of completion. Individual elements, namely the polychromed porch, the great west arch, the external gables and, presumably, the four full-size figures housed on the main buttresses, would all have enriched the area around the doors, the ceremonial entrance to the church.

Central Porch, Interior.   The central porch, known as the 'Blue Porch',[4] retains the greatest evidence of paint and the broadest of palettes. The pale copper blue that gave the porch its name can be found in abundance, as well as multi-layered traces of richer colour of various periods (pls. III-V). The most extensive survivals are on the tympanum, the focal point of the porch, above the main doors, which would almost certainly have housed an image of the Virgin Mary (see p.40). However, the rich palette extends across the central section of the porch, on north and south elevations, ribs and across the vault, with evidence of retouching throughout. The west doors also retain evidence of many repaintings; however, the original red ochre finish still exists.[5] The survival of bands of a copper alloy, above and below the central capital of the trumeau, indicate further effects that would have been used to enhance the richness of the central porch.

---

[4] The earliest known reference is in the Clerk of Works Book for 1671. I am grateful to Roy Spring, formerly Clerk of the Works and currently Fabric Records Clerk to the Dean and Chapter, for this information.
[5] I am grateful to Catherine Hassall for analysing the door samples: Hassall 2000.

In the north and south arcaded recesses, paint traces are largely in a simple palette of copper blue and red ochre, which probably date from early schemes (pl. V). In the south recess, however, there is also evidence of richer colour. Vermilion and copper resinate green survive in the angle on either side of the sinister boss of the central niche and the niche back and, although these deposits could relate to the painting of the capital, it is more likely that they are the remains of colouring from the niches themselves. The presence of more exotic colour here confirms that these niches once housed sculptures, for which the remains of iron fixings exist. Whilst the green provides the background colour for the central niche, the red is found in the southernmost niche, suggesting an alternation. This would continue that found on the tympanum, where the central niche with its vermilion background is flanked by niches of copper resinate green (pl.II).

As most of the sculpture within the porch today is 19th-century, the survival at the apex of the tympanum of a group of four carved heads set within quatrefoils is particularly important (pl. IV). The larger heads are identified elsewhere as St Peter and St Paul (see p.43). All heads retain a considerable amount of polychromy, in the depths of the carving and on sheltered portions. The dexter eye of the sinister head (St Paul) is particularly finely painted, delicately delineated with a double sweep of the brush in a rich red ochre. The irises are painted with finely ground azurite, which is found in no other location on the front. In the deeply cut grooves of the beard many traces survive, which close examination show to be gold leaf, applied up to four times.

The rest of the polychrome within the porch is on architectural elements. The inner and outer archivolts framing the tympanum retain the most, with nearly all mouldings bearing some evidence of paint (pl. III). Tin leaf, now badly oxidised, was discovered both here and around the voussoirs of the west doors. The resinous mordant to which the tin is adhered is also found within mouldings on the side elevations, as well as on the ribs of the vault above. The east face of the great west arch also retains some fragments of oxidised tin. It would appear that all elevations within the central section of the porch employed tin leaf to decorate the architectural surfaces.

On the side elevations of the central section there is evidence of a later copper blue (pl. V). Years or even centuries after the initial painting there was a return to the palette of the early scheme. Similarly, it is noticeable elsewhere that after many changes of colour, certain mouldings were repainted to match earlier decoration (pl. III).

Central Porch, Exterior. The great west arch that frames the porch is decorated with raised white bands, 2.5 cm wide, which spanned each arris along the soffit and chamfered faces (pl. V). Although the bands are no longer complete, they represent the most continuous decoration to survive anywhere on the west front. As this is an important location, it was originally thought that the bands might have been decorated with metal leaf. No evidence was found to support this supposition, however, and it appears more likely, given that the bulk material consists of calcium sulphate, that an organic lake once enriched the great west arch. Thompson describes how 'when lakes were made by precipitating the alum solution with chalk, the calcium sulphate was formed automatically along with the lake'.[6] A lake pigment is particularly prone to fading on exposure to light. As Cennini wrote in Italy, in the late 14th or early 15th century, 'the air is its undoing'.[7] Nevertheless, organic pigments, used as glazes, have at times been detected on exterior polychromy,[8] where their best chance of surviving is in the depths of carved surfaces. The outer stones around the arch would have been especially vulnerable.

In the niches of the porch gables, traces of red ochre and copper green were exposed after cleaning. Both colours were found in niche no. 180, though it is unclear if they belong to the same decorative scheme. In the back of the opposite niche (no. 182) only the copper green is found. These deposits survive largely within recesses in the stone, towards mortar joints, or where cement deposits smeared over the stone have given protection.

North Face of the North Turret.   Outside the porch, the largest group of paint traces is on the lowest tier of niches on the north face of the north stair turret (pl. VII). The majority are in the arch heads, with the central niche (no. 167) retaining the most paint and the richest traces of colour. Niche no. 166 retains an original full-size medieval figure, still bearing traces of polychromy. Yellow ochre occurs extensively, whilst copper blue fragments are also found. It is impossible to tell whether the two colours belong to the same scheme.

Red, yellow and large areas of white are clearly visible on the architectural elements, with faint traces of copper blue-green. Some of the white may be the remains of an altered limewash ground, now missing upper layers, or it may have been left exposed to add white to the palette; elsewhere white traces may be oxalate deposits produced by a reaction between lichen and limestone.[9] Apart from this white, paint analysis has revealed that the principle pigment is red ochre, with yellow ochre, some white lead, carbon black and a copper blue-green, all found above the level of the capitals. Several extremely fragmentary traces of vermilion, found in niche no. 167, overlying white lead, further enrich the palette. The copper blue-green also appears lower down on the backs of niches nos. 166 and 167, as well as on the triple attached shaft on the dexter side of no. 166. Although only surviving as a turquoise stain on the stone, this

---

[6] Thompson 1956, p.119.
[7] Cennini, p.27.
[8] At Wells Cathedral a yellow lake was identified in the niche of the Coronation of the Virgin (Sampson 1998, p.119) and at Amiens Cathedral, in the Portail de la Mère Dieu, red lake was found (Weeks 1998, p.102).
[9] In 1996 Helen Howard, Courtauld Institute of Art, carried out an investigation of the thick white deposits found in parts of the front, in order to establish whether the material was based on lichen or paint. Both were found: Howard 1996.

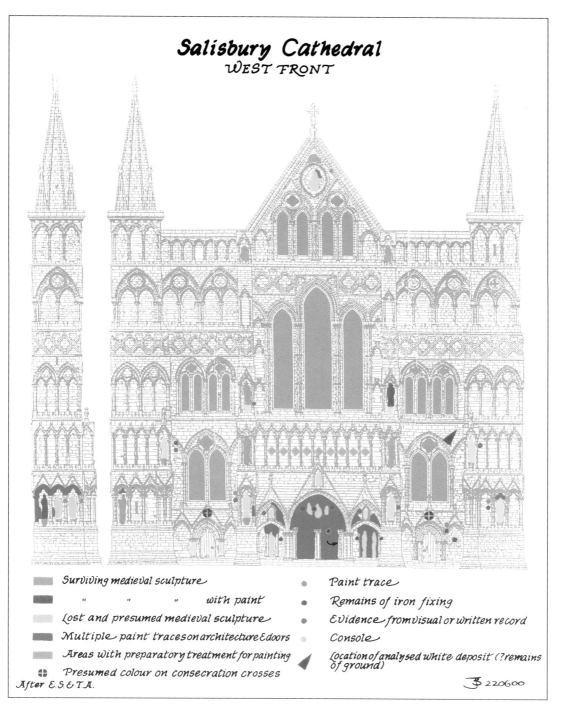

Salisbury Cathedral
WEST FRONT

Surviving medieval sculpture

" " " with paint

Lost and presumed medieval sculpture

Multiple paint traces on architecture & doors

Areas with preparatory treatment for painting

Presumed colour on consecration crosses

After E.S. & T.A.

Paint trace

Remains of iron fixing

Evidence from visual or written record

Console

Location of analysed white deposit (?remains of ground)

220600

I Medieval figure sculpture and polychromy.

II   Colour reconstruction of the tympanum and surrounding stonework in the central porch.

It is based on evidence from the analysis of surviving paint and comparative medieval polychromy. All reconstructions can only offer a suggestion of how the porch was decorated, as the available evidence is but a shadow of what once existed.
a. Early scheme based on extensive use of copper blue and red ochre, possibly completed in time for the 1258 consecration.
b. The development of a richer polychromy with the introduction of orpiment, copper resinate green and indigo.
c. The polychromy at its most opulent, with the lavish use of vermilion and gold, alongside earlier colours and indicating the use of decorative devices such as stencilling (perhaps mid- to late 15th century).

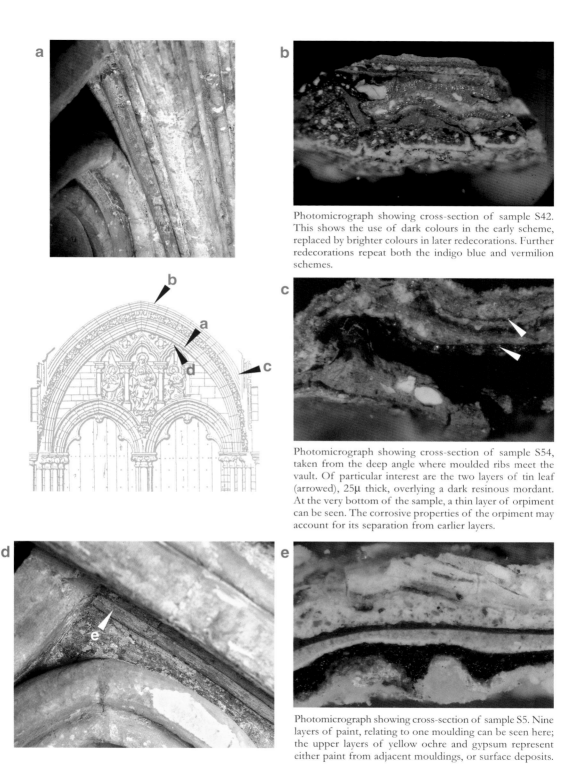

Photomicrograph showing cross-section of sample S42. This shows the use of dark colours in the early scheme, replaced by brighter colours in later redecorations. Further redecorations repeat both the indigo blue and vermilion schemes.

Photomicrograph showing cross-section of sample S54, taken from the deep angle where moulded ribs meet the vault. Of particular interest are the two layers of tin leaf (arrowed), 25µ thick, overlying a dark resinous mordant. At the very bottom of the sample, a thin layer of orpiment can be seen. The corrosive properties of the orpiment may account for its separation from earlier layers.

Photomicrograph showing cross-section of sample S5. Nine layers of paint, relating to one moulding can be seen here; the upper layers of yellow ochre and gypsum represent either paint from adjacent mouldings, or surface deposits.

III Polychrome on and around the tympanum in the central porch.

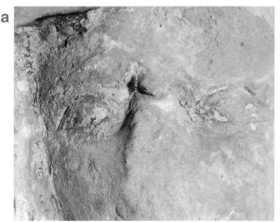

Close-up, showing the surviving painted detail on the eyes of St Paul.

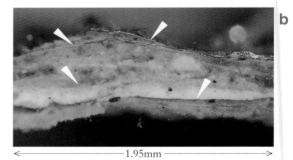

Photomicrograph of cross-section of sample S9, taken from the beard of St Paul, showing four layers of gilding.

IV   Carved heads on apex of tympanum, central porch.

a

Detail of western face of great west arch, showing remnants of decorative bands, which may once have been glazed.

b

Photomicrograph of cross-section of sample S144, showing later copper blue and earlier resinous mordant for tin leaf.

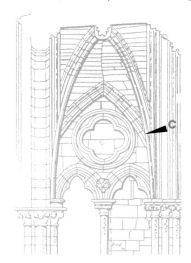

c

c

b

Location of sample S144, where later copper blue is found.

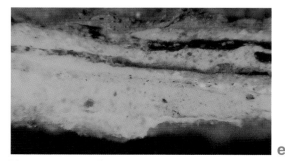

d

Northern recess, central niche. Detail of copper blue on boss.

e

Photomicrograph of cross-section of sample S74, showing successive layers of the early copper blue, with later repaints where a richer palette is employed.

V   Central porch polychromy.

VI The central porch and its surroundings, as they may have appeared in the 15th century.

All available evidence has been studied, including fragments of paint found on the doors. The reconstruction may incorporate colour of different periods. It is unlikely that redecoration was always total, so that different palettes and styles of painting could become juxtaposed. Large areas shown as plain colour are likely to have borne further decoration; in places perhaps even carved features. Ashlar lining has been assumed, on the basis of evidence elsewhere in the cathedral.

An impression of the porch in the medieval period
Eddie Sinclair & John Boden

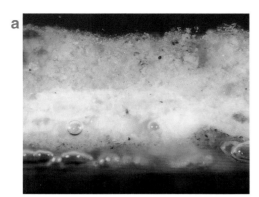

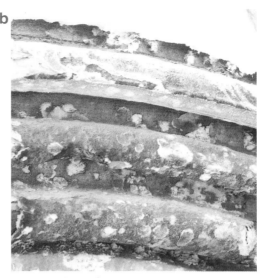

Photomicrograph of cross-section of sample S19, showing white lead ground and yellow ochre top coat.

Lichen and polychromy on voussoirs.

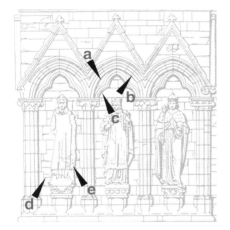

vermilion

Photomicrograph of cross-section of sample S158, showing layers of yellow ochre, red ochre, vermilion and carbon black.

Detail of niche back showing faint copper blue/green traces. This copper pigment is also found on the adjacent triple shaft.

Detail of yellow ochre, sinister side of deacon's drapery.

VII North face of north turret (niche nos. 166-68).

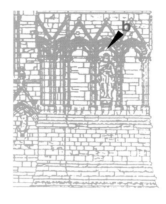

Apex of niche no. 195.

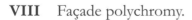

a Traces of polychromy in the back of niche no. 22, Christ in Majesty, in the gable. Pink paint consists of a mix of finely ground vermilion and orpiment.

VIII   Façade polychromy.

Trace of red 'line', possible remnant of ashlar lining.

copper pigment is consistent with findings in the niches of the blind arcading in the central porch. As discussed below, copper blue is fundamental to the Salisbury palette and occurs in several layers and applications, making it difficult to date.

The red ochre does not match that found in the porch or in niche no. 195 (see below). It is possible that it is of a different period than the early red in the porch, perhaps applied when later sculptures were inserted. The vermilion that overlies this red may be of an even later date; within the porch, vermilion belongs to the later schemes. In niche no. 167 it is found in a similar location to the red in niche no. 195 (see below), which is possibly the remains of a masonry pattern. By the period when vermilion would be found in such a location, these masonry patterns were no longer fashionable, however, and some grander form of decoration must be imagined. If the vermilion were a repaint, then it might well have disappeared from other more exposed low-level niches, such as no. 195.

Other Niches.   Moving on to the western face, four niches retain fragmentary evidence of colour, while St Paul in niche no. 95 is the only sculpture to retain traces of paint. Both red and yellow ochre survive on the carved locks of hair, on the small remnant of medieval head (to which a 19th-century face is attached). Niche no. 169 is the most northerly on the west face to house an original full-size figure. Although no paint survives on the figure itself, traces of copper green were found on the canopy roof. Overlying a white ground that must once have been calcium carbonate, now altered to calcium sulphate, the paint sits in recessed pockets in the surface of the stone. The copper-based paint appears particularly green here, but a pigmented preservative (see below) could be partly responsible for this. Faint traces of a similar copper pigment were also found on the triple attached shaft on the sinister side of niche no. 178.

Niche no. 195 is the most southerly to show evidence of paint (pl. VIII). Traces of red ochre have been found in the angle between the inner roll and the niche wall, and the angle between the inner roll and the niche roof on both sides of the upper cusp. This red is a very finely divided pure iron oxide, which compares closely both in colour and composition with that on the central external consecration cross at the east end of the cathedral and that found on the niche backs of the pulpitum.[10] It is darker and finer than that found on the north elevation, but matches again in colour, texture and composition the early red primer in the porch and in niche no. 180, one of the porch gables. The red in niche no. 195 and on the consecration cross overlies a white ground, which is also found in the porch. The ground from niche no. 195 consists principally of calcium carbonate, although in the upper part of the layer calcium sulphate and calcium oxalate were found.[11]

[10] Catherine Hassall analysed the paint on the pulpitum in a recent survey carried out by McNeilage Conservation Practice: McNeilage 1999.
[11] Howard 1996.

Just down from the apex of the niche, along the sinister angle, the paint has the suggestion of a deliberate lower edge. If so, it could suggest that this is the remains of ashlar lining, such as exists in the cloister and within the cathedral. However, the surviving 'line' is only 8 mm long and it may be chance that gives it an apparent edge. This remnant may take the form of a line because it clings to mortar residues, where there is usually more 'key' for the colour to adhere to, within the protected angle of the niche back.

The survival of paint 90 feet up in the gable, in niche no. 22, was a remarkable discovery (pl. VIII). Protected by the moulded frame of the quatrefoil vesica, three of the plain ashlar blocks bear traces of a thin reddish-pink coloration. This survives particularly well in the depths of the tooling from the claw chisel and over mortar joints. Analysis revealed that a mix of finely ground vermilion and orpiment had been used. Both rich and vibrant colours, they would have provided a fitting background for a figure of Christ. It says much about the quality of the paint that it has survived in such an exposed spot, although it is surprising that white lead was not used as a ground for this iconographical focal point.

Angel Corbel.   Inserted into the wall of the blind arch to the right of the south-west door is a small angel corbel with a polygonal top, which once supported a sculpture (no. 208). Yellow ochre, a pinkish red iron oxide, vermilion, copper green, white lead, calcium carbonate white and carbon black were identified on or adjacent to it. The most complex sample consisted of a white ground, with a yellow ochre primer, over which a pale pink limewash had been applied. The white ground was a mixture of chalk and fine white lead. The copper green was also observed on the edges of the surrounding ashlar blocks, disappearing beneath mortar smears. The paint, though belonging to the same palette identified elsewhere, does not tie up with any of the repaints found within the porch. The presence of paint in the lower horizontal joint indicates that the sculpture was painted *in situ*, after insertion, though the date remains unknown.

Techniques

It has to be remembered that what remains is merely a shadow of what once existed. The richest effects would have been reserved for the sculpture, which has for the most part disappeared. Painting would have been an extremely complex, sophisticated business. A thematic consideration of the recent findings is presented here.

Grounds.   Throughout the survey, paint was found frequently in weathered or damaged pockets.[12] Stone may be cut and stock-piled for some time before erecting

---

[12] Report, Phase 3b (Polychromy), p.17.

or even painting. An examination of the polychromy from the roof bosses of the west walk of the cloister at Salisbury has revealed the presence of dirt beneath the lowest paint layer, suggesting that they were left unpainted for some time.[13] At Exeter priming was also often noted in weathered holes.[14] It appears as though uneven surfaces were filled with plaster; perhaps mortar from joints was smeared across the surface, prior to the application of primers. The choice of materials for these initial preparations is crucial, though at times it appears as though the primer is applied directly to the stone.

Whilst the soft ground of the earliest schemes employs bone white and calcium carbonate, as well as white lead, the latter dominates subsequent schemes. The extensive use of white lead in the porch, both in primings and in decorative coloured layers, has played a large part in ensuring the survival of the paint. The scarcity of paint beyond the porch may be due partly to the fact that cheaper calcium carbonate grounds were employed, although these are not always in evidence. At Wells Cathedral, different grounds were used according to the importance of the location.[15] It would be uneconomical to treat large areas of polychromy with white lead preparations and cheaper grounds would have been a natural choice for less important positions.

The discovery of white lead as a ground in the back of niche no. 167 on the north elevation (pl. VII) suggests that a sculpture of importance was housed here; none was identified in neighbouring niches. White lead is also found in the preparation of the pierced quatrefoils above the west doors, which suggests that this, too, was an area of particular importance. The treatment here could resemble that identified on the Portail Royal at Chartres, where a lead white ground was laid directly on to the stone. The surface of the limestone was probably wetted with limewater and rubbed with some sort of polishing tool (see below).[16] As noted above, however, no trace of white lead was found in the iconographically important location of the gable. The later angel corbel also uses white lead as a ground.

The survival of a white ground in many protected corners of the architectural elements could indicate that these surfaces were limewashed (pl. I).[17] It is not possible to know at what point such a coating was applied, or how extensive it was, but it would be very much in keeping with 13th-century practice, as for example in the cloisters or within the cathedral itself, where ashlar lining, described above, is painted in red iron oxide over a white calcium carbonate ground.

Preparations. After the application of a white calcium carbonate ground, the relevant architectural stonework of the western elevation was primed with red ochre

[13] Sinclair 1995, p.109.
[14] Sinclair 1992, p.12.
[15] Sampson 1998, pp.118–19.
[16] Nonfarmale and Rossi-Manaresi 1987, p.274.
[17] Howard 1996, p.6.

prior to the application of coloured layers. This is discussed below. Within the porch it is most noticeable sitting in the depths of the tool marks, where later paint layers have flaked away. The north elevation may have received a different treatment. The extensive use of yellow ochre here suggests that this may have been applied as a base coat over the white. The presence of yellow in the hollow mouldings reinforces this possibility, as it is an unlikely choice of colour for such a location. The dominant colour on the heads of the niches is red, but it is not clear how this worked with the yellow, although they appear to belong to one scheme. In one of the rarer, more complex paint sections the red overlies the yellow (pl. VII), suggesting that it may indeed have been applied as a general base coat. If so, it is puzzling that more does not survive.

As mentioned, yellow ochre appears also on the drapery of the deacon martyr in niche no. 166, again on the north turret (pl. VII). This might represent the same technique in use on figurative sculpture. However, it does not appear to overlie a white ground and was perhaps here being used as a pore filler.[18] The coarse stone required preparation before it could receive paint. It is too crude for a top coat and would not throw the figure into strong enough relief, particularly against possible backgrounds of red or blue. Often the draperies of full-size figures of this kind would be white with decoration applied as additional layers, for linings, hems and cuffs.[19] Yellow ochre might also be an undercoat for gilding, but an extensive use of gilding in this location would be surprising. Such costly materials were reserved for the most important sculptures. At Exeter the fabric rolls of 1341-42 list the purchase of gold and silver for the painting of St Peter, the dedicatee of the cathedral, in the gable of the west front.[20]

With little in the way of figurative sculpture surviving on the west front, it will never be known whether what survives on the north elevation is typical of the treatment elsewhere. The main approach to the cathedral was from the north, so it is possible that this location received special or different treatment. The red and yellow ochre on the head of St Paul (in niche no. 95) may once have been primings or base coats, but the stone here has become polished and the paint is now an integral part of the substrate. At Exeter, too, the red ochre ground appeared polished and perhaps these initial coats were applied according to ancient recipes, in which preparatory layers are rubbed and pressed into the stone 'until as smooth as glass'.[21] The treatment observed on the quatrefoils could represent an early stage in this technique. On St Paul, it is not clear which colour was the base coat, red as used in the porch, or yellow as on the north elevation. It is likely, though, that further layers were applied.

[18] The yellow ochre on the bodies of the figure sculptures from the Gallery of Kings at Notre-Dame in Paris (c.1220–30) was identified as a pore filler: Brodrick 1993, p.19.
[19] The effect is illustrated in a reconstruction of a figure at Wells: Sampson 1998, pl. 7.
[20] Erskine 1983, p.269.
[21] Eraclius, 'How a column is prepared for painting': Merrifield 1999, p.230.

Pigments.   A broad palette of colours has been found, all typical of the middle
ages. The widest range occurs within the porch, with the use of copper blue, indigo,
azurite, ultramarine, red lead, vermilion, red ochre, white lead, chalk, bone white, carbon
black, verdigris, copper resinate green, orpiment, yellow ochre, tin leaf and gold leaf.
As discussed, the great west arch that frames the porch retains portions of a white
band consisting largely of calcium sulphate, which may be the substrate for an organic
lake pigment, now faded and no longer detectable. Beyond the porch, the surviving
evidence is of a simpler palette of calcium carbonate white, carbon black, copper
blue, and red and yellow ochre. Richer pigments also occur, however, with the
identification of localised fragments of white lead grounds, as well as vermilion and
orpiment.

By far the most common colour is a copper-based pigment, which appears within
the porch on every elevation. It is not possible to tell whether it was originally green
or blue. In the porch it tends towards blue (pl. V), but elsewhere appears more green.
Different conditions may have altered the copper pigment and the presence of a
preservative has also affected it optically (see p.160). The fact that it was used in great
quantities suggests that it was cheap, apparently applied like a wash over clusters of
mouldings, ribs and vault. However, the painter must have employed certain skills of
technique for any to survive at all after seven hundred years.

There are many recorded medieval recipes for synthetic copper blues, but none so
far matches that found at Salisbury, which appears in association with white lead, as
well as the more usual chalk ground. A comparison of copper blues from different
locations proved particularly interesting.[22] Detailed analysis revealed that the porch
blue and the blue found in the early scheme on the cathedral's pulpitum were identical
in dispersion, consisting largely of lead, calcium and copper with similar ratios of lead
to chalk, as well as displaying very distinctive characteristics in cross-polarised light.[23]
This suggests that the porch and the pulpitum were painted from the same pot, although
not necessarily at the same time. The blue in the porch also appears in several repaints
(pl. V), which would appear to have utilised the same stock of paint; a freshly synthesised
batch, even from the same recipe, would be unlikely to provide such a perfect match,
particularly when viewed at chemical or microscopical level.

More costly mineral blues were reserved for sculpture. Azurite was used to paint
the irises of the eyes of the small carved heads at the apex of the porch tympanum
(pl. IV) and the fragment of an original fleuron on a tympanum capital retains the
only trace of ultramarine.

Orpiment or 'gold-pigment', with its mica-like sparkle, was used as a substitute for
gold,[24] but as sulphide of arsenic it was known even in the middle ages for its corrosive

---

[22]   I am grateful to Catherine Hassall for looking at a variety of copper blues.
[23]   Personal communication from Catherine Hassall.
[24]   On the west front of Exeter Cathedral orpiment was used on crowns and headresses: Sinclair 1991, p.123.

properties. Where it is found in the porch, it seems to have been used pure and in thin layers (pl. III), but it is also found in the back of the vesica, no. 22, in the gable, where it is mixed with vermilion to make a pink (pl. VIII).

Media.   Media analysis is particularly problematic on exterior paint, where little of the binder will remain. Paint that has already been attacked by weathering and the passing of time is also contaminated by lichen, air-bound pollutants and, at Salisbury, a 19th-century pigmented preservative (see p.160). This appears to have affected much of the paint on the lower levels. Samples from locations beyond the reach of the preservative, such as the gable, were too small to give reliable results.

In the porch the indications are that a drying oil/colophony mix was used as a binder, and analysis of samples from the north elevation also suggests this.[25] Close examination of the best paint traces in the porch shows thick substantial layers, which are still physically tough and retain a degree of gloss. These features would seem to confirm the use of oil, at least in some of the layers, though samples from the north elevation are far more deteriorated and seem to be of a quite different character. Media analysis confirms the presence of resin both in the mordant for the tin leaf[26] and in the copper resinate glazes. The binder for the early copper blue scheme could be proteinaceous.

Repainting

Within the porch, up to sixteen layers of paint have been observed, which appear to represent approximately six repaintings. In between major campaigns of work, retouching would have been carried out where necessary, as can be seen in some cross-sections (pl. V). The early copper blue was re-applied up to three times prior to the onset of richer schemes. These introduced orpiment, verdigris and copper resinate greens (pls. II, V). This palette was superseded, in turn, by a lavish use of vermilion, applied over a thick, distinctive yellow ochre primer and used alongside gold leaf (pls. II, III). A look at cross-sections of the paint shows how different colours were employed over the years (pls. III, V). Capitals painted naturalistically at first with copper resinate green were later gilded. Hollow mouldings, which in the early schemes were picked out in black, were later painted with indigo.

Tin leaf also belongs to later schemes (pl. III), though how it was used remains a mystery. It may have been laid around the mouldings in bands, to create a 'barber's pole' effect, such as occurs on 15th-century church rood screens.[27] It could then have been embellished further by lacquering to imitate gold, or decorating with coloured

---

[25] I am grateful to Dr Spike Bucklow, Hamilton Kerr Institute, for carrying out this analysis for me.

[26] On the west front of Lausanne Cathedral, where tin is used to create patterns on the drapery, the mordant is also thought to be colophony: Brodrick 1993, p.21.

[27] Hulbert 1987, pp.277–79.

glazes of translucent pigments to create 'lustres'. Such glazes may also have been applied to define the great west arch that frames the porch.

With so little paint surviving beyond the porch, it is not possible to tell whether any repainting took place. If most of the sculpture on the wider façade was added in the 14th century, as argued above (see pp.62-69), the original painting of it would also be of this date. The vermilion that overlies the red and yellow ochre on the north elevation may be a repainting (pl. VII), contemporary with the later repaints within the porch, where vermilion is so extensively used. The low-level niches were easily accessible for repainting.

Date

It seems likely that important elements of the 13th-century scheme, notably the central porch, would have received some painted decoration by the time of the consecration in 1258. Sculpture would be seen as incomplete without the final touches of colour, though a shortage of funds might dictate a simple decoration. The copper blue may have provided a temporary solution until richer more costly schemes could be afforded. If there were around six schemes, that would suggest a repainting every fifty years. This is rather a long time for paint, particularly exterior paint, to survive and explains also the evidence for simple retouching.

As mentioned, there are links with the polychromy found in datable parts of the cathedral. The copper blue in the porch is identical in its particulate structure to that found in the first painting of the pulpitum. The red iron oxide both in niche no. 195 and in the porch relates closely to that found on the early decorative scheme on the pulpitum and the consecration cross. Although red iron oxides are common, they occur in many varieties and samples from these four locations match very well. No other similar traces have been found elsewhere on the front. The external consecration crosses may date from as early as the 1220s and the pulpitum was probably completed by 1236, when the choir stalls that abut them were begun.[28] This suggests that niche no. 195 was occupied and painted early on. At an early date, the use of masonry pattern might have been an appropriate option, as found on the west front of Wells.

Of particular help with dating is the presence of minute survivals of ultramarine, found in three out of the four above-mentioned locations. This usually indicates an early date. At Bourges Cathedral in France it appears only in the first decorative scheme of 1225;[29] later, azurite was used instead. Features where ultramarine occurs are not likely to be of the 14th century. Only one trace was found in the central porch at Salisbury, on a capital, but the presence of such a costly material on such a feature suggests that it was also used for more important sculptures.

---

[28] T. Tatton-Brown, 'The Salisbury Cathedral Consecration Crosses', *Transactions of the Monumental Brass Society*, xvi, 2, 1998, pp.113-16; *Cal. Close 1234–37*, p.279, 18 June 1236.

[29] Rossi-Manaresi and Tucci 1984, p.84.5.2.

Orpiment, appearing some time after the copper resinate green had enriched the porch, may have been introduced at the same time as it was employed in the gable, belonging to a later phase of work. The orpiment in the gable appears in a mixture with vermilion, unlike in the porch, where it occurs in a pure form. Orpiment and vermilion appear together, with a white lead, as a glaze over gold leaf on a wall painting examined at Farleigh Hungerford Castle, Somerset.[30] This dates from the early 15th century and shows how these colours may have been used, though here in the gable, with such fragmentary paint survival no trace of metal leaf has been observed. At Toro, in Spain, pure orpiment is found almost exclusively instead of gold in the original scheme of the west portal, *c.*1298, before it was replaced with gold leaf in 1408.[31]

Conclusion

The recent discovery of colour on the west front of Salisbury Cathedral radically changes our perception of this majestic building. The façade may never have been completely painted, but colour will have defined key points, emphasising the splendour of the cathedral, adding to its impressiveness and reminding us today that this was not a sombre building. The addition of colour, built up perhaps over a period of time, would have begun with the different effects achieved by the different stones.[32] The dark grey-black of the polished Purbeck marble would have contrasted strongly with the white limewashed ashlar, which may itself have been decorated originally with a fictive masonry pattern.

Against all this, pockets of rich polychromy would have stood out, jewel-like. Additional materials, such as metal, would also have embellished the scene, set within the consecration crosses above the porches and in the central porch, where metal bands still survive. Even incomplete, with perhaps only the eight or nine identified areas painted, such a façade would present an awe-inspiring sight. On entering the close, the view from the north approach would have been of the three lower niches, brightly painted and occupied with sculpture. From the west, abundant colour in and around the porch (pl. VI) would have led the eye up along the line of finished sculptures on the central buttresses and beyond into the gable (pl. I). With a background of orpiment and vermilion, this crowning image must indeed have been glorious.

---

[30] Howard, Manning and Stewart 1998, p.60.

[31] Katz 1998, p.31.

[32] In describing the building of Lincoln Cathedral by Bishop Hugh, the author of the Metrical Life of St Hugh, writing in around 1220, enthuses how 'the work is supported by another costly material consisting of black stonework [Purbeck marble], as though it is not content with thus having just one colour': Erlande-Brandenburg 1995, pp.131–34.

Photography and the West Front in the mid-Nineteenth Century

ANTHONY HAMBER

The conservation of the west front of Salisbury Cathedral during the 1990s has highlighted the value of mid-19th-century photographs of the building as records of its state both before and immediately after the restoration carried out under George Gilbert Scott, between 1866 and 1869. This essay is in many respects a joint collaboration with my co-authors, for together it has proved possible to put into context the significance of a number of photographs taken in the 1850s and 1860s.[1]

The history of photography in 19th-century Salisbury remains largely unwritten. The scale and scope of the medium in and around the town during the 1840s may never be known.[2] It is unfortunate, given the proximity of his home in Lacock, that the pioneer William Henry Fox Talbot did not select the cathedral as a site for one of his photographic campaigns. No Daguerreotypes have yet been located either, although the building would have been a natural subject. A Daguerreotype of the west front of Wells Cathedral, dating to the late 1840s and now in the Canadian Centre for Architecture in Montreal, underlines the probability that such images were taken.

In 1841 a licence for a Daguerreotype studio in Southampton was issued by Richard Beard (1802-1885), the holder of the licence, to John Frederick Goddard (c.1795-1866). The building of this studio, the Photographic Institution in Portland Terrace, commenced in November 1841 and it opened in May of the following year.[3] The railway between Salisbury and Southampton opened in 1847. The 1849 Post Office Directory for Southampton listed a George Marks as having a Daguerreotype studio on the premises of a bookseller and printer at 180 High Street.

---

[1] I should like to thank Tim Ayers and Tim Tatton-Brown for their help in explaining the significance of a number of the images discussed in this essay and for answering my flow of questions and queries. Roger Taylor was, as ever, most generous in supplying me with details of photographic images of Salisbury Cathedral from his database of mid-19th-century photographic exhibitions. Philippe Garner of Sotheby's most kindly had copy negatives made of a number of the images by Roger Fenton discussed below, which appeared in the sale of the collection of Marie-Thérèse and André Jammes at Sotheby's, London in October 1999.

[2] In 1985 Martin Norgate's *Photographers in Wiltshire* (Wiltshire Monograph No. 5, Wiltshire County Council Library & Museum Service, Trowbridge) was published. Two years later Peter Saunders's *Salisbury in Old Photos* (Alan Sutton, Gloucester) was published and this was followed by a number of books by Peter Daniels.

[3] K. Adamson, 'More Early Studios', *The Photographic Journal*, January 1988, pp.32–36.

It is likely that photographs were displayed at various *conversazioni* held in Salisbury during the 1840s. The meetings of national and provincial scholarly organisations provided another channel. Between 24 and 31 July 1849 the Archaeological Institute of Great Britain and Ireland held its annual meeting there. Charles Robert Cockerell (1788-1863), architect, archaeologist and a key figure in the Institute, gave a paper on the sculpture in the cathedral and Robert Willis (1800-1875) a lecture on its architecture. No evidence has been found to show that photographs were either exhibited in the 'temporary museum' or used by speakers. This does not match the experience of other comparable academic societies. When the Somerset Archaeological and Natural History Society held its annual meeting in Taunton in September 1849 the exhibits in the 'temporary museum' included a 'Daguerreotype by Claudet', shown by the antiquarian John Britton (1771-1857).[4] At the following year's annual meeting, held in Frome, the Revd E. Dighton showed a 'Daguerreotype view of the leaning Tower of Pisa'.[5]

By the early 1850s photographs were clearly being collected in Salisbury. In October 1852 an exhibition of 'Local Industry, Amateur Productions, Works of Art, Antiquities, Objects of Taste, Articles of Virtue, etc.' was opened in the Council Chamber, Law Court, Grand Jury Room and Crown Court. James Brown of Silver Street, a tobacconist by profession, included 'Photography on Glass and Paper, by the Calotype or Talbotype Processes with Collodion etc'. H. Neale Jnr of the Canal exhibited 'A Series of Pictures from Nature, taken by Talbot's Photographic process called Calotype; the whole of them printed from paper negatives.'[6] Unfortunately, the subject matter is not known. A similar exhibition took place in 1862.[7]

By the mid-1850s professional photographers were beginning to advertise their services. One of the earliest was John Clarke, a miniature painter and photographer of 89 Strand, London, who started advertising in the *Salisbury Journal* in July 1854.[8] He used the premises of Mr Webb, Gunmaker, at 38 Catherine Street, where 'specimens may be seen'. Like the majority of photographers active in Salisbury during the first half of the 1850s, he was 'itinerant', working between the spring and early autumn. It seems likely that such people took the opportunity to photograph the cathedral to add to their portfolios of commercial images, selling them both locally and elsewhere.

William Thomas Pitcher was one of the most prominent commercial photographers in the mid-Victorian city. In June 1855 he was elected to serve on the committee of the Salisbury Literary and Scientific Institution and he became Honorary

⁴ *Proceedings of the Somerset Archaeological and Natural History Society*, 1–2, 1851, p.25.

⁵ *Ibid.*, p.41.

⁶ There were at least three editions of the catalogue and the Salisbury Library holds a copy of the third edition, *Catalogue of the Salisbury Exhibition of Local Industry, Amateur Productions, Works of Art, Antiquities, Objects of Taste, Articles of Vertu, Etc., Opened on the Twelfth of October, 1852,* James Bennett, Salisbury [1852].

⁷ The copy in the British Library was destroyed in the Second World War.

⁸ Clarke is listed as a London photographer and in 1858 he had moved premises to 140 Strand. See M. Pritchard, *A Directory of London Photographers 1841–1908*, Watford, 1994, p.46.

60 William Russell Sedgfield (1826-1902), *West Front of Salisbury Cathedral from the North-west*, Calotype, signed 'R. Sedgfield. March 1853'. Hardwicke Knight.

Secretary in February 1856. The following month F. A. Blake, a bookseller of Blue Boar Row, advertised that specimens of Pitcher's photographs were on display. However, it is not clear to what extent he photographed the cathedral and this is true of other local photographers in the 1850s and 1860s. Few advertised extensively since their clients would naturally come across their images in local shops. When advertisements do appear they are frequently unspecific. In 1857 James Miell, photographer, in Catherine Street, was offering 'Views of Salisbury' and his services included 'Views taken of Buildings'.[9] Miell is known to have produced both *cartes de visite* and stereoscopic views of the cathedral.

It is fortunate that a number of the most significant contemporary architectural photographers visited Salisbury and worked there. The two most important were William Russell Sedgfield and Roger Fenton. Sedgfield (1826-1902) was born in Devizes

[9] *Brown's Stranger's Handbook and Illustrated Guide to the City of Salisbury*, Salisbury and London, 1857, p.46.

61 William Russell Sedgfield, *No. 382 Salisbury Cathedral. The West Door*, Albumen print, stereoscopic view. Author's collection.

and became probably the earliest commercial photographer in Wiltshire. In 1842 he contemplated acquiring a licence for William Henry Fox Talbot's Calotype process and began taking photographs.[10] In March 1853 he took the west front of the cathedral (fig. 60). The image was advertised to be included in Part V of an early photographic publication entitled *The Photographic Album*, published by Joseph Cundall of London. It was mentioned and praised in the journal *Notes and Queries*, following a letter from an anonymous Fellow of the Society of Antiquaries, regarding the ability of paper negative photography to capture high levels of detail.[11]

In 1854 Samuel Highley of London began publication of a series of Sedgfield's photographs under the title, *Photographic Delineations of the Scenery, Architecture, and Antiquities of Great Britain, and Ireland.* The stated intention was to publish six parts. The first three appeared during 1854, containing five or six prints and a title page, and costing one guinea each. No image of Salisbury was included, but Sedgfield did exhibit a view of the west front at a number of photographic exhibitions in this year, including that of the Photographic Society of London and at another in Dundee, as well as probably the following year in Brussels. By 1857 he had extensively photographed the cathedral. In an advertisement placed in *Brown's Stranger's Handbook and Illustrated Guide to the City of Salisbury*, Sedgfield listed six mounted photographic views, each costing 4s., and 'a great variety of Stereographs of the Cathedral, Cloisters, Old Sarum, &c.'

---

[10]   Knight 1998, I, p.19.
[11]   *Notes and Queries*, 13 August 1853, p.157.

62 Anonymous, *No. 142 Salisbury Cathedral. West End*, King's English Landscape and Architectural Series, Albumen print, stereoscopic view. Author's collection.

This probably included two views of the front, which formed part of a series known as *Sedgfield's English Scenery* (fig. 61).

The stereoscopic view and the *carte de visite* became increasingly popular formats from the late 1850s, and a number of anonymous views of the west front appeared (fig. 62).[12] However, it is difficult to calculate the level of dissemination of such images and what contemporary impact they may have had. It is unlikely that any were taken specifically to document the state of the building. Similarly, no images by amateur photographers can be shown at this date to have had an archaeological purpose.

In 1869 Brown and Co. of Salisbury and Simpkin, Marshall and Co. of London jointly published the Revd H. Armfield's *The Legend of Christian Art Illustrated in the Statues of Salisbury Cathedral*.[13] The book included a photographic frontispiece, a general view of the west front, although different copies have variant images (fig. 63). Sedgfield is not credited as the photographer in the text, but is named in Brown's advertisement. The earlier image was taken while Redfern's campaign was still in progress. One of the medieval figures that he subsequently replaced is still *in situ* (no. 150a).[14] Other copies of the book have a variant image, which provides valuable clues as to the order in which the sculptures were carved and installed. It is not known whether Armfield had a particular interest in photography, but documentary work was being carried out

[12] During the late 1850s and early 1860s there was a high degree of photographic 'piracy'. This resulted in many *cartes de visite* and stereoscopic photographs being produced without any indication of the photographer or publisher.

[13] Armfield was a minor canon of Salisbury Cathedral and Vice-Principal of the Salisbury Theological College.

[14] I am grateful to Tim Ayers for pointing this out to me.

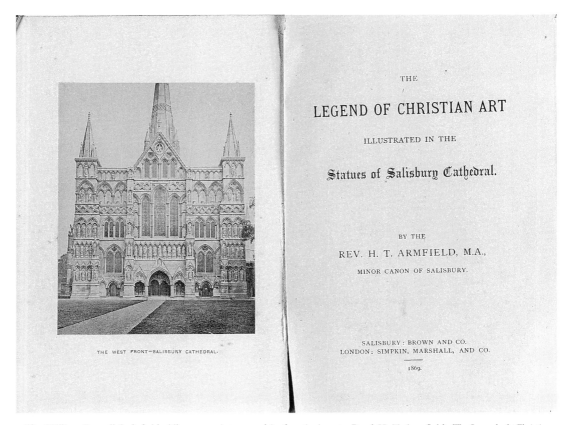

THE

LEGEND OF CHRISTIAN ART

ILLUSTRATED IN THE

Statues of Salisbury Cathedral.

BY THE

REV. H. T. ARMFIELD, M.A.,

MINOR CANON OF SALISBURY.

SALISBURY: BROWN AND CO.
LONDON: SIMPKIN, MARSHALL, AND CO.

1869.

THE WEST FRONT—SALISBURY CATHEDRAL.

63   William Russell Sedgfield, Albumen print, pasted in frontispiece to Revd H. T. Armfield, *The Legend of Christian Art Illustrated in the Statues of Salisbury Cathedral*, Salisbury and London, 1869.

at the cathedral during the 1860s. At a meeting at the Society of Antiquaries on 24 November 1864 the Revd D.J. Eyre exhibited photographs of chalices, patens, episcopal staffs and rings, from tombs of bishops of Salisbury. It is unclear who had taken them.

Roger Fenton (1819-1869) was one of the most significant figures in British photography from the early 1850s until his retirement from the profession in 1862.[15] During the second half of the 1850s he documented many of the Gothic cathedrals of England. The date of his photographic campaign, or campaigns, at Salisbury remains unclear. However, it was one of the cathedrals that he covered particularly well. The *Sarum Almanack Advertiser* for 1861 includes an advertisement by the London publisher Victor De La Rue for *Views of the Principal Cathedrals & Churches of England, photographed from Nature by Roger Fenton*, each image costing 10s. 6d. There were 13 of Salisbury, more than for any of the other 11 listed cathedrals. Fenton took at least three views

[15]   Hannavy 1975; *Roger Fenton*.

64   Roger Fenton (1819-1869), *Salisbury: the West Front*, Albumen print, from *The Works of Roger Fenton. Cathedrals.* Francis Frith, Reigate [*c.*1863]. Sotheby's.

of the west front in and around 1858: a general view from the south-west; a full-frame view, square on to the façade (fig. 64), and a detail of the porch (fig. 16). He exhibited, amongst six views of the cathedral, a view of the 'west porch' at the 1859 exhibition of the Photographic Society of London. The full-frame view was also published in 1862, as a large (34 x 41.5cm) plate in *The Works of Roger Fenton. Cathedrals.* These two magnificent images include much now-lost evidence for missing medieval figures.

It is curious that photographs do not seem to have been used to document the restoration work at the cathedral in this period. George Gilbert Scott (1811-1878) was appointed to survey and report on the cathedral in 1858 and the results were presented to the Dean and Chapter in 1862. Restoration was then carried out on the west front between 1866 and 1869. Scott's professional use of photography remains largely unresearched. His office may have had a collection of photographs, but no record of it has been found. The Royal Institute of British Architects holds some of Scott's sketchbooks, which include a number of photographs that have been tipped in. In his *Personal and Professional Recollections*, published in 1879, Scott recalled that he had made use of photographs of Chichester Cathedral, taken prior to the collapse of the tower there.[16] He was also a member of the committee of the Architectural Photographic Association (APA), formed in 1857.[17] The local secretary was none other than William Osmond Jnr, of the Salisbury firm of architectural masons, William Osmond & Co., which was involved at the cathedral from 1818 until the 1880s.[18]

In conclusion, no evidence has yet been found to indicate that photography was used as a professional tool to record contemporary work on the west front. However, photographs taken by Sedgfield and Fenton (amongst others) are now clearly understood to be extremely important documents for historians of the medieval sculpture and architecture. It is hoped that additional mid-19th-century photographs may be uncovered and that these will add further to our knowledge.

[16] Scott 1879 (1995 edn), pp.309, 480.
[17] See R. Elwall, 'Foe-to-Graphic Art: The Rise and Fall of the Architectural Photographic Association', *Photographic Collector*, 5, no. 2, 1984, pp.142–63.
[18] It is not clear what success William Osmond Jnr had in increasing APA membership in the Salisbury area. None of the leading Salisbury architects, such as John Peniston, his son, John Jnr or grandson H. Peniston, is listed in the 1858 membership list.

Conservation and Repair, 1994-2000

MICHAEL DRURY AND NICHOLAS DURNAN

1. Background to the Conservation and Repair Programme

The demands made by the programme for the conservation and repair of the west front between 1994 and 2000 have been met by the specialist skills and expertise of many craftsmen and women, conservators and consultants.[1] The programme has presented challenges of conservation and repair that have necessitated the development of appropriate techniques, specific to the need of this particular project, although the lime method which formed the basis of the masonry conservation policy was already well tested.

Although the record indicates that the project began in 1994, it was preceded by many years of fund raising and preparatory planning. It formed part of a sequence of work that had already included the repair of the spire, from 1988 to 1993, and the tower, completed in 1996. Both these projects were made possible by Salisbury Cathedral Trust's appeal funds raised between 1988 and 1992. On the west front, appeal funds were augmented annually by consistently high levels of grant aid from English Heritage, sustained throughout the project. Over this period English Heritage has supported the Dean and Chapter's own fabric fund at a similarly generous level of grant aid, enabling the cathedral's major repair programme to progress elsewhere, independent of the Trust. Much still needs to be done throughout the cathedral and the campaign continues.

Originally constructed in a relatively rapid and almost unbroken campaign, as explained elsewhere in this volume, the front was last worked over systematically by George Gilbert Scott between his appointment in 1858 and his death in 1878. In 1963 the medieval statue known as St Augustine of Canterbury (no. 124) partly fell and the remainder was removed for reasons of safety (fig. 65).[2] Thereafter Laurence Bond and his successor Alan Rome, Cathedral Architects, reported on the west front's deteriorating condition in their quinquennial reports. Continuing falls of stone prompted the erection of scaffolding shelters at the foot of the façade to protect visitors and passers-by. In 1982 Roy Spring, Clerk of Works from 1968 to 1996, implemented a trial conservation exercise on the main northern buttress, using lime

---

[1] See Appendix II for a list.
[2] 'The West Front', *Spire*, The Friends of Salisbury Cathedral, 36th Annual Report, May 1966, p.14.

65 The remains of the figure known as St Augustine of Canterbury (no.124), which was removed in 1963 for reasons of safety (*Spire*, May 1966, p.14).

66 Roy Spring and Iain Lunn working on lime-method trials to the northern buttress in 1982 (*Salisbury Journal*, 19 August 1982).

techniques developed for the west fronts of Wells and Exeter Cathedrals by Robert and Eve Baker (fig. 66). Twelve years later, with work on the spire completed and the conservation and repair of the tower well advanced, a seminar was held to address the specific problems that the west front presented and to help the project team towards the commencement of the £3 million project in the following year.

2. Attitudes to Conservation and Repair Today

The seminar held on 25 February 1994 was the starting point in the formulation of a policy for conservation and repair. Informed on that occasion by leading experts in their fields, the Dean and Chapter's consultants began to develop a set of proposals.[3] The experts included Peter Kidson, who presented a paper on the history of the west front; Warwick Rodwell, who addressed questions relating to its archaeology; and Martin Caroe, who spoke about the architectural control of a major west front project from his experience at Wells and Rochester. Eddie Sinclair considered the implications

[3] Policy 1995.

of surviving medieval polychromy and Nicholas Durnan offered a review of the current masonry conservation techniques that might be appropriate. Chaired by Hugh Dickinson, Dean of Salisbury Cathedral from 1986 to 1996, other contributions came from members of the Chapter, the Salisbury Cathedral Trust, the Fabric Advisory Committee and the Cathedrals Fabric Commission for England, from representatives of English Heritage and from amenity groups, including the Society for the Protection of Ancient Buildings (SPAB) and the Victorian Society. These contributions fuelled the debate on attitudes towards building conservation generally and to the conservation of Salisbury Cathedral's west front in particular.

The resulting policy of the consultancy team on the west front and elsewhere has been one of conservation and repair. In the current context of architectural conservation, this is perhaps the first and most important distinction to make. Ours has not been a philosophy of restoration, nor one of preservation. Such distinctions remain relevant in building conservation today, for to distinguish between restoration, preservation and conservation acknowledges the historical evolution of sensitivities towards the care of ancient buildings.

The centenaries of William Morris's death in 1996 and John Ruskin's in 2000 remind us of developments in this field over the last hundred years. Attitudes have changed, as attitudes to architecture have changed, and the world of conservation has seen the same technological advances that have altered our lives fundamentally in other ways. With a wide array of techniques available, there was an obligation upon the team to think carefully about what we were trying to achieve. We concluded that our basic aims had not, in fact, changed fundamentally from those that Ruskin and Morris might have propounded.

'Take proper care of your monuments,' wrote Ruskin in the *Seven Lamps of Architecture*,[4] 'and you will not need to restore them. Watch an old building with an anxious care; count its stones as you would the jewels of a crown … do this tenderly, reverently, continually and many a generation will be born to pass away beneath its shadow.' Morris adapted this philosophy in the manifesto he wrote for the SPAB and his raging against the restoration of our cathedrals was the starting point in the formation of that society. 'Do not let us talk then of restoration. The thing is a lie from beginning to end,' Ruskin had written in 'The Lamp of Memory'. In his and Morris's view, to restore (even if it could be done without conjecture) was to return something to the way it would have been at an earlier time, by necessity a destructive process in that it meant the loss of later work.

To preserve, on the other hand, has come to mean the arrest of change. This may be an appropriate philosophy for a historic building that no longer serves an ongoing purpose, a building one might visit to appreciate the values of an earlier era. Indeed it has been central to the policies of such organisations as the National Trust. It is less

[4] J. Ruskin, 'The Lamp of Memory', in *The Seven Lamps of Architecture*, 1880.

appropriate for a cathedral, however, whose continuing mission is dependent upon its very vitality, its ability to change as the demands put upon it change, in order to continue to fulfil its original purpose. Conservation rather than preservation is the necessary course of action if the cathedral's capability to fulfil such an ongoing purpose is to be ensured.

Does this imply that conservation is a philosophy of change? It does not. Conservation is based fundamentally upon a respect for what has been left to us by those who went before. The conservation process involves careful recording, an archaeological interpretation of that record informing a commensurate approach to the needs of the fabric. This approach values all surviving medieval fabric as witness to the cathedral's history. It accepts replacement work by the generations that followed as a valid reflection of its own era, the building becoming, as a result, an index of changing times. The current campaign of repair will not be the last. Our work will, in its turn, be seen as one of many past campaigns. It will contain much that is of our time and recognisable as such. Accept this and you accept the principle of ongoing conservation.

To Morris and his followers, architecture was, first and foremost, an art. It is timely, in a period when developments in the science of building conservation proliferate, to remember this and to consider the architecture of a structure such as the west front as something more than the sum of its collective parts. With this in mind, we see more clearly that such edifices are vulnerable to collective loss in a qualitative rather than a quantitative sense. Building conservation must therefore balance science and art for, if there is no art in conservation, there will in time be less art in our historic architecture.

3. Development of the Conservation and Repair Policy

The policy document was approved by Salisbury Cathedral's Fabric Advisory Committee early in 1995, some twelve months after the initial seminar. The intervening period had been one of inspection and analytical work, carried out on a scaffold erected to cover the first phases of work. Small areas of cleaning and pointing were undertaken and one Victorian statue was conserved, with its medieval niche, as a full-scale trial. This was the figure of Bishop Brithwold (no. 187b) (fig. 67).

The development of a well-defined philosophy was fundamental to the preparation of the conservation and repair policy. The authenticity and integrity of the west front were central and it was established that every effort should be made to preserve as much original material *in situ* as possible. This meant, in practice, the acceptance of weathered and damaged stones, where their retention was not structurally or aesthetically detrimental. A high value was set on the ancient surface and its patina, seeking to preserve the sense of age and history that the front expresses, whilst clarifying the original design through sensitive and selective cleaning and repair. For

67   The figure of Bishop Brithwold (no. 187b), before and after conservation as a full-scale trial in 1995.

example, worn lichen-covered surfaces were accepted as contributory to the dignity of the whole, if the stone was sound, whereas black soot crusts, which are visually disfiguring and potentially harmful, were removed or reduced.

Where stones had reached the end of their life, the need for replacement with new geologically similar stone was accepted. A meticulous study of the original forms ensured continuity with the original design. Where carved ornament was lost, the study of similar well preserved features elsewhere provided the basis for replacements. In terms of practical masonry conservation and repair treatment, there was an emphasis on materials and techniques that would be compatible both with the historic craftsmanship and with the physical and chemical properties of the ancient stone and mortar. Such methods are a proven form of repair and their use will facilitate future conservation and repair work. Thus the quality and durability of the work depends to a large degree on the craft skills of the masons, carvers and conservators. The appropriate technology was not always traditional, however, and advantage was also taken of recent advances, including laser cleaning. Primary consolidation has been carried out using ethyl silicate as a last resort in a very few instances, where lime methods were unable to hold the repair prior to conservation.

4. The Process and the Project Team

For the purposes of the project the west front was divided into five phases, with work progressing from south to north, allowing approximately one year for each. Although the procedure for each was broadly similar, there were exceptions. Phases One and Five, for example, hardly fitted the usual perception of the west front at all, comprising the side elevations of the flanking turrets and the rear, east-facing elevations of the structure. After twelve months of trials, Phase One, containing no statuary, offered the opportunity to test skills and methodology further, before turning the corner on to the west front proper.

A clear working procedure was adopted from the outset to ensure that the complex programme would be effectively carried out. The individual specialists and consultants all played their part, working ahead of the craftsmen and women, phase by phase. First, the existing photogrammetry donated by Laings Construction was enhanced at 1:20 scale by John Atherton Bowen, an archaeological draughtsman working under the auspices of Tim Tatton-Brown, the Cathedral Archaeologist (Appendix III). These drawings, delineating the west front stone by stone, were annotated by Jerry Sampson as part of the archaeological recording process. Stone and mortar types and dates were noted, together with archaeological and historical information relating to the structure and statuary. Much of this is recorded in the catalogue at the end of this volume.

Although the team was aware from the outset of the problems presented by statuary, it was perhaps concern for surviving polychrome decoration that shaped the process more than any other. A painstaking archaeological survey technique was developed in Phases One and Two, preparing the way for work on the interior of the central porch, as part of Phase Three. The wealth of surviving evidence here, from a sequence of medieval decorative schemes, presented a specific challenge. This was complicated further by an overlying discoloured surface layer (see below), thought to have been applied initially as a preservative.

The meticulous search for evidence of surviving polychromy formed part of the recording archaeologist's brief, his discoveries being followed up by detailed analytical work and appraisal by the specialist polychromy consultant, Eddie Sinclair. Her work on the decorative schemes is described elsewhere in this volume. Further specialist reports were commissioned on art-historical aspects of the west front's statuary, Tim Ayers contributing invaluable work on that of the medieval period and Emma Hardy on that of the 19th century. Summaries are found in earlier chapters.

Before the schedule of work was prepared, the first phase of masonry conservation was carried out - including holding repairs to the statuary, the removal of cement pointing and the preliminary cleaning of stone surfaces. The cleaned surface facilitated the scheduling stage, during which Michael Drury, the Cathedral Architect, his assistant Elizabeth Ozmin and Nicholas Durnan, the Consultant Conservator, decided on the level of stonework replacement and conservation treatment (fig. 68). Structural matters

68 Consultants on the scaffold at the top of the southern spirelet in 1995, prior to commencement of scheduling. From left to right: Elizabeth Ozmin (Assistant to the Cathedral Architect), Nicholas Durnan (Consultant Conservator), Jerry Sampson (Recording Archaeologist) and Tim Tatton-Brown (Cathedral Archaeologist). Photographed by Michael Drury (Cathedral Architect).

relating to the fabric and scaffolding design were handled by Andrew Waring, Consulting Structural Engineer.

The Dean and Chapter's consultants worked closely with English Heritage throughout the project, invaluable assistance being offered at various stages by their architects, quantity surveyors and specialist conservators. A particularly significant contribution was made by their Cathedrals Architects (Mrs Corinne Bennett OBE, succeeded by David Heath), both during and after the preparation of detailed project documentation, which included marked up drawings at 1:50 scale. These were passed to the Consultant Quantity Surveyor (initially Derek Slatter, succeeded by Jeffrey Weeks, both of Dearle and Henderson, Wilson, Colbeck, now known as Dearle Henderson Consulting) for costing and advice prior to the Dean and Chapter's approval for each phase. The Canon Treasurer, responsible for fabric matters, was (and remains) June Osborne, who succeeded John Stewart in 1995. Andrew Robertson succeeded Roy Spring as the Dean and Chapter's Clerk of Works in 1997.

5. Geology and Stone Supply
The west front is constructed primarily of local stone, known generically as Chilmark although the precise location of the medieval quarries remains unknown. Many were

certainly outside the parish of Chilmark. Medieval workings and natural outcropping suggest that much early material was extracted in and around Tisbury (fig. 69).[5] Certain elements like shafts and abaci were originally of Purbeck marble. These were largely replaced during Scott's restoration with Devonshire marble.

Chilmark/Tisbury Stone. The geological survey of the front suggests that the stone types are similar to those of the central tower, which were studied by Donovan:

> All the stone … has been obtained from the Upper Jurassic (Portlandian Stage) of the Vale of Wardour, and is known generically as 'Chilmark Stone'. It is composed of calcium carbonate (lime) with a variable, usually subsidiary proportion of sand grains, hence it is sometimes called a calcareous sandstone and sometimes a sandy limestone. Analysis shows a range of about 10% to 40% for the proportion of sand. The mineral glauconite (an iron silicate) is present as scattered grains and gives the rock its greenish or yellow colour. The stone has appreciable porosity, up to 30% by volume.
>
> The mediaeval work is carried out in a fine-grained variety of Chilmark Stone. Grain size is usually <100 micron. The stone generally appears homogeneous and even textured. A minority of blocks show the bedding marked by slight differences of colour and grain size. Cross bedding is sometimes present. Fossil shell fragments are present in some blocks. Chert nodules are occasionally seen.
>
> The repairs and replacements by George Gilbert Scott (1863-1876) were carried out with stone of a different variety from the medieval stone. Grain size is coarser, around 200-300 micron. The stone is usually conspicuously laminated on a millimetre scale, the laminations being due to variation in grain size. Calcite veins up to about 1 mm wide occur in a few blocks.[6]

Most of the 19th-century stone came from the 'Lower Building Stones', but it was reported in 1895 that an 'upper and oolitic freestone has been obtained by means of galleries at Chilmark; it was employed in the West Front of Salisbury Cathedral, and has lately been worked again'.[7] Not all of it has proved as durable as the medieval material (see below).

Ideally, for reasons of durability, workability and matching characteristics, a stone more akin to the original should be used for future repairs. Neither of the two supply-quarries operating today provides stone that is directly comparable, however. One is an open quarry on the south side of the Nadder Valley in Chicksgrove, the other a mine that continues earlier underground workings on the north-east side of the

[5] Tatton-Brown 1998.

[6] D.T. Donovan, 'Salisbury Cathedral, Interim Geological Report on Stone Decay', unpublished report for the Dean and Chapter, Salisbury Cathedral, November 1991.

[7] H.B. Woodward, *The Jurassic Rocks of Britain*, 1895, pp.312–317. He is quoting W.H. Hudleston, *On the Geology of the Vale of Wardour*, 1883, pp.167–68.

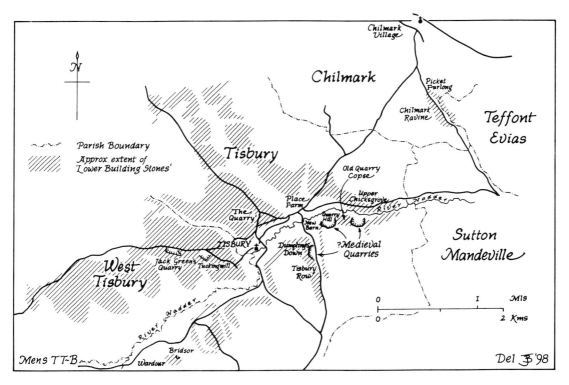

69   Map of Chilmark and Tisbury, showing the location of quarries.

Chilmark ravine. The mine tends to yield material that is relatively soft, greenish and sandier, the quarry's output being typically harder, whiter, shellier and more intractable.

Further investigation into stone supply was instigated as part of the west front programme. Mapping, sampling and thin-section analysis were undertaken by the British Geological Survey and this could provide the means to improve supply. The quarries that supplied the original builders may not yet all have been identified. Medieval stone was almost certainly taken from open workings and these are likely to have been in the Tisbury area. Their location would not only answer questions posed by archaeologists and historians, but might also help to resolve the cathedral's current stone supply needs.

Purbeck Marble.[8]   This is obtained from the very base of the Cretaceous strata and occurs in a narrow band running west from Swanage, Dorset, across the whole of the Isle of Purbeck:

[8] A very hard limestone that can be cut and polished is popularly known as a marble, but, geologically, the term should be reserved for metamorphic materials, originating from calcareous sediments, such as limestones and dolomites, that have been subjected to heat and pressure. The resulting structure is a coarsely crystalline calcite, having a granular texture with little foliation and no cavities or fossil remains.

True marble is not found in England, although a number of partly crystallised limestones occur which are hard and capable of taking a high polish … [Purbeck marble] occurs in two thin bands, usually not more than 30-50 cm in thickness, 2.5-3.5 metres apart, near the top of the Upper Purbeck beds. It is a hard, partly metamorphosed limestone, originally formed from the deposition of freshwater gastropods Viviparus cariniferus (formerly Paludina cariniferus) and Viviparus inflatus. The two beds may differ, the upper having a grey-green to blue colour while the lower stone, with a red brown tint, may sometimes contain the larger mussel shell, Unio porrectus. Visually the marble can be confused with other Purbeck beds, e.g. Purbeck burr, a softer limestone containing shell fragments of Viviparus shells, found below the marble beds, and in particular with material from the younger Lower Cretaceous Wealden beds from east Sussex and west Kent where thin beds of Sussex marble (containing the gastropod Viviparus sussexiensis) were worked in the mediaeval period. The presence of V. cariniferus, however, indicates that the stone is from the Purbeck strata. Published data indicates that gastropod shells and skeletal particles have inverted to calcite and are surrounded by a micritic sediment (fine microcrystalline calcite) together with some cavities, filled with a ferrous iron (ferroan) calcite cement. Other impurities, including glauconite and possibly clay minerals, may be present.[9]

Devonshire Marble.   This stone, like Purbeck, is not a true marble, but a limestone of the Devonian System:

The Devonian System has yielded limestones which had wide use. The principal beds occur in the middle Devonian in a belt extending from Plymouth across to Torquay, Devon. Babbacombe, Petit Tor, Ippledon, Ogwell, Kitley Green and Ashburton are widely known names of Devon 'marble'. They range from almost white to black. They are mostly veined or mottled and corals, stromaporoid (an extinct form of reef-building organism), and other fossils commonly contribute to the figuring. Natural exposures and polished slabs left unattended weather to a uniform pale dull grey. Internally however the limestones show a remarkable range of colours ranging from dark grey to almost black, commonly with white and yellowish streaks, veins and blotches. Grey to white, dove, pink and red, green and yellow variations may all be seen.[10]

The variety of Devon marble used in the Scott campaign at Salisbury has become known as Ashburton, but the material is certainly not the dark charcoal-grey stone normally associated with this name, characterised by thin pink and white veins textured with fossil corals. Ashburton might have offered a stronger contrast with the Chilmark, as did the Purbeck originally. The colour of the stone chosen by Scott varies, but is

[9]   J. Price, 'Removal and Conservation Problems of a Twelfth-Century Screen with Notes on Purbeck Marble', in proceedings of the IIC Bologna Conference, *The Conservation of Stone and Wallpaintings*, London, 1986, pp.142–47.
[10]   J. Ashurst and F. Dimes, *The Conservation of Building and Decorative Stone*, London, 1990, p.90.

generally a pale dove grey with pinkish tendencies. Its visual incompatibility was noted from the start, as the Dean and Chapter reported in 1869:

> The decayed shafts, capitals and bases of the numerous windows have been thoroughly restored. These were originally of Purbeck marble, a material peculiarly liable to decay. It was therefore resolved by the recommendation of Mr Scott, to employ in repairing them a variety of the Devonshire marble as being more durable and less costly than the Purbeck. The juxtaposition of these two kinds of marble, differing as they do in external appearance, offend the eye. In order to soften the contrast a process of rubbing and oiling the surfaces of both is now being employed, under the sanction of Mr Scott, with a view of assimilating, as nearly as possible, the colour of the new to that of the old material. The result of the experiment has, thus far, been highly satisfactory.[11]

6. Condition and Causes of Decay

The appearance of the front before repair and conservation began was typical of a limestone structure that had not been cleaned for over a century. The higher exposed parts were rain-washed clean, with abundant lichen and algae growth, except for the undersides of the deeply moulded arcading and tracery. The pale green of the Chilmark/Tisbury stone was clearly displayed, contrasting with the light grey of the Devonshire marble shafts. The lower half of the front, being more sheltered, had collected more soot crusts, which extended to the statues and ashlar below weatherings. Many sheltered areas were a yellowy brown, the result of a discoloured surface treatment, probably applied in the 19th century (see below).

The condition of the stonework depended on whether it was rain-washed or sheltered, exposed or protected, plain or sculptural, simple bold moulding or intricate and deeply undercut, medieval stone or 19th-century replacement, south or north side, and so on. Overall, there was a loss of carved and moulded detail, and the sharp lines and deep mouldings of the original design were obscured by the colour and texture of the surface accumulations. Decay was clearly visible, especially to the medieval statues on the south buttress and the north turret, and to hoods and canopy mouldings over most of the front. The Chilmark/Tisbury ashlar and much of the plainer carving were in remarkably sound condition, whereas the sculptural and ornamental elements and the deeply undercut 13th-century mouldings were prone to severe decay.

Barely any of the original Purbeck marble had survived. Drawings show that many of the shafts were already missing in the 19th century and those that remained were probably in a similar condition to the medieval Purbeck shafts in the cloister today. Scott chose to replace them with Devonshire marble because it was supposed to be more durable, and it has so far proved to be so.

[11] Dean and Chapter, 'Report on the Restorations', *The Builder*, 6 May 1869, p.384.

The Chilmark stone of Scott's restoration is less durable than the original, being more prone to laminating and surface cracking, so that much has required replacement in the current programme. An additional factor in this decay was determined by Scott's 1866 specification, which instructed 'all new stone work and building of old stone to be built in Roman cement and pointed with Portland cement in equal proportions of sand and cement, all grouting to be done in Roman cement'.

The main cause of decay, however, has been the chemical change of the calcium carbonate binder in the stone to calcium sulphate, as a result of atmospheric sulphurous acids from the burning of fossil fuels. Analysis of the stone from many parts of the cathedral has revealed the presence of the soluble salt calcium sulphate, which eventually breaks down the stone surface through repeated cycles of crystallisation. This process of sulphation causes gypsum skins, exfoliation of surfaces, deep soft powdery layers, the cracking and falling away of large pieces of stone, and the disfiguring soot crusts that have built up in sheltered areas.

The eight medieval figure sculptures remaining on the front were repaired during Scott's restoration. All have 19th-century heads, except one, and even this has a 19th-century face (no. 95). Several of the statues have restored arms and hands. Five were in a very weak and friable condition, showing signs of accelerating decay. John the Baptist (no. 145) and St Paul (no. 95) on the south buttress had suffered much surface loss in the last hundred years, especially the Baptist. This figure was carved from a thin slab, approximately 150 mm thick, and rested precariously upon two worn and decayed ankles. The pair of medieval statues on the upper tier of the central buttresses (nos.19a and 26a) was also in an alarmingly fractured and friable condition.

The 19th-century statues varied in condition, depending on location. Some were severely laminated and some were near perfect, but the majority displayed some kind of decay and loss of detail. As the statues are face-bedded, lamination has been a particular problem, causing losses to arms, attributes and protruding drapery.

7. Architecture and Sculpture Conservation

The majority of the masonry conservation work was carried out by the conservators of the Works Department (see Appendix II). They have worked alongside specialist conservators for specific tasks like polychromy and metal conservation, and for specific areas presenting complex conservation problems, such as the west porch. Multidisciplinary skills were required of them.

The policy for the conservation of both architectural and sculptural stonework has been to retain as much original stone as possible and to use materials that are physically and chemically compatible with the existing stone and lime mortar (see Appendix I). The following methodology was used for both the architectural and sculptural stonework, differing only in scale and subtlety of application:

· Recording condition of stone and becoming familiar with the decay patterns and qualities of the different stone types.
· Removing or reducing unwanted and potentially harmful accretions.
· Repairing fractures and cracks using non-ferrous pins and dowels, and repairing decayed surfaces using lime mortars.
· Applying consolidants to friable stone.
· Applying protective coatings to stone surfaces.
· Recording all conservation interventions.

The wide range of techniques, combined with the scale of the project, enabled work to continue throughout the year. Only during frosty weather did cleaning and mortar repair work have to stop. Conservation was also carefully co-ordinated with masonry replacement. The typical sequence was for the conservation team to clean the stonework and remove cement. They were followed by the masons, who then cut out and replaced the most severely decayed stone. Once new stones were in place, the conservation team returned to carry out repairs and apply protective coatings to the architectural and sculptural stone surfaces.

Masonry Conservation.   The first conservation process was the recording of the condition of the stone, on 1:20 scale drawings (fig. 70). Through this process the architect and conservator became familiar with the actual condition of the stone. This was followed by a series of cleaning operations, to reduce surface accretions that were either visually or physically detrimental to the appearance and condition of the stonework. A balance had to be struck between maintaining the surface patina, developed through the ageing process of the stone, and the removal of harmful materials. The sensitivity of the conservator was paramount in this.

Cleaning began by dry brushing with bristle brushes, to remove or reduce loose dirt, algae and lichen. This was followed by ammonium carbonate poulticing, to soften the black soot crusts that had accumulated in sheltered areas. After brushing and poultice cleaning were complete, the remaining stubborn soot crusts were cleaned using the Jos Vortex System, which involves a fully controllable wet calcite abrasive. On copings and weathering surfaces that had accumulated ingrained dark lichens and algae, a low-volume water pressure washer was used.

Cleaning revealed a 19th-century hard grey cement pointing, which was carefully removed by hand, using a hammer and tungsten chisels. Fortunately, in most cases this was merely a thin layer over the original 13th-century creamy white lime mortar, on average less than 6 mm thick, but around 19th-century replacement stonework the cement mortar was deep and very difficult to remove without damaging the stone; so it was usually left.

Condition in 1994 prior to Repair & Conservation

KEY:
∴ Soot Crusts
/// Friable Surfaces/Exfoliation
✕ Sugaring Surfaces
⌒ Cracking
≡ Scott Preservative?
⌐ Portland Cement

Zinc alloy sword

St. Paul

Lead pen

Victorian shellac adhesive

St. Luke

70 A small section of the record drawing at 1:20 scale, showing (a) a condition drawing, and (b) conservation and repair.

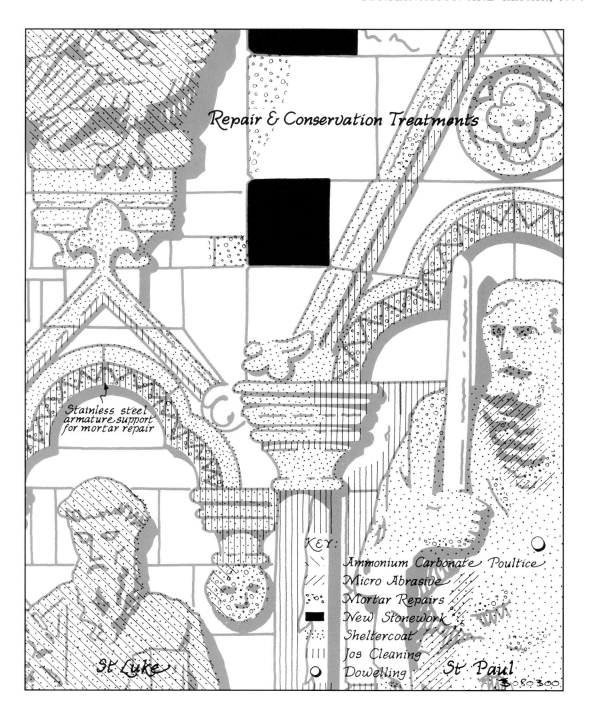

Repair & Conservation Treatments

Stainless steel
armature support
for mortar repair

KEY:
Ammonium Carbonate Poultice
Micro Abrasive
Mortar Repairs
New Stonework
Sheltercoat
Jos Cleaning
Dowelling

St Luke

St Paul

With the cement and other accretions removed, the actual condition of the stone and joints was clearly visible. Conservation work ceased whilst stonework replacement was carried out. Only where a stone was so decayed that it no longer had any meaning, or was not performing its function, was it replaced. More often a stone might be found that had not wholly decayed; usually stones were partially decayed and partially sound. In this situation there was the option of either piecing-in the decayed area with new stone or removing the decayed surface and applying a lime mortar repair.

After stone replacement and piecing-in were complete, the conservation team returned to apply conservation and repair treatments. Decayed areas that had been designated for lime mortar repair were prepared and filled with a mortar composed of Chilmark, Portland and local greensand stone dusts, Buxton non-hydraulic lime putty and a natural pozzolanic additive (see below). Depending on the type of stonework and the amount of decay or stone loss, the mortar repairs were used either as cappings or to restore the lost form. Deep repairs required building up in several layers and some required non-ferrous armatures. Very exposed areas and weathering stones were repaired using moderately hydraulic lime mortar.

Limewater surface consolidation treatment (a clear solution of calcium hydroxide/putty lime) was applied locally to sheltered surfaces that displayed a powdery quality. Following mortar repair and limewater treatment, one application of sheltercoat composed of finely sieved Chilmark, Portland and local greensand stone dusts, Buxton non-hydraulic lime putty and casein was given to vulnerable areas of carved stonework and moulded masonry (fig. 72).

Comprehensive conservation and repair records were compiled as work proceeded (figs. 70, 71). The conservators, carvers and masons recorded their own interventions on 1:50-scale stone-by-stone drawings. There were two drawings for each area of stonework: a condition record, showing areas and types of decay, cement pointing and repairs, and iron fixings; and a conservation and repair record, showing cleaning methods, stone replacement and treatments.

Conservation and Repair of Statues.   At the policy-making stage it was resolved to conserve all the statues on the west front *in situ*, whatever their condition. It was felt that their meaning derived largely from their location and architectural setting. The conservation techniques were thus designed to be repeatable in the future, as in the earlier sculpture conservation programmes at Wells and Exeter Cathedrals.[12]

The first stage of the practical conservation work, after condition records had been made, was to apply holding repairs to vulnerable areas using lime mortar. These consolidated vulnerable surfaces in preparation for cleaning. Further temporary

[12] N. Durnan, 'Conservation of Exterior Sculpture', in *Stone Conservation – State of the Art*, ed. P. Burman, Donhead (Dorset), forthcoming; idem, 'An Assessment of the "Lime Method" of Conservation of Exterior Limestone Sculpture', in *Sculpture Conservation, Preservation or Interference*, ed. P. Lindley, Aldershot, 1997, pp.83–94.

protection was provided by specially designed wooden canopies fixed above the statuary. Areas of soot crusts were then cleaned with ammonium carbonate poultices, followed by a dry microabrasive system using fine aluminium oxide powder. Lichen and algae were removed or reduced using wooden and plastic modelling tools.

The most challenging aspect of the statue repair and conservation process lay in dealing with severely decayed and deteriorating surfaces. Many of the statues were missing parts of their anatomy and attributes. Our policy from the start was not to make conjectural repairs, but only to repair lost forms when we were sure of the original sculptors' intentions. There was not enough detail in early photographs to guide such a process, so no conjectural repairs were made to any statue during the programme.

The modelling and repair of statues with lime mortars using these criteria requires considerable skill and sensitivity. Knowing how far to go depends upon really coming to understand the three-dimensional forms of each statue. Both the medieval and Victorian statues have been treated in the same way, with equal respect for their integrity (fig. 72). On completion of the mortar repairs, each figure was sheltercoated to give further protection and to reintegrate the sculptural forms (figs. 73-76).

Two statues defied the most ardent attempts at conservation *in situ*, those at the top of the north and south central buttresses (nos. 19a and 26a). Both showed enthroned figures in mass vestments originally, but had been heavily restored as

71 Senior Conservator David Henson completing the conservation record for the 19th-century statue of the Blessed Virgin (no. 181b) above the west porch.

72 Sculpture Conservator Christina Kaye applying mortar repairs to the 19th-century statue of St Thomas of Canterbury (no. 196).

73   St Birinus (no .166) before and after conservation.

angels during Scott's restoration. The combination of poor quality 19th-century Chilmark, rusting iron fixings, numerous structural fractures and deep friable stone led us reluctantly to the conclusion that both statues should be removed. They have been conserved and kept close to their original location, however, and can now be seen in a special exhibition at the west end of the nave roof.

8. *Innovative Conservation and Repair Techniques*

Purbeck and Devonshire Marbles.   Before the west front programme began, conservation trials were carried out to a cluster of Purbeck shafts in the south walk

74   St Alban (no. 192) before and after conservation.

of the cloister by conservator Mike Burleigh (1994). As a result, a lime/casein repair mix was developed that set hard enough to take a polish, adhered well to the stone surface and could be coloured to emulate the distinctive markings of the stone. Lias lime (hl2) from Somerset was found to be superior to putty lime for such work, in controlling the malleability of the mortar and avoiding the fine hair-line cracks that appear in putty lime/casein mortars. These lias lime/casein mortars were subsequently used to repair both Purbeck and Devonshire marbles across the front.

Mike Burleigh also tested a range of wax surface protective treatments for Purbeck. Renaissance (microcrystalline) wax was found to be the most suitable, in terms of

75   St Lucy (no. 152) and St Agatha (no. 153) before and after conservation.

penetration, clarity and colour enrichment. It has been used to protect all the Purbeck and Devonshire marble surfaces. It was also used elsewhere. Above and below the central capital of the trumeau of the great west door there are bronze bands, seemingly unique in medieval architecture in Britain. Careful study by metals conservator Andrew Naylor led him to conclude that they were originally polished. Why bronze was chosen, rather than the much cheaper gilded stone, remains a mystery. The present black and green patina contains the original metal surface and thus was only lightly cleaned and then waxed to protect it from further corrosion.[13]

Ethyl Silicate Consolidation Treatment.   The decay and fragility of small areas on 11 statues (such as fingers and locks of hair) necessitated the application of a consolidant (or stone strengthener) prior to the application of lime treatments. Ethyl silicate was selected, as it had a good track record on exterior sandstone and trials indicated that the sandy limestone at Salisbury was equally susceptible to such treatment.

[13]   The bronze was cleaned using Prelim conservation standard abrasive paste, treated with benzotriazole solution (3 per cent by volume in mineral spirit) and protected with two coats of Renaissance wax.

76 Noah (no. 59) before and after conservation.

The clear solution is applied by pipette, brush or fine spray to a dry surface and its low viscosity enables it to penetrate deep into the stone, where a curing process by reaction with moisture takes place lasting up to 28 days, depending on weather conditions. At the end of this time silica has formed within the pores of the stone, but the stone is still permeable. As a result, stones previously too friable to take a lime mortar repair become strong enough to receive one. The permeable nature of the treated area ensures a sympathetic interface between mortar and stone. This combination of a synthetic material and a traditional one has produced successful results, allowing the retention of features that would otherwise, in the last resort, have been lost.

Putty Lime and Hydraulic Lime Mortar.   Lime mortars have been used extensively both for the repair of decaying stone surfaces and for repointing. In general, the lime mortars have been putty based, with the addition of Trass, a naturally occurring pozzolan to aid setting and increase durability. Since the beginning of the repair programme, in 1994, the availability of reliable hydraulic limes has been of great interest to us. Trials were carried out using the French Saint-Astier range.

Complementary to these was the testing of Metastar (metakaolin – calcined Cornish china clay) pozzolans as an alternative to Trass.

As a result of the trials, the Saint-Astier moderately hydraulic lime (NHL 3.5) was introduced for the repair and repointing of particularly exposed areas, and for large-scale mortar repairs to architectural detail. It has durability and minimal shrinkage, whilst retaining a similar permeability to putty lime mortars. The majority of the lime mortar repairs to the architectural detail and to the statuary have, however, been carried out using pozzolanic putty lime mortars, Trass being retained as the pozzolanic additive.

9. Conservation and Polychromed Masonry

Little medieval polychromy survives on the exterior elevations of English churches and cathedrals, so the survivals at Salisbury are very important. The majority are concentrated within the west porch, where virtually every medieval stone retains some remnant and trace of colour. Details of the condition, pigments and location of the paint are dealt with elsewhere in this volume. This section concentrates on how the unique cleaning and conservation problems were addressed.

The main task, and the one presenting the greatest challenge, was the removal or reduction of the so-called 'Scott preservative' a brown surface treatment probably applied during or soon after Scott's restoration. It appeared to have had no preservative effect, was discoloured to a rather unsightly brown and in many places had blistered away from the stone, taking the top surface with it. It was decided to remove or reduce this where possible. On architectural stonework, it was reduced using a combination of ammonium carbonate poultice and gentle microabrasive cleaning. However, in the porch the extensive polychrome survivals under the preservative layer necessitated special techniques. Three separate analyses of the preservative were carried out, by the Historic Building and Site Services of Bournemouth University (1994), by Sandberg (1998) and by The Getty Conservation Institute (1999). Each produced a different result (casein, natural resins and wax/oil respectively), aged natural organic materials being notoriously difficult to identify. The analyses were useful in suggesting possible components of the preservative, but did not solve the problem of how to remove it.

A series of cleaning trials was carried out, initially by polychrome conservator Ann Ballantyne (1997) and then in October 1998 by the polychrome and sculpture conservator Christopher Weeks, who had extensive experience of cleaning and conserving polychromy on stone at Amiens Cathedral, using lasers and microabrasive techniques.[14] It became apparent that the preservative was so inextricably bonded to the upper surface of the stone and polychromy that complete removal would be impossible. The carefully controlled and recorded trials were highly successful and showed that the use of a microabrasive, combined with the NdYAG laser (fig. 77)

[14] Weeks 1998.

was the safest method for cleaning the polychromy and carved surfaces, and reducing and lightening the preservative layer.[15]

77 Conservator Christopher Weeks cleaning medieval stonework within the west porch using the NdYAG laser.

As a result, we proposed to use this combination of techniques for both poly-chromed and non-polychromed stone surfaces. However, the English Heritage Building Conservation Research Team expressed concerns regarding the safe use of lasers for cleaning polychromy, with the result that the laser was excluded from the range of techniques. The trial area executed in October 1998 remains undisturbed by subsequent intervention, however. Future monitoring may be of immense value to conservators who are considering the use of the NdYAG laser for cleaning historic surfaces with traces of polychromy.

After the trials had been fully discussed, the agreed treatment for the polychromy and associated stone surfaces within the porch was implemented as follows:

- Polychromed surfaces were cleaned using a combination of gentle dry brushing and microabrasive.
- Areas of previously painted stone surface, where the original polychromy no longer existed, were cleaned with the laser in combination with microabrasive.

Continuous assessment of the overall visual balance between stones holding polychromy and non-polychromed stones resulted in the preparation of specific cleaning criteria:

- Potentially damaging accretions (soot, preservative, and general dust and grime) were to be removed or reduced, to minimise the adverse effect that they might be having.
- Polychrome and stone surfaces were to be cleaned to enable the condition of stone and polychromy to be assessed, and to enable appropriate conservation treatment to be applied.
- The porch was to be cleaned to similar levels as the west front elevation, so that the architectural and sculptural decoration would 'read' clearly, and so that the

[15] The laser was an 'R10' NdYAG, manufactured by Lynton Lasers of Wilmslow, Cheshire. It operates at 1064 nm with a pulse length of 6–9 ns; beam delivery is through four fibre-optic cables, allowing an average energy of 1J per pulse.

colours of the surviving polychromy could be more clearly seen, both at close range and from the ground.

Both sturgeon glue and acrylic resins were used as adhesives and consolidants for refixing detached paint flakes and strengthening friable paint layers.[16]

Before work began and during the work itself, comprehensive written, drawn and photographic records were compiled by the conservation team. Archaeological records prepared in the preceding years were collated and examined. Each stone was numbered and recorded separately. Along with this comprehensive record, the opportunity for testing an innovative video recording system was allowed.[17]

10. Masonry and Carving

The repair and conservation of the spire, tower and west front during the last ten years have enabled the masons and carvers in the Salisbury Cathedral Works Department to develop an intimate knowledge of the medieval mouldings and ornament found here.

The masonry department is divided up into five specialist areas: sawyers, setters out, banker masons, fixer masons and carvers. Each has an important role to play in replacing a stone. The process begins with the setter out, who uses the schedule drawings that specify which stones are to be replaced, and then measures and draws the required profiles. The making of these templates is a painstaking task, first because each stone is different and secondly because, where old stones are very decayed or worn, the original profile has to be calculated by studying adjacent sounder stonework. The accurate reproduction and the fitting of the new stone depend entirely on the setter out's skill. The templates are first drawn at full size on cartridge paper and then transferred to tough semi-transparent orange plastic. The banker masons apply these to the sawn stone (fig. 80) and work to the profiles.

The stone arrives from the Chicksgrove quarry in three to four tonne blocks (fig. 78), which are stacked in the masons' yard before sawing. The primary saw scants the blocks (cutting two opposite faces) in preparation for the secondary saw (fig. 79), which cuts and profiles each stone to size. It is then ready to go to the banker masons and carvers (fig. 80), who work the stone using a combination of pneumatic chisels and hand tools. Chicksgrove is a hard stone and requires the use of tungsten chisels. The surface is left to a tooled finish, just as it was by the medieval masons. Some of the complex 13th-century moulded stones present a time-consuming challenge. The most detailed can take up to eight weeks to work.

The worked stones are then stacked in the masons' yard on wooden pallets, protected from frost, before being taken up the west front by the fixer masons. The

[16] The majority of refixing was effected with B72 acrylic co-polymer at 5 per cent solution in acetone.
[17] MuSIS 2000, a multi-spectral CCD imaging system manufactured by Art Innovation, Hengelo, The Netherlands.

78 Blocks of Chicksgrove stone in the masons' yard.

79 Sawyer Gary Price sawing Chilmark stone.

80 Mason Robert Hawes carving a new cross for the west porch gable.

81 Fixer masons Jonathan Parsons and David Vanstone setting new weathering stones in place.

82 A newly carved plinth stone, by Henry Gray, supporting the medieval statue of St Paul (no. 95).

83 Jason Battle carving a new angel in Chicksgrove stone for niche no. 26, with a half-size plaster maquette in the foreground.

old stone is carefully cut out and the internal condition of adjacent stone is assessed before the replacement is fixed (figs. 81, 82). The new stonework is bedded and pointed with lime mortar. If necessary, the stone is grouted using a proprietary lime/bentonite/pulverized fuel ash (pfa) product. Once the mortar and grout is set, any necessary trimming-in is done.

The carvers are responsible for preparing full-size clay models of the carving to be replaced, which is invariably in such poor condition that comparisons with similar carvings elsewhere are necessary. Once approved, the models are copied to stone. The head carver Jason Battle was given a unique commission to design and carve two replacement angels for medieval statues that had been removed (see above). A lengthy consultation process with the Dean and Chapter and advisory bodies was required to achieve agreement on their final form. Working from half-size maquettes in plaster, two statues of angels in Chicks-grove stone have been made (fig. 83), which are expressive and sensitively carved with contrasting textures for flesh and drapery. They are intended to fit within the medieval architectural context and to complement the existing medieval and Victorian statuary on the west front.

11. *Glass Conservation*

The windows of the west front contain some of the best of Salisbury Cathedral's surviving medieval glass, with additional material of later dates from elsewhere. This is not described in detail in the present volume, as it is comprehensively covered by Sarah Brown in the recent publication '*Sumptuous and Richly Adorn'd*', for the former RCHME.[18] All of the west front glass has been carefully taken down, conserved and returned behind new isothermal glazing, as part of the recent programme. The

[18] RCHME 1999, pp.97, 99.

windows were considered as an entity, comprising ferramenta and oak sub-frames as well as glass, the conservation and repair of each element being given due regard. Some of the deep oak sub-frames and ferramenta are thought to be ancient survivals and have been retained where possible to support the isothermal glazing, a new system being developed to support the original glass.

12. Public Access and Information

During the conservation a tour programme was set up, enabling visitors to see work in progress on the scaffold. The processes were explained by specially trained guides. The Dean and Chapter, and their consultants, were particularly pleased to be able to offer visitors this opportunity, compensating for the front's shrouded appearance and allowing them to experience something of the conservation process.

The polychromy within the porch was seen as an especially interesting part of the work and a full-size coloured reconstruction of the tympanum was fixed to the front of the scaffold at the same level as the original, within. The reconstruction showed Eddie Sinclair's carefully deduced recreation of the last medieval decorative scheme. Exhibition boards outside the west porch also gave illustrated and written information about both the history of the front, and the repair and conservation programme. Information leaflets for visitors, grant aided by the Conservation Unit of the Museums and Galleries Commission, were also available.

13. Records

The written, drawn and photographic records are now stored in duplicate, one copy being with the Cathedral Architect, Michael Drury, and a second with the Cathedral Fabric Records Clerk, Roy Spring. Interested parties can access the record from either source by prior arrangement. The photographs and coloured drawings are carefully stored under appropriate environmental conditions.

14. Inspection, Monitoring and Maintenance

Regular inspection and monitoring of the condition of the west front are essential for the continued well being of the fabric. Many of the problems that have occurred since Scott's restoration could have been avoided through regular maintenance. It is now accepted that materials like stone and glass are continually changing, especially in the modern polluted environment. It is only through monitoring these changes that the appropriate intervention can be made. 'Little and often' is the maxim whereby historic buildings are now maintained and this type of programme was introduced on completion of the major conservation and repair programmes on the west fronts of Wells and Exeter Cathedrals.

The west front will now be inspected every five years and the results will form part of the Cathedral Architect's quinquennial report. As there is a large area of stonework, the front will be divided in two and one half will be inspected every two-and-a-half years. The upper levels will be inspected first, two-and-a-half years after completion of the repair and conservation programme. The inspection will concentrate on the following parts of the fabric: stone surfaces of statues, carvings and architectural detail; and the conservation treatments of repointing, mortar repairs, ethyl silicate consolidation, waxing and sheltercoat. The medieval polychromy within the porch and elsewhere on the front will also be closely monitored. Levels of growth of algae, lichen, moss and plants will be recorded.

Much of the decay of the stonework and glass is due to air pollution. The recording of atmospheric pollutants like nitrogen dioxide and sulphur dioxide in the vicinity of the west front will be carried out in cooperation with Salisbury District Council Environmental Health Department. This information will be of use to future repairers and researchers, and for comparing past and current levels of atmospheric pollutants.

15. Summary

The intention of the conservation and repair process has been to ensure the integrity of the west front's overall appearance and to respect the venerable surface of the ancient fabric. A degree of contrast was intended to reinforce the architectural balance, the statues now being more clearly defined within their niches, the dark Purbeck and Devonshire marble shafts more clearly set off against the pale Chilmark, Tisbury and Chicksgrove stones, and the architectural detail and mouldings more legible, as intended by the medieval designers.

As a result of the work, the stone surfaces are refreshed and healthy, while still showing their age and honestly revealing repairs where they have been necessary. The work has been a logical development of the approaches and techniques developed for the conservation and repair of historic stonework during the last 25 years, combining ethics, aesthetics and tradition, and integrating these with modern scientific and technological advances.

APPENDIX I

Repair and Conservation Techniques for Architectural and Sculptural Stonework

Repair and Conservation Technique	Purpose	Location/ Stone type	Procedure	Equipment	Materials	Result
Cleaning – dry brushing	Reduction of algae and lichen	All areas	Gently dry brush stone surfaces	Variety of natural bristle brushes		75% reduction in algal/lichen deposits
Cleaning – Jos Vortex system	Reduction of soot crusts	All architectural surfaces holding soot crusts	Hand-held Piccolo nozzle working across and downwards over surfaces	Jos Vortex system with Piccolo and Micro nozzles	White Calcite abrasive 5-300 micron	90% reduction of soot crusts
Cleaning – ammonium carbonate poultice	Reduction and softening of soot crusts before Jos cleaning	All areas	Poultice applied to dampened stone surfaces 2.5% w/v ammonium carbonate in tap water		Ammonium carbonate, Sepiolite, paper pulp	30–40% reduction of soot crusts
Cleaning – microabrasive	Reduction of soot crusts and 'Scott' preservative	Sculpture and polychromy		Sandmaster Microabrasive System	Aluminium oxide powder – 17 micron	95% reduction of soot crusts, 50% reduction of 'preservative'
Cleaning – laser	Reduction of soot crusts and 'Scott' preservative	Architectural and sculptural stonework in porch excluding polychromy	Hand-held gun with fibre-optic cable at distance of 50–100 mm from stone surface	Phoenix NdYAG, 1–15 Hz repetition rate, average fluence 0–0.7 J/cm2		98% reduction of soot crusts, 75% reduction of 'preservative'
Cement removal	Removal of cement pointing from joints	All areas	Cutting out by hand using hammer and tungsten chisels			98% reduction from medieval joints, 10% reduction from Victorian joints

Repair and Conservation Technique	Purpose	Location/ Stone type	Procedure	Equipment	Materials	Recipes
Mortar repairs – architectural	Fill voids, protect vulnerable areas, restore lost form	All areas excluding 'marble'	Remove friable stone, key surface, apply, compress and texture mortar	Dental tools, hammer and chisels, spatulas	Lime putty, sand, stonedusts and pozzolanic additives	Typical recipe Lime putty 1 Graded stonedust 2 Sand 0.5 Trass 10%
Mortar repairs – sculpture	Fill voids, protect vulnerable areas, restore lost form	Statues	Remove friable stone, key surface, apply, compress and texture mortar	Dental tools and spatulas	Lime putty, sand, stonedusts and pozzolanic additives	Typical recipe Lime putty 1 Graded stonedust 2 Sand 0.5 Trass 10%
Mortar repairs – 'marble'	Fill voids, protect vulnerable areas, restore lost form	Purbeck and Devonshire 'marble' elements	Remove friable stone, key surface, apply and rub down mortar	Dental tools, hammer and chisels, spatulas	Moderately hydraulic lime, casein, sand and stonedusts	Typical recipe Hydraulic lime 1 Graded stonedust 3 Casein 0.25 Earth pigment
Mortar repairs – weatherings	Fill voids, protect vulnerable areas, restore lost form	Strings, coping and weatherings	Remove friable stone, key surface, apply, compress and texture mortar	Dental tools, hammer and chisels, spatulas	Moderately hydraulic lime, sand and stonedusts	Typical recipe Hydraulic lime 1 Graded stonedust 2 Sand 0.5
Repointing	Fill open joints, replace cement mortar	All areas	Apply, compress and texture mortar	Pointing irons and spatulas	Lime putty, sand, stonedusts and pozzolanic additives	Typical recipe Lime putty 1 Graded sand 2 Stonedust 0.5 Trass 10%
Limewater consolidation	Consolidate powdering surfaces		Apply 40 applications by means of spray	Metal dustbin, wood/polystyrene float, syphon tube	Putty lime and tap water	
Sheltercoat – architectural	Fill microcracks and protect sheltered areas from sulphation	All mouldings, ornament and sculpture	Applied and compressed by brush	Soft bristle brushes	Lime putty, stonedusts, sands and casein	Typical recipe Lime putty 1 Graded stonedust 3 Thinned with tap water/ skimmed milk 50/50
Waxing – 'marble'	Fill microcracks, protect surfaces and enrich stone colour	All 'marble'	Applied by brush, heated in and mechanically polished.	Brushes, hot air gun, rotary polishing brush	Microcrystalline wax, Renaissance wax	2 coats of Renaissance wax followed by 2 coats of microcrystalline wax

APPENDIX II

Personnel on the West Front Project

Masons and Carvers (Salisbury Cathedral Works Department)
Brenda Aldridge, Colin Avery (head mason), Tonia Batchelor, Jason Battle (carver), Steve Beer, Paul Bloomfield (head mason), Gaetan Chapel, Rachel Cooke, Simon Elloway, Shea Finney, Robin Golden-Hann, Henry Gray, Piers Hanley, Robert Hawes, Clive Hunter, John Lane, Gareth Lewis, Jonathan Parsons, Sarah Pennel, Simon Pickett, Chris Sampson (head mason), Leigh Silvester, Roger Stephens, Mark Thompson, Bradley Townsend, Tom Trenchard (carver), Gordon Tucker, Gordon Utting, David Vanstone, Gerry Wilson

Sawyers (Salisbury Cathedral Works Department)
Douglas Ford, Gary Price, Peter Townsend

Conservators (Salisbury Cathedral Works Department)
Rowan Adams, Kate Anstead, Phil Arnold, Gary Birkwood, Tody Cezar, Chris Daniels, Anthony Evans-Pugh, Katherine Hallett, Kate Hardy, James Harford, Alison Henry (sculpture), David Henson (Senior Conservator), Sarah Heyatt, Danielle Horne, Richard Humphries, Linda Johnson, Christina Kaye (sculpture), Damian Kaye, John Macaulay, Elizabeth McCrimmon, Nell Pickering, Andy Pullen, Mark Sidebottom, Marianne Suhr, Helen Thompson, Christina Young, Helena Zakiewicz
Christopher Weeks (west porch), Ann Ballantyne (west porch)

Glaziers (Salisbury Cathedral Works Department)
Kathy Crouch, Sam Kelly (head glazier), Vicky Smith, Trevor Wiffen (head glazier), Celine Zuretti

Specialist Conservators
Christopher Weeks (polychrome conservation, west porch), Ann Ballantyne (polychrome conservation trials, west porch), Andrew Naylor (bronze conservation, west porch)
Medieval glass conservation was undertaken by Goddard & Gibbs, initially under the control of their specialist conservator Drew Anderson and later with the assistance

of Canterbury Cathedral Stained Glass Conservation Studio under the supervision of Dr Sebastian Strobl.

Hoist Operators (Salisbury Cathedral Works Department)
Lynn Court, Gordon Gay

Labourers (Salisbury Cathedral Works Department)
Steve Melon, Mark White

Works Department Management
John Croad (General Manager), Ted Hillier (Works Foreman), John Martin (Works Manager), Alasdair Murray (Finance Manager), Mark Robertson (Estimator/Surveyor), Michael Statezney (Works Manager)

Dean and Chapter
The Very Revd Hugh Dickinson (Dean, until 1996), The Very Revd Derek Watson (Dean); Revd Canon June Osborne (Canon Treasurer); Christopher Owen (Chapter Clerk), Roy Spring (Clerk of Works until 1996), Andrew Robertson (Clerk of Works)

Project Team and Consultants
Michael Drury (Cathedral Architect), Elizabeth Ozmin (Assistant to the Cathedral Architect), Tim Tatton-Brown (Consultant Archaeologist), Andrew Waring (Consulting Engineer), Jeffrey Weeks (Quantity Surveyor), Nicholas Durnan (Consultant Conservator), Eddie Sinclair (Polychrome Consultant), Jerry Sampson (Recording Archaeologist), John Atherton Bowen (Draughtsman), Nigel Tucker (Safety Planning Supervisor)

APPENDIX III

Scale Drawings of the West Front

The following is a record of the fabric of the west front prior to the conservation programme of 1994-2000, made by John Atherton Bowen. The 18 numbered drawings record the front and turrets from top to bottom and from left to right, beginning with the north, west and south faces (drawings 1-6), and continuing with the east face or back (drawings 7-12), the buttress flanks with adjacent wall sections (drawings 10, 12, 13, 15, 16, 18), and the central porch (drawings 14, 16-18). The interior west wall of the nave was not fully recorded. The drawings were made to a scale of 1:20 (as marked) but are here reproduced at approximately 1:100.

1

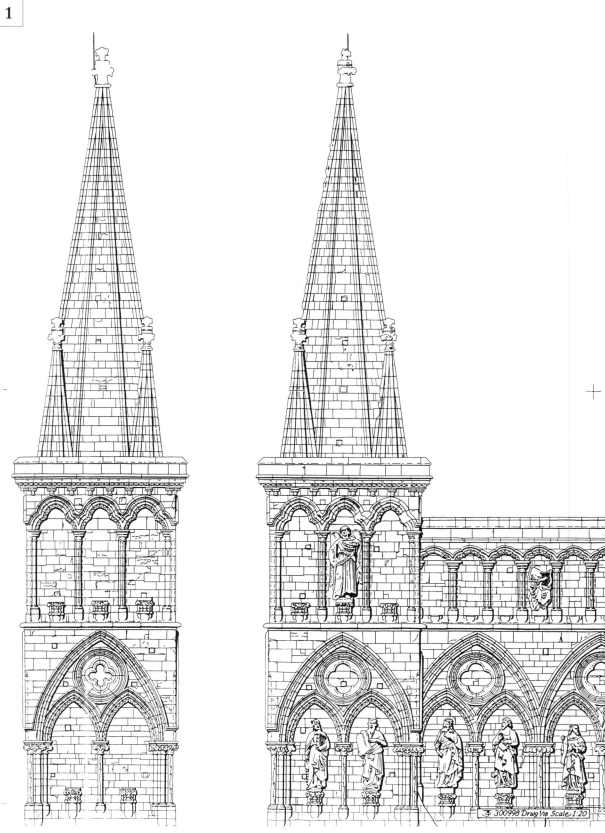

300998 Drwg'ns Scale 1:20

300998 Drwg 9he Scale 1:20

3

3 30099B Drwg No Scale 1:20

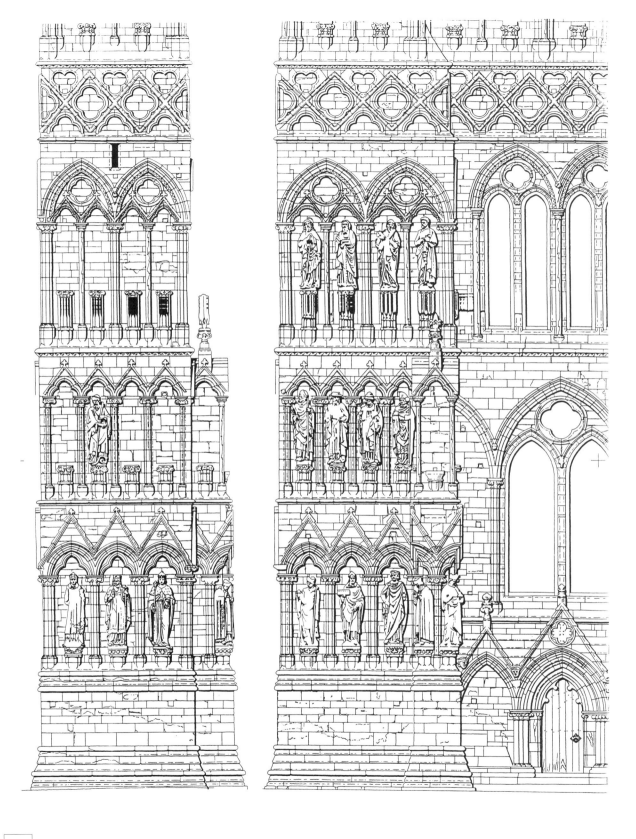

4

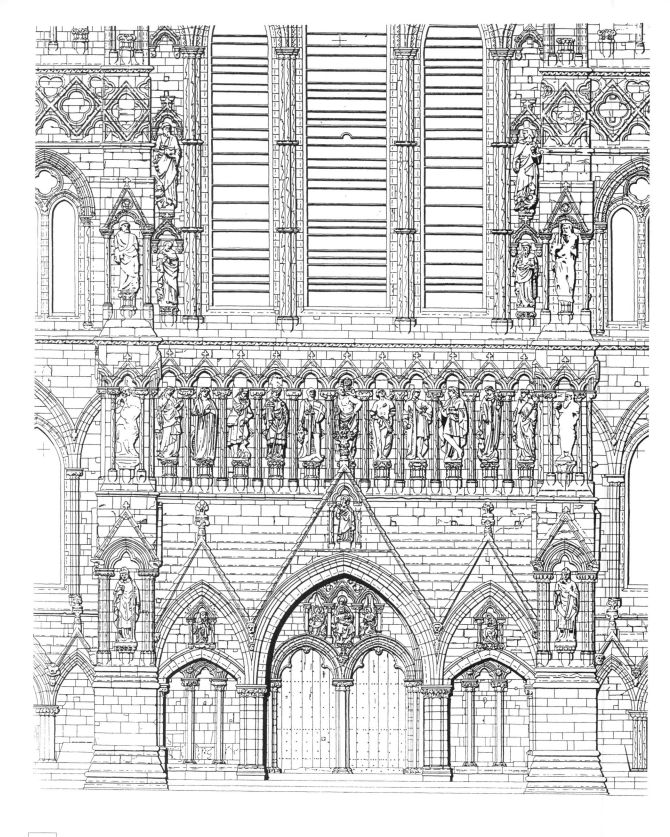

5

6

300998 Drwg 6/18 Scale 1:20

John Atherton Bowen
Assisted by R Read & A Patton

3 300998 Drwg 7ns Scale 1:20

300998 Drwg 8/18 Scale 1:20

9

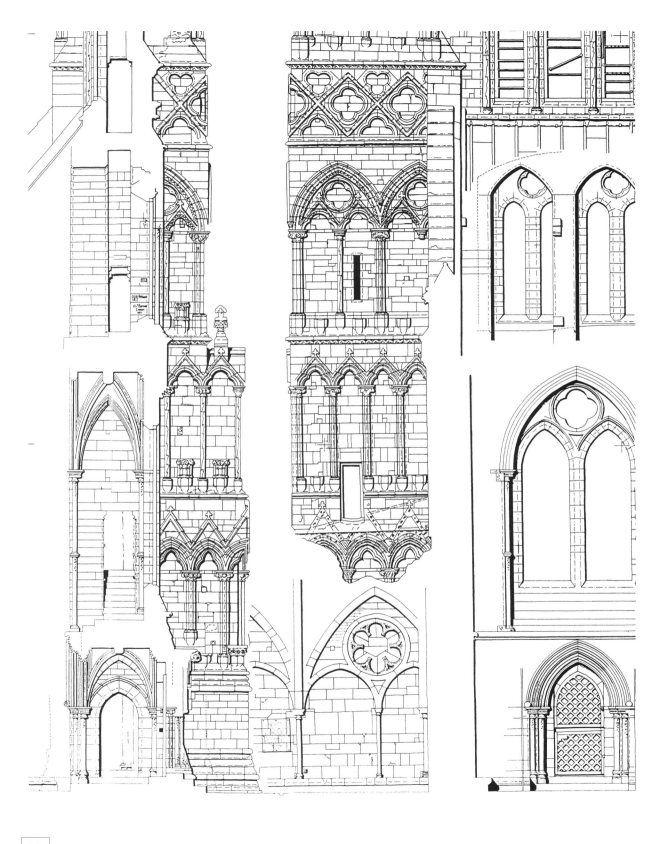

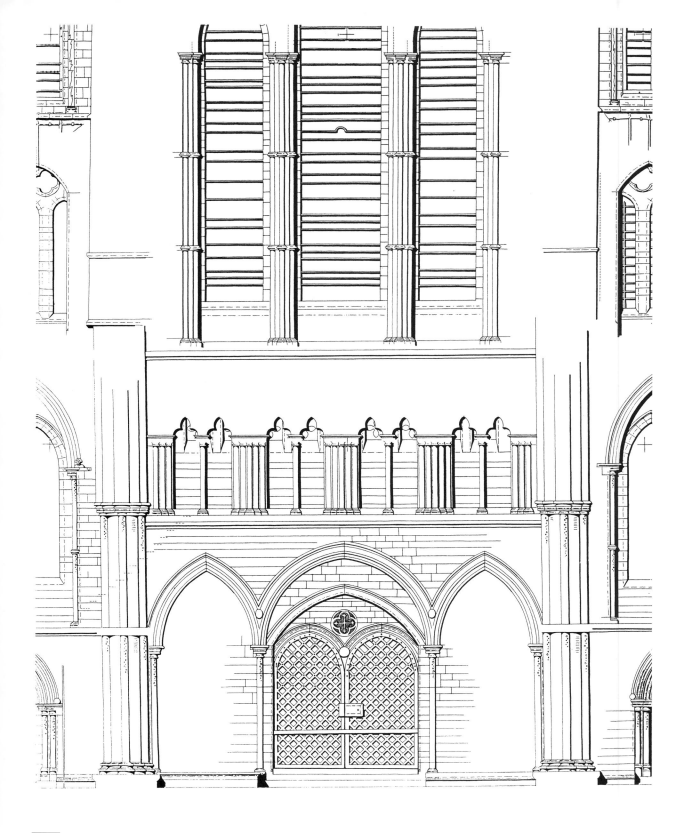

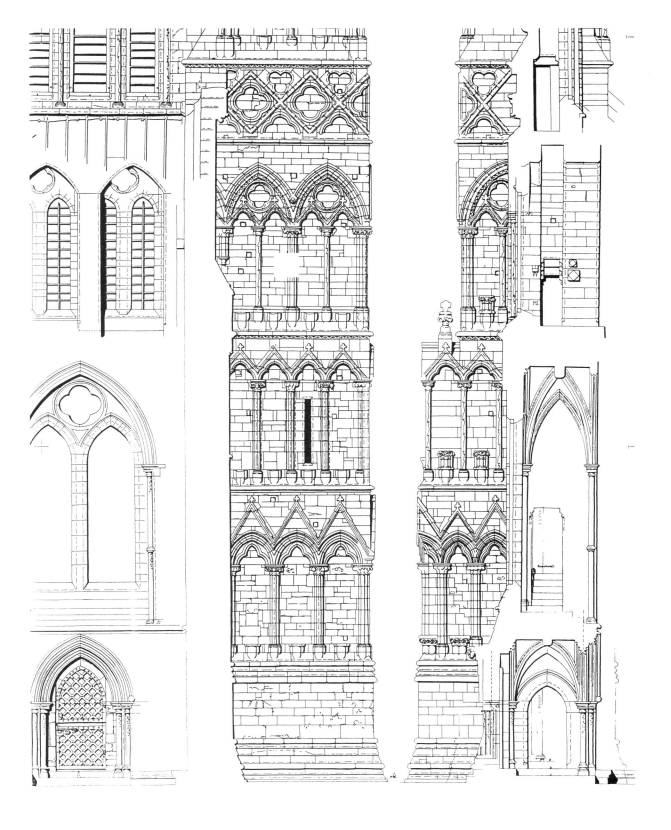

12

John Atherton Bowen
Assisted by R. Read & A. Patton

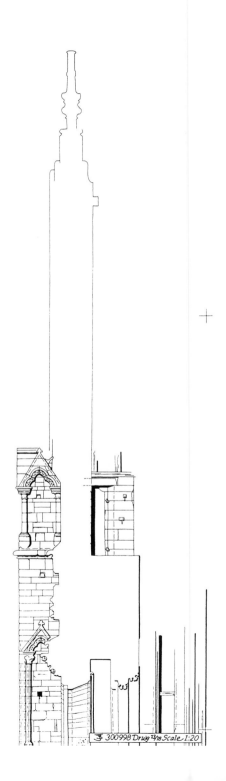

300998 Drawing Scale 1:20

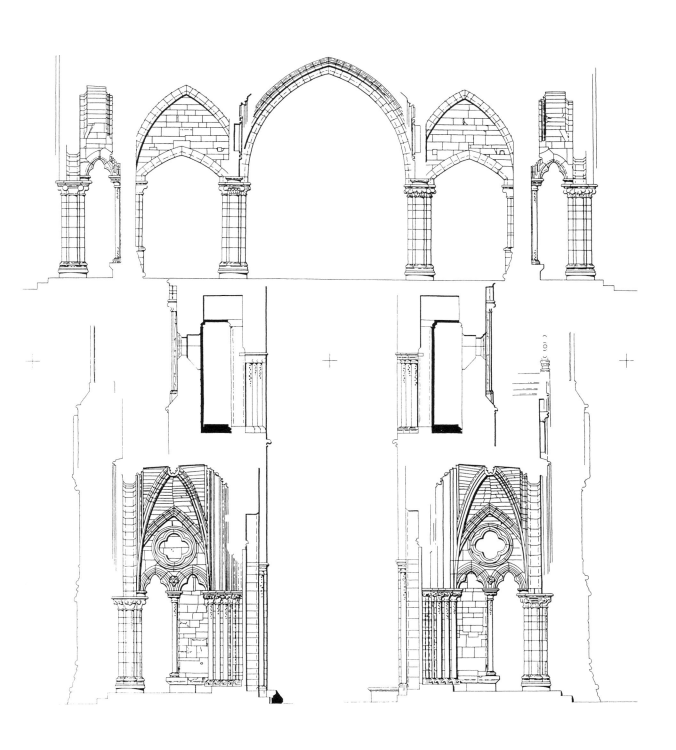

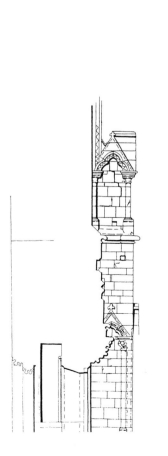

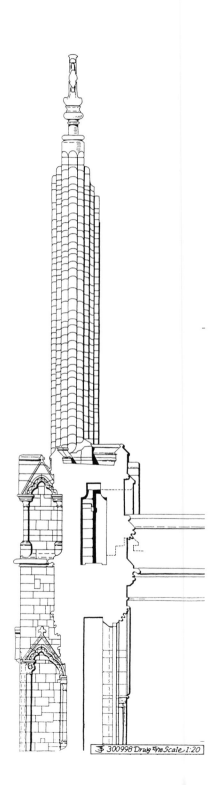

300998 Drwg Fns Scale 1:20

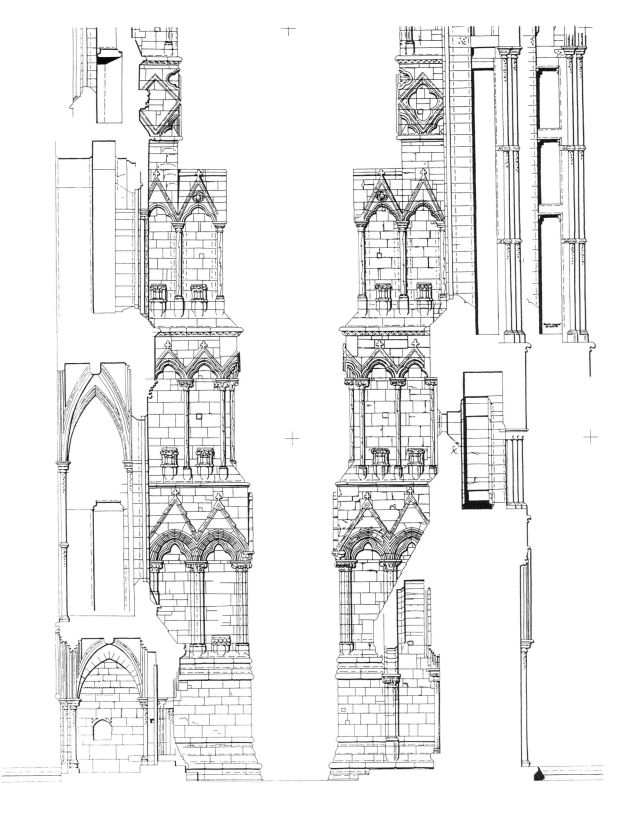

16

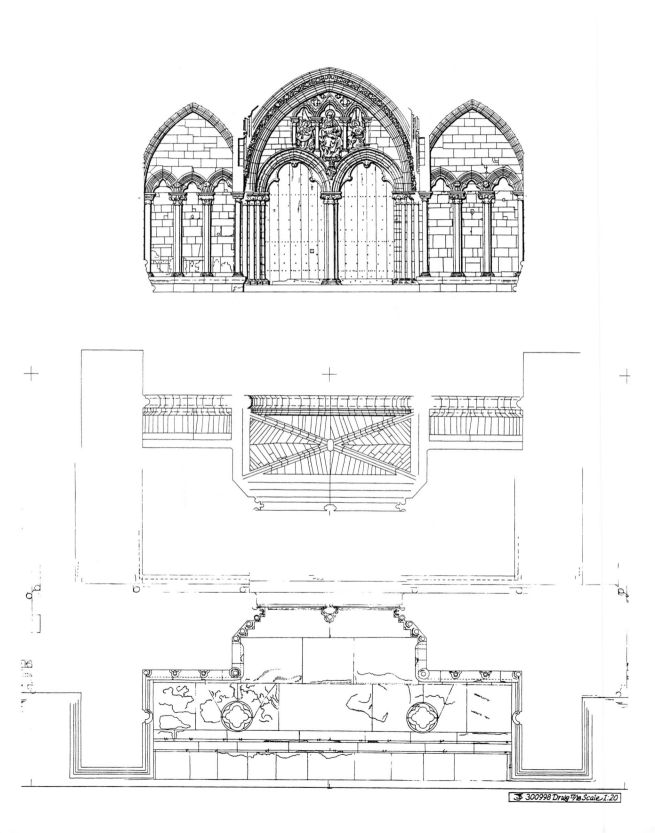

300998 Drwg Nº Scale 1:20

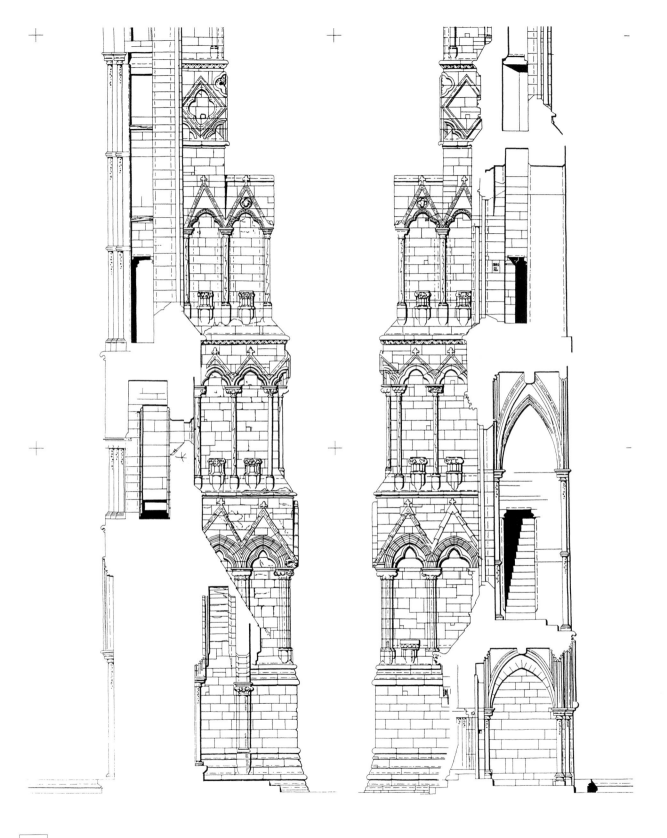

18

300998 Drwg no. Scale 1:20

John Atherton Bowen
Assisted by R.Read & A.Patton

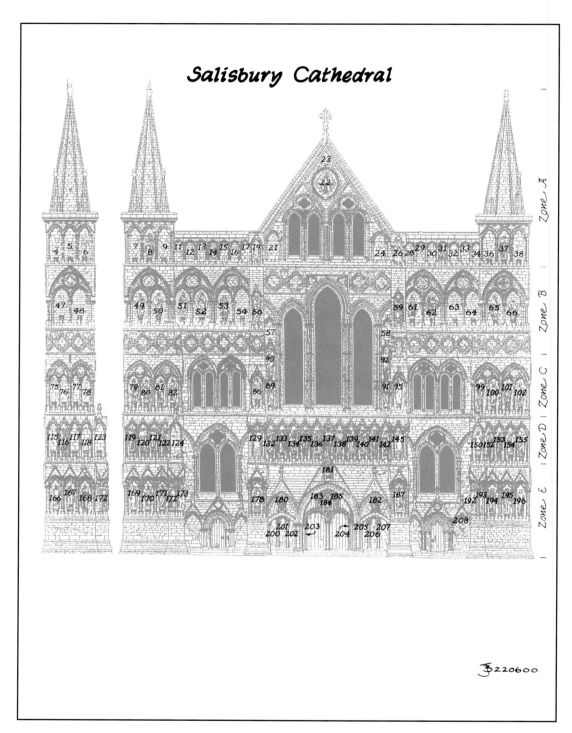

1 West front elevation: system of niche numbers.

Illustrated Catalogue of the Sculpture

The numbering system for the niches is shown opposite. The medieval sculptures are then catalogued first, including lost figures, followed by the Victorian and later sculptures. Where it is known that a medieval figure has been replaced by a later figure, the identifying niche numbers in the catalogue entries are qualified by the addition of a and b, respectively (e.g. 22a, 22b). Previous identifications for the medieval figures are given in brackets after the present identification. Their date is discussed in the main text (see pp.47-50, 62-69). The later figures are identified mostly according to Armfield's guide.[1]

Abbreviations

H, height; W, width; D, depth

The Middle Ages

19th and 20th Centuries

(continued overleaf)

[1] Armfield 1869b.

Peter G.J. Marsh is acknowledged for illustrations of the following sculptures (taken 2000): 86 (p.196), 95 (p.197), 8, 14 (p.211), 22b, 31 (p.212), 37 (p.213), 49/50, 51-53 (p.214), 56, 59 (p.216), 61/62 (p.217), 65/66 (p.218), 79-82 (p.219), 89 (p.220), 90 (p.221), 91, 92 (p.222), 99-102 (p.223), 116 (p.224), 119-22 (p.225), 125 (p.227), 132-42 (p.228), 150b (p.232), 152-55 (p.233), 166-68 (p.235), 169-71 (p.236), 172 (p.237), 173, 177 (p.238), 180b (p.239), 181b, 182b (p.240), 183b-185b (p.241), 187b, 192 (p.243), 194-96 (p.244).

THE MIDDLE AGES

19a. **Enthroned Prelate** (Christ, Angel)[2]
Pale Tisbury/Chilmark stone, with Chilmark additions
Probably 2nd quarter 14th century, with additions of
*   1866-69*
H (medieval part), 131 cm; W, 67 cm; D, 23 cm

Until recently this figure was in Zone A, at the top of the north central buttress, within a hollow-backed niche. It rested uncomfortably on the stub of a shaft, of 13th-century origin and trefoil section, rising from a sloping sill. It was attached to the wall by a modern dowel,[3] but originally had the two iron hooks and a ring, at shoulder height, that are found elsewhere on the front (fig. 29). The hooks had survived, but the ring had dropped off.

The sculpture is made of a single thin block of limestone, with harder chert inclusions standing proud of the level of the surface by about 3 to 5 mm. The original front plane of the block is clearly evident, since the front facets of all the major projecting folds over the legs (from the tops of the knees to the base of the sculpture) are in the same plane. Evidently the carver has worked from a masoned slab, drawing the main lines of the design on to the surface and then carving back.

Before conservation, the stone was badly weathered, particularly the upper body, which had become very fragile. The back was also in a poor state. The head and neck, right arm from mid-upper arm (including hanging sleeve) and left arm from the elbow (with palm) were restored by Redfern, *c.*1866-69, but the head and right hand are lost. The lower edge includes a slot, probably for lifting and supporting the figure. At Wells such slots were cut by G. P. White's masons to support sculptures while the lias abaci beneath them were renewed. Here, however, the block beneath appears to be medieval. Perhaps the slot relates to the original installation of the sculpture. Grooves have been observed on 13th-century figures in the Resurrection tier on the west front at Wells, probably to ensure that the stone did not break free of the lifting tackle – and also possibly on the 15th-century angels from the west face of the nave gable.

No. 19a, Enthroned Prelate. CI (403/67 (34a)).

The severely decayed state of the stone led to the removal of the present sculpture in 1998 and the carving of a modern replacement. At present the original is displayed in the nave roof space.

The lower corners of the medieval sculpture are gone, but they appear in an earlier photograph to have been cut away to allow for the bases of the niche sideshafts.[4] Although this figure and its pair (no. 26a) fit their niches badly at the foot, the back of both benches is cut to the curvature of the recess and the composition suits the height. It may be that a measurement was taken across the full width of the niche before the sculpture was carved on the ground, but that the trefoil shaft, its necessary support, was either ignored or overlooked. This seems more likely, on balance, than that the figures were made for

---

2   Cockerell 1851, p.96; Armfield 1869b, p.7.
3   Done at the restoration in 1982.
4   CI 403/67 (34a), 1966.

another location, and later moved. No other suitable location suggests itself for such a pair of figures.

The figure is seated on a bench-like throne, the top angled at about 45 degrees. The upper body now has few distinguishable characteristics (there is a diagonal ridge to upper sinister), but sways slightly to sinister, like its pair. The tallness of the upper body may have been intended to counteract foreshortening in the view from the ground, as in many of the figures on the earlier west front at Wells. The lower part is better preserved and the legs are taken slightly to dexter and the feet to sinister, again like its pair. Above the knees, drapery is pulled tightly across and pouchy folds hang off them, between the legs and on both sides.

Redfern restored this figure and its pair as angels, with palm and crown, and Armfield described them as such.[5] In spite of the surface losses, it is clear that this was not the original intention. Cockerell's suggestion of Christ and his mother is equally ill founded. Both were vested for the mass. There are multiple hemlines: the chasuble looping across the lower legs and the squared up edge of the dalmatic against the bench to either side (both also visible on no. 26a), and the alb below. The end of the stole is also unmistakably shown on the present figure. The two were therefore churchmen and the thrones on which they sit demonstrate their high rank. They could have been bishops, given the dalmatic, which would have been appropriate to a cathedral, the bishop's seat; or perhaps representatives of yet higher rank, archbishops or popes. The headgear on the lost heads would have helped to clarify this, but both were lost by 1802.[6] The pull of the drapery folds running back from the left forearm, and the angle of the upper arm with the forearm, suggest that the hand was raised, probably in a gesture of benediction. The buskins are acutely pointed.

Of their style, little can be said beyond observing that they share with the other surviving figures on the front a dramatic sense of swing and movement. Among seals, a similar pose is found, for example, on the second great seal of Edward III, 1327.[7]

22a. Lost Figure: Christ

The mandorla implies the presence of a sculpture of Christ. That the niche was occupied is confirmed by traces of paint within the mandorla itself, which show that the whole was finished and decorated in the middle ages (see p.124, pl.VIII).

23. Eagle of St John
(Dove of the Holy Spirit, Pelican in Piety)[8]
Tisbury/Chilmark stone, with Chilmark additions
Probably 2nd quarter 14th century, with additions of 1866-69
H, 80 cm; W, 112 cm; D, 24 cm

No. 23, Eagle of St John. CI (403/66 (33a)).

In the great gable, above the central mandorla. The medieval sculpture is in one piece of limestone. It is weathered but relatively well preserved, with only a part of the halo (originally, the slate dowel alone survives) and the upper wing pieced-in at the restoration of 1866-69. The method of fixing is not visible, but there are no fixings present behind the lower two-thirds of the block and it appears that the slab was secured by inserting part of the upper third of the stone (by at least 10 cm) into the ashlar of the wall. Three 6 mm stainless steel dowels were inserted in 1998. The lower edge rests on the top of the mandorla.

The sculpture shows a bird facing to dexter, with formidable curving beak and huge talons, the head haloed, the wing originally above, a phylactery with

5 Armfield 1869b, p.7.
6 BL, Add. MS 29939, ff.39 (no. 4), 40 (no. 13).
7 *Age of Chivalry*, cat. no. 670.
8 Cockerell 1851, p.96; Armfield 1869b, p.15.

scrolling terminals below, angled slightly downwards. No doubt this originally bore an inscription, either in relief (some relief is visible, but may be the result of decay) or in paint. Christ was almost certainly represented enthroned within the vesica directly beneath the bird; traces of medieval paint have been located within its shelter. It is in relation to this that the bird must take its meaning. Various writers have thought that it was the dove of the Holy Spirit, but the scroll and the formidable claws and beak strongly suggest that it is the symbol of St John the Evangelist, as Blum proposed.[9] A general comparison can be made with the Evangelistic eagle in the nave vault at Tewkesbury Abbey, Gloucs., which dates probably from the 1330s or 1340s.[10] A Pelican in Piety would be pecking its breast.

It will be argued that John appeared in person on the great north buttress, where he was identified again by the eagle attribute on his dexter shoulder (no. 129), of which the outspread talons remain. The repetition of the symbol would have underlined John's role as the author of the Book of Revelation, as well as of one of the four Gospels, and perhaps also the position of the cathedral as a likeness of the Heavenly Jerusalem, which is described in it. It is in Revelation that the four beasts associated with the Evangelists are described, anticipating the Second Coming (Revelation 4, 6-7). The presence of the bird above Christ in the mandorla therefore identifies this figure as a Majesty, albeit in an abbreviated form. It is the only surviving medieval sculpture to have been placed in a location not intended or provided by the 13th-century planning (although there were once others in the central porch), but it was added perhaps to clarify the meaning of this isolated figure.

26a. **Enthroned Prelate** (Virgin, Angel)[11]

Pale Tisbury/Chilmark stone, with Chilmark additions
Probably 2nd quarter 14th century, with additions of
* 1866-69*
H, 150 cm (c.127 cm, medieval part); W, c.61 cm max;
* D, c.25 cm max*

[9] Blum 1996a, p.629.
[10] Morris 1974, p.146.
[11] Cockerell 1851, p.96; Armfield 1869b, p.7.
[12] CI 403/66 (32a), 1966.
[13] BL, Add. MS 29939, f.40 (no. 13).

No. 26a, Enthroned Prelate. CI (403/66 (32a)).

Until recently this figure was in Zone A, on the west face of the south central buttress, within a hollow-backed niche. The sculpture rested awkwardly on the stub of a shaft, of trefoil section and 13th-century origin, which rose from an angled sill (see no. 19a). The original fixing survived at shoulder height, with two iron hooks set in lead plugs, one in the back of the niche and the other in the back of the sculpture. A neat recess around the wall fixing facilitated the dropping of an iron ring over the hooks, to join them.

The figure is in a single piece of limestone, bearing many shells, and is in very poor condition, with heavy surface loss and major cracks. The sculpture was better preserved some decades ago,[12] but it had already lost head and arms by 1802.[13] The present head and neck, the left arm (now lost, but still present in the illustration mentioned above) and the whole right arm (supporting a crown, now very damaged), are restorations by Redfern (1866-69). The lower edge has a central slot, perhaps for lifting and/or supporting the figure. In the 1960s two copper restraining straps were fixed horizontally around the statue. The severely decayed state of the stone led to the removal of the sculpture from the building in 1998, and the carving of a modern replacement. At present the original is displayed in the nave roof space.

The figure is seated on a bench-like throne, with the top angled at about 45 degrees. The tall upper body swings to sinister and had parallel folds stretched across it. The legs are swung to the figure's right and angled to give movement to the pose. At the knees there are pouchy folds centrally and to sinister. For a discussion of identity and style, see no. 19a.

---

86. St Peter

Tisbury/Chilmark stone, with Chilmark additions
Probably second quarter 14th century, with additions of
*   1866-69*
Figure: H, 204 cm (175 cm, medieval part); W, 61.5 cm;
*   D, 26 cm*

In Zone C, on the west face of the north central buttress, in a hollow-backed niche. Within the spandrel of the gable above, a quatrefoiled roundel centres a tonsured head carved in high relief, integral with the 13th-century fabric. The figure sculpture now stands on a tall base with a stiff-leaf capital, of 19th-century date, probably copied from that once beneath the equivalent figure on the south central buttress (no. 95). Pre-restoration photographs suggest that the original console was of similar form (fig. 16). The figure has a down-turned copper hook in the back, unlike the upturned medieval fixings of iron, no doubt because it was taken down in 1866-69, when the base was renewed. An upturned iron hook in the back of the niche at shoulder height suggests that the hooks-and-ring system was used originally.

The figure is carved from a single piece of sandy limestone, with several calcite veins (cf. no. 169) running lower dexter to upper sinister, across the trunk. There is much loss of surface, especially at the front, but this figure is better preserved than some of the others, perhaps because the hollow of the niche

No. 86, St Peter.

gave it more protection. The upper neck and head, parts of the right arm and attribute (keys) and the whole front of the left arm (with book) were restored by Redfern (1866-69), although the piecings-in to the left and right arms are lost. The sculpture was conserved and sheltercoated in 1982 by Iain Lunn, the coating making some details difficult to interpret.[14]

The figure wears robe and mantle, the feet being covered, and formerly held an attribute in his right hand at chest height, against the body. The upper arm drops vertically, and the lower arm is foreshortened; the hand is turned sharply at right-angles. Although Redfern restored the front of the hand (lost), the profile of the original fingers remains, clasping an object(s) that had a large flattened circular lower terminal(s), with a raised centre and wide outer ring. There are traces of a vertical dowel hole directly above the hand, with what may be rust deposits, for an attribute in iron. This could be either medieval or Victorian; but in the figure's dexter side there is an original hole (1.25 cm diameter) for further securing an attribute. This hole is not far above that in the hand, but off slightly to one side. There is no good evidence for the original left arm and hand, which had gone by 1802.[15]

Cockerell and the Victorian restorers identified this figure as St Peter and were almost certainly right.[16] The substantial round terminal could be a sword pommel, of the kind represented on early 14th-century brasses,[17] or it could be the ferrule or loop at the end of a key, or keys. The latter is more likely, given that the fixing hole in the body is close to the hand and off vertical. Redfern restored the figure with a book in the left hand, which may well also have been correct, as Apostles commonly hold books. Peter was as popular at Salisbury as elsewhere; the altar to the north of the Trinity Chapel was dedicated in 1225 to St Peter and all Apostles, and there were relics of his cross and hair by the end of the middle ages.[18]

It will appear from the discussion of no. 95 that the equivalent figure on the front of the south central buttress was St Paul, who often accompanies Peter. Peter usually appears to the viewer's left in such pairings. The two were conceived together and are similar in style, turned towards each other, one swaying off the left hip (Peter) and the other off the right (Paul). Such pairings occur also in the zone below (nos. 129, 145), and the two seated figures in Zone A were also obviously both conceived and made together (nos. 19a, 26a). This very much suggests that they were executed by the same workshop working to an integrated design for the west front, and that the sculptures were specifically designed for the niches that they occupy. These two sculptures, and almost certainly the other carvings surviving on the central pair of buttresses, were all from the same campaign.

The contrapposto of Peter is complemented by the arrangement of drapery folds. The turned-over V-shaped neckline of the mantle sets up a rhythm that is picked up by two substantial pouchy folds swinging to right and left, and by the lower hem. Cascades of undercut and sinuous folds fall from the right hand and left hip, where the thin and soft-looking material of the mantle is gathered up. Below, the robe falls vertically from Peter's right knee and diagonally off his left knee to his right foot, with relatively deep undercutting between. This rather slim and narrow-shouldered, highly mannered figure contrasts strangely with the ponderous 19th-century head. There may be the remains of original locks of hair on the figure's dexter shoulder, although the sheltercoat has made them hard to interpret; if so, this would confirm that the head was turned towards St Paul on the south.

This figure and the St Paul belong in the soft style that distinguishes all of the surviving west front sculpture, and the dynamic curves reflect the English Curvilinear Decorated style of architecture. In various respects – necklines, pouches, soft material – the figures compare with the less agitated Evangelist figures remaining in the choir at Edington, Wilts., c.1351-61 (fig. 36).[19] At Salisbury itself, some of the mannerism, and the pouches, are apparent in the little mourning crocket angels above the tomb of Bishop Martival (d. 1330) (fig. 38). In monumental brasses, the slim swaying figures and pouchy drapery of the

[14]   Policy 1995, p.25.
[15]   BL, Add. MS 29939, f.39 (no. 5).
[16]   Cockerell 1851, pp.96–97.
[17]   Coales 1987, figs. 86–88.
[18]   Wordsworth 1913–14, pp.559–60 (altar); Wordsworth 1901, pp.4, 8, 9, 10, 33–34 (relics).
[19]   *BoE Wilts.*, p.209.

Seymour style, *c*.1335-50, almost certainly made in London, offer a general comparison.[20]

95. St Paul

Tisbury/Chilmark stone, with Chilmark additions
Probably 2nd quarter 14th century, with additions of
*   1866-69*
Console (now removed): H, 49.5 cm; W, 37 cm; D, 26.5 cm
Figure: H, 205 cm (excluding 19th-century sword); W, 69
*   cm; D, 28 cm*

In Zone C, on the west face of the south central buttress, within a hollow-backed niche. The gable above contains, within a quatrefoiled roundel, a tonsured head in high relief, integral with the 13th-century fabric. The figure stood until recently on a tall base, with the remains of a stiff-leaf console of the 13th century. Piecing-in at the front and a copper dowel to mend the foliage on the dexter side must have been 19th-century restorations. This was the only 13th-century console on the front, although photographs of the 1850s suggest that it once had a counterpart in niche no. 86. It probably provided the inspiration for the general design of Scott's upper tier of consoles. The figure is fixed with two lead-set iron hooks, at chest height, in the wall and the back of the figure, with a ring over, as found in both Zone A and D. The hook in the wall has been more extensively recessed than the others that are visible. The ring appears to be the medieval original, a wide staple with an estimated width of about 12 cm.

The figure is carved from a single thin block of sandy limestone, which retains an almost vertical edge at the sinister side. It is thicker than some of the other medieval figures, because the niche is hollowed out, and also therefore modelled in higher relief than Zone D, with some carving round the back. The upper body is slightly hollowed out at the back, as elsewhere, to lighten it for lifting.[21] Before conservation the sculpture was in a state of extreme decay. The spalled surface of the front was unstable and powdery, while edges of earlier spalled surface or original carved surface were exfoliating. There is more original surface at the sides, but the back of the head was coming away. Traces of medieval paint were found here (see

No. 95, St Paul.

[20]   P. Binski, 'The Stylistic Sequence of London Figure Brasses', in Coales 1987, pp.103–16, figs. 99 (*c*.1337), 102, 104.
[21]   Sampson 1998, p.110.

p.123). Redfern pieced-in the face, the right arm from the shoulder and the front of the drapery hanging from it, the left arm and attribute of a book (both now lost), and the top of the right hand with the quillons of a sword, for which a metal blade was provided (zinc alloy). The renewals are in a rather shelly Chilmark stone (a fairly good match for the medieval block), possibly trough bed, which would suggest a date in or before the second half of 1867 (see below, no. 8). There is a shallow hole at the centre of the bottom edge of the sculpture, for lifting and/ or supporting the figure (see no. 19a).

This is almost certainly St Paul, a universal figure who was as popular at Salisbury as elsewhere; the cathedral had a relic by the mid-15th century.[22] While Redfern has renewed the face from the mouth upwards, part of the medieval carving of the hair survives, both in the beard and the fall of the long locks behind the shoulders. One hallmark of the medieval figures is the remarkable distance to which they were carved around the back. Paul wears a mantle and robe, which covers the feet. So much of the surface is lost that it is difficult to reconstruct the form of the drapery. An attribute was held in the right hand, of which the two lower fingers survive at right-angles to the vertical. The object was almost certainly a sword: below the fingers remains part of a pommel, once ball-shaped,[23] as on the brass of Sir William Fitzralph, c.1331-38, at Pebmarsh, Essex.[24] The left arm was angled back and down slightly, to support something, as Carter's pre-restoration drawing suggests.[25] As Apostle and author of the Epistles, Paul probably supported a book, like Peter.

As discussed, this figure is Peter's pair. The head was turned towards him, as shown by the position of the medieval beard. The right hand clasped an attribute in an exactly similar way (just as the figures in the zone

below do). The two are found very commonly together and from an early date, and share a feast day (29 June).[26] English examples are discussed by Park in relation to the pair on the Thornham Parva retable, which flank the Crucifixion, as do many others.[27] In style, the figure is also Peter's counterpart, with a folded over edge of the mantle at the neck and substantial pouchy folds swinging to left and right. Again, sinuous and undercut drapery fell originally off the sinister hip.[28] Beneath, the robe falls to the ground, but with a substantial fold structure angling down to his left foot. There can be no doubt that these two figures, paired in subject matter and style, were made by the same sculptor or workshop, at the same time.

---

124. **Lost Figure: Clerical Saint** (Dean or Bishop Poore, St Augustine of Canterbury)[29]
Console: H, 25 cm; W, 48 cm; D, 30 cm

In Zone D, on the lesser north buttress, against a flat-backed niche. Only the console on which the figure stood remains, above a stub of trefoil section and 13th-century origin. This seems to have been heightened by 18 cm when the console was added. There is an upturned corroded ferrous metal hook, set in a lead plug and recessed in the wall, at about shoulder height for the lost figure. The figure must have been as thin as those that survive in other niches in Zone D.

The figure was taken down in 1963, for safety reasons, and is reported to have disintegrated on removal.[30] A published photograph shows it laid out on the ground (fig. 65).[31] No trace of it remains; it is not in the Salisbury Museum, as Blum has claimed.[32] It was drawn, however, by Carter in 1802 and illustrated, rather small, in Prior and Gardner's survey

[22] Wordsworth 1901, pp.3, 8, 9, 34.
[23] CI 403/66 (30a), 1966.
[24] Coales 1987, fig. 91.
[25] BL, Add. MS 29939, f.40 (no. 12).
[26] *Golden Legend*, I, pp.342–48, 351, 354; *Lexicon* 1994, 8, col. 128; Réau 1959, III, 3, pp.1035–40, 1083–85.
[27] Norton, Park and Binski 1987, pp.40–41. eg *Age of Chivalry*, cat. nos. 345 (Newport chest, Crucifixion), 574 (Gorleston Psalter Crucifixion), 593 and 596 (Grandison ivories); Tristram 1955, pp.26, 87, 154, 184, 245, pls. 46, 51a, 53b (murals at Idsworth and Selling, Kent, and Chalgrove, Oxon.).
[28] BL, Add. MS 29939, f.40 (no. 12).
[29] RIBA, Library, Cockerell Papers, Box 6, CoC.1/83, [p.ii]; Cockerell 1851, p.97; Armfield 1869b, p.10.
[30] Spring 1987, p.36.
[31] 'The West Front', *Spire*, The Friends of Salisbury Cathedral, 36th Annual Report, May 1966, p.14.
[32] Blum 1996a, p.628.

No. 124, Clerical Saint (lost). CI (A73/1828).

of English medieval sculpture.[33] It is also recorded in other photographs, including a number of close ups.[34] The latest shows the sculpture after pieces had begun to fall off. The earliest reveal that Redfern had added a mitre and renewed the right hand, in the act of blessing; Carter had drawn the figure bare-headed and Cockerell confirms this.[35] The photographs also seem to show that the figure was wearing a chasuble, with amice. The right arm was raised and the left was held across the body, with an extended index finger, suggesting that the figure was pointing to something in the other hand, like St John in this same zone (no. 145); these figures have similar plain bases, and visual rhyming of the figures in Zone D will be noticed in relation to the attributes of the two St Johns.

The identity of the figure is uncertain, the vestments now suggesting nothing more precise than a clerical saint. He was turned to the north, as discussed in relation to no. 169. This intention may have suggested the remarkable triangular composition. The figure's left foot is shown at the front of the base, decisively angling the figure towards the north side, although the trunk is flatter to the wall, so that it could be attached there. Compositions in which a sharp angle is formed centrally to the front by crossing the legs, are also a feature of some of the early figures on the west front at Exeter, dated to c.1342-47.[36]

The Salisbury figure had a large head, with wide cheekbones, a square jaw and curling hair; the loss of this face is greatly to be regretted, as it was the only medieval example to survive into the present century. From the photographs, it recalls some of the square-jawed clean-shaven types by the Majesty Master in the De Lisle Psalter miniatures (before 1339); found also widely in stained glass, as in Wells Cathedral choir clerestory (c.1340); and rather later, possibly documentable to c.1382, in one of two English alabasters at Santa Croce in Gerusalemme, Rome.[37] Unlike the ribby drapery represented in Rome, however (found also on other early alabasters), that at Salisbury was arranged in big pouchy folds, with sinuous hemlines falling from the left wrist and, less certainly medieval,

[33] BL, Add. MS 29939, f.39 (no. 3); Prior and Gardner 1912, fig. 390.
[34] CI, A73/1827 and 1828.
[35] RIBA, Library, Cockerell Papers, Box 6, CoC.1/83, [p.ii], 'a clergyman without a mitre'.
[36] Allan and Blaylock 1991, p.102.
[37] Sandler 1983, pls. 21, 22; Woodforde 1946, pl. IV (for the date, see Ayers 1996, pp.299–302); Lindley 1990, p.104, fig. 6.

the right arm. This combination is familiar from the other figures on the west front. The plain base is similar to that for nos. 129 and 145 in this zone, tending to confirm that all four were made at the same time.

---

129. St John the Evangelist
(Virgin of the Annunciation)[38]
Tisbury/Chilmark stone, with Chilmark additions
Probably 2nd quarter 14th century, with additions of
1866-69
Console: H, 23 cm; W, 66 cm; D, 30.5 cm
Figure: H, 200.5 cm (170 cm, medieval part); W, 62.5
cm; D, 14.5 cm

In Zone D, on the west face of the north central buttress, in a flat-backed niche, on a shaft of trefoil section and 13th-century origin. The figure stands on a plain console, similar to the others surviving in Zone D (nos. 124, 145), spreading from a trefoil necking to a wide and irregularly shaped top. The figure is attached to the wall at chest height by two upturned hooks, set in lead plugs, one in the back of the niche and the other in the back of the figure, with a large oval ring dropped over to join them. While the hooks are of iron, the ring which joins them is of copper alloy, thus the hooks are probably original, but the ring probably of 1866-69. There is a notch out of the centre of the lower edge, where the figure may have been supported during a previous restoration (see no. 19a).

Distinguished by its thinness, the sculpture is made from a single piece of limestone, with chert inclusions on the sinister side (cf. no. 19a). The right foot has been refixed in an original medieval repair, apparently with squared edges – implying the insertion of a new piece of stone during carving. The joint was repointed in 1982 using lime mortar and no indication of the original medium can be seen. Before recent conservation, the figure was in poor condition, with heavy surface loss on the upper body and a crack at the sinister elbow. The right arm, part of the right side to the waist and the veiled head, from the lower neck, were pieced in by Redfern, 1866-69. The whole had been conserved and sheltercoated previously in 1982, making some detail difficult to interpret.[39]

[38] Armfield 1869b, p.11.
[39] Policy 1995, p.25.

No. 129, St John the Evangelist. CI (63/45 (35)).

The figure wears robe and mantle, with bare feet emerging below. It swings dramatically off the dexter hip, so that the lower body is substantially to dexter of centre and the upper body is over to sinister. Neither Carter nor Cockerell gives any clues to the original disposition of the right arm, which was lost by 1802, but they confirm what is still just visible that the left fell limply to the figure's side, overlaid by a band of some sort in its lower part.[40]

The bare feet suggest an Apostle and it is likely, therefore, that the claw on the dexter shoulder belongs to the eagle attribute of John the Evangelist (Catalogue fig. 2). As elsewhere, the feasts of this universally popular figure were celebrated with honour in the cathedral and by the mid-15th century there were relics; another image of the saint is recorded, in or adjacent to the altar north of the Trinity Chapel, dedicated to the Apostles, which was sometimes itself associated with him.[41] This identification of the present figure was conjectured by Cockerell in 1851.[42] The band across the left arm may then be the end of a phylactery, bearing the first words of St John's Gospel, 'In principio erat verbum', clarifying his identity further and laying stress on his Evangelistic status.[43] Standing St Johns often carry a phylactery, as in the choir of Edington Priory, Wilts., *c.*1351-61 (fig. 36).[44] That figure has an eagle at his feet, as elsewhere in English art of this period, including a Book of Hours in Baltimore (*c.*1340-50).[45] The bird is more commonly found at John's shoulder when he is seated, to receive dictation of the Gospel, as on one of the Grandison ivories (*c.*1330-40) or an early 14th-century roof boss in Norwich Cathedral cloister.[46]

The mannered pose in this case was determined partly, at least, by the need to convey John's attention to the bird. The position of the feet in the Salisbury

2   Detail of the figure in niche no. 129. CI (A97/444).

figure also suggests that he is turned in this direction. The bird and the pose led the Victorians to restore the figure as a Virgin of the Annunciation and, even if they were wrong, the compositional similarity of such images as the Virgin in stained glass from Hadzor, Worcs., *c.*1330-50,[47] suggests that the pose could well have been inspired by an Annunciation. Another reason to dismiss the Victorian identification is the absence of the Angel Gabriel, who appeared originally in another light at Hadzor. At Salisbury, the two could easily have made a pair across the central buttresses, but do not. It has been argued that, since the 13th century, the focus of Marian imagery on the west front at Salisbury had been the porch.

[40]   RIBA, British Architectural Library, Drawings Collection, H10; BL, Add. MS 29939, f.39 (no. 6).

[41]   Wordsworth 1901, pp.3, 7, 14, 34; Wordsworth 1913–14, pp.559–60.

[42]   Cockerell 1851, p.97.

[43]   For other attributes, see *Lexicon* 1994, 7, cols. 112–13.

[44]   *BoE Wilts.*, p.209. For other standing figures of the Evangelist with such scrolls, see the Sherborne Cartulary, *c.*1146 (*English Romanesque Art*, cat. no. 46), or the Norwich Ante-Reliquary Chapel murals, *c.*1300 (Tristram 1955, p.230, pl. 11a; D. Park and H. Howard, 'The Medieval Polychromy', in *Norwich Cathedral, Church, City and Diocese, 1096–1996*, ed. I. Atherton *et al.*, London/Rio Grande, 1996, pp.392–400, fig. 141).

[45]   Baltimore, Walters Art Gallery, MS W105, f.13; Sandler 1986, no. 117. Also ibid., no. 78, ill. 199 (Tiptoft Missal); Tristram 1955, p.245, pl. 51b.

[46]   *Age of Chivalry*, cat. no. 594; A. Whittingham, *Norwich Cathedral, Bosses and Misericords*, Norwich, 1981, E1, p.17 and ill. p.15. For another standing example, see the former high altarpiece of the Marienkirche, Rathenow, *c.*1370–80: *Die Parler*, II, pp.542–43.

[47]   *Age of Chivalry*, cat. no. 740.

Instead, the counterpart to the present figure on the south central buttress is St John the Baptist (no. 145), who appears very often in medieval art with his namesake; according to the Golden Legend, the date of the death of the Evangelist coincided with the feast of the Baptist's birth.[48] The sculptures are directly complementary in pose, for John holds up to his right shoulder the clipeus of the *agnus dei*; one relates the life of Christ in his Gospel and the other foretells it. In a similar way, the Apostles Peter and Paul (nos. 86, 95) are paired in the niches above.

The style and arrangement of the drapery is still visible, in the lower part of the figure particularly, but it is clearer in Carter's and Cockerell's drawings. The mantle was caught up under the original right elbow and lower left arm to create a broad apron, with swags and sinuous hemlines falling from each hip. As in the other figures on the west face of the front, particularly the similarly dressed Peter and Paul, there is a counterpoint between these vertical falls and wide horizontal pouches of cloth across the body. Below the apron, a bold fold structure falls vertically towards the ground, while another is angled off his right hip towards the left foot.

The apron fold and/or the fan-like fall off the right hip find parallels in England from the mid-1320s, among the weepers on Aymer de Valence's tomb (d.1324), but also later, as in the Virgin of the Annunciation in the Vicars' Hall, Wells Cathedral (perhaps *c*.1350; fig. 39).[49] On the continent, similar features are found on French sculpture of the second quarter of the 14th century and the fan-like drapery at the dexter hip appears on the west front sculpture of Cologne Cathedral, probably in the second half of the century.[50] Such conventions could persist over a long period.

145. St John the Baptist

Tisbury/Chilmark stone, with Chilmark additions
Probably 2nd quarter 14th century, with additions of
1866-69
Console: H, 30.5 cm; W, 54 cm; D, 30.5 cm
Figure: H, 184 cm (166 cm, medieval part); W, 69 cm; D,
15 cm

In Zone D, on the west face of the south central buttress, against a flat-backed niche, on a trefoil shaft of 13th-century origin. The figure stands on a plain console, rising from a trefoil necking to a roughly rectangular top with rounded corners, similar in its plainness to those of nos. 124 and 129 in this zone. The figure stands slightly away from the wall and is not entirely square to the front. It is fixed into the niche at mid-chest height, although the method is hard to see, for a substance, perhaps lead, has been poured over the fixing; but an iron ring may be visible, of the kind joining upturned hooks in the medieval fixing for other figures, including John the Evangelist in this zone.

The figure is very thin, carved from a single piece of sandy limestone, worked around the sides and towards the back, and slightly hollow at the rear, to reduce its weight to a minimum. The squareness of the original block is apparent at the upper sinister side. The figure has weathered very badly to the front, retaining hardly any original surface, although there is some to the dexter side, at the feet and around the head and shoulders, where long locks of hair remain to sinister. The head above the beard, the left hand and the right arm supporting an *agnus dei* roundel were pieced-in by Redfern, *c*.1866-69.

Like its counterpart on the north buttress (no. 129), this figure has the weight on its right hip and is turned to dexter. This is evident in the position of the feet on the sloping base and in the angle of the surviving lower part of the medieval head. Like its counterpart, again, the figure had an attribute at right shoulder height, a roundel, which was held in the right hand. The upper left arm fell vertically and the surviving medieval stonework of the sleeve indicates that the left hand was directed across the body and

---

[48]   *Golden Legend*, I, p.335; Réau 1958, III, 2, p.713. They appear together on the north portal of the west front of Rouen Cathedral.
   [49]   *Age of Chivalry*, cat. nos. 526–27. The hall was completed by 1348 (Colchester 1982, p.212).
   [50]   *Fastes du Gothique*, cat. nos. 7, 8 (1329); *Die Parler*, I, pp.159–68.

upward slightly, no doubt pointing to the attribute in the right hand. The bare lower legs and feet remain visible. Drawings by Carter and Cockerell reveal that the figure was wearing an animal skin, with the hind legs of the pelt tied across the chest and the head falling between the legs to knee height (fig. 32, Catalogue fig. 3).[51] The furred edge to this skin is still visible where it was pulled tight by the extended right arm. A vent in the side of this or some undergarment also remains visible to dexter.

There can be no doubt that the restoration of the figure as St John the Baptist, holding the *agnus dei*, is correct. John was as popular at Salisbury as elsewhere and the cathedral had, by the mid-15th century, a relic of his hair.[52] Carter and Cockerell show that the west front figure always held a clipeus and he is obviously dressed in the camelskin by which the Baptist is commonly identified in English medieval art.[53] The most interesting aspect of the iconography is its very literal depiction of the animal skin, although this is now best recorded by the antiquaries. Carter shows the camel's head between the legs, and Cockerell the hooved feet of the animal at the chest. The head makes its first recorded appearance in stained glass of the mid-14th century (fig. 41). By the end of the century this type is found on works associated with the most powerful men in the kingdom:[54] in stained glass from Winchester College Chapel, *c*.1393, where the saint is addressed by William Wykeham;[55] and in the image of John as sponsor of King Richard II on the Wilton Diptych, in the same decade.[56] There is another example locally, in a limestone sculpture from the reredos of the Guardian Angels' Chapel, Winchester Cathedral, dated tentatively by Lindley to the late 14th century.[57] The camelskin with head is also found in undateable (but late medieval) lead pilgrim badges, discovered in Salisbury, from Amiens, where the cathedral claimed to possess the head of the saint.[58]

No. 145, St John the Baptist. CI (403/66 (31a)).

[51] BL, Add. MS 29939, f.40 (no. 11); RIBA, British Architectural Library, Drawings Collection, H10. The hind legs across the chest are visible in Fenton's photograph (fig. 16). See also Cockerell 1851, p.97.

[52] Wordsworth 1901, p.33 (relic); pp.8, 9, 10 (feasts); Wordsworth 1913–14, p.562 (altar). Tristram 1955, p.26, for a growing number of surviving representations in the 14th century.

[53] Norton, Park and Binski 1987, p.41. On French 14th-century depictions, see Gillerman 1994, pp.185–86.

[54] Rushforth 1936, p.235, n. 4. It is not in the earlier glass at Grappenhall, Cheshire, as Rushforth maintained.

[55] *Age of Chivalry*, cat. no. 613.

[56] *The Wilton Diptych*, pl. 2.

[57] Lindley 1987, pp.164–65; Lindley 1990, pp.102, 106, fig. 4.

[58] Spencer 1990, p.40, figs. 108–109.

It is difficult to make much of the figure style, but the contrapposto is common to the other surviving figures on the two central buttresses. The dancing pose is accentuated by the left foot, which appears to be slightly raised. The hair of the beard is dense, with fine strands, although there is a possibility of 19th-century recutting. In its draping and fastening the camelskin most resembles that on the Wilton Diptych.

3 Pencil drawing of St John the Baptist, niche no. 145, by C. R. Cockerell, before 1851. RIBA, British Architectural Library, Drawings Collection, H10.

These iconographical and stylistic similarities raise the possibility that the Baptist figure, and the others related to it, could be later than is argued above in the text. To recap, the group comprises John's counterpart the Evangelist, Peter, Paul and the lost figure on the lesser north buttress, which are closely associated in their fixings and/or consoles. On an alternative hypothesis, they could all be later than the lost figures flanking the central porch in Zone E, which stood on ballflower bases and must therefore have dated to the first half of the 14th century. They would then represent yet another stage in the accumulation of figure sculpture on the front. As a circumstantial attraction to this theory, towards the end of the 14th century the patron of the scheme, the chapter, regained leadership after almost a century, when the deanship passed at last to a resident officer.[59] On the present balance of evidence, however, it seems more likely that the big figures in Zones C, D and E were added at the same time. As argued above, there is also circumstantial evidence for a possible *terminus ante quem* of 1341. Only for the St James, with its taller base, is there evidence good enough to argue a later date (no. 150a). It would be sensible, however, to retain an open mind on the question.

150a. **Lost Figure: St James**
(Bishop Roger of Salisbury, William Longespee Earl of Salisbury, St Bridget)[60]

The best records of this figure are a sketch by Carter of 1802 (fig. 32), a small Buckler drawing of 1811 (Catalogue fig. 4), Cockerell's description published in 1851 and Fenton's photograph of *c*.1858 (fig. 64).[61] It is described in Armfield's guide, published 1869, as an 'old mutilated figure unrestored'. It can be seen, now without a head, in the pasted-in photograph that serves as a frontispiece to his *Legend of Christian Art*, in the same year.[62] In another copy, however, the frontispiece shows the present occupant of the niche, St Stephen (no. 150b), so the medieval sculpture must have been removed around this time. The medieval

[59] Edwards 1949 (1967 edn), p.85.
[60] RIBA, Library, Cockerell Papers, Box 6, CoC.1/83, [p.ii] (Roger of Salisbury); Cockerell 1851, p.97 (Longespee); Armfield 1869b, p.12 (Bridget).
[61] BL, Add. MSS 29939, f.40 (no. 14); 36392, f.89; Cockerell 1851, p.97.
[62] Armfield 1869a, frontispiece.

4 Pencil drawing of St James formerly in niche no. 150, by J. Buckler. BL, Add. MS 36392, f.89.

console was also taken down and a stiff-leaf base substituted.

Carter and Buckler show a figure in a tall hat, spreading to a rounded top, centering a badge at the front. The figure had a forked beard and wore a long coat, without a belt, with folds falling straight to the ground. Buckler draws and Cockerell describes a scrip or purse, slung over the figure's left shoulder and hanging at his right hip. The figure has been variously identified, but was undoubtedly St James, with a pilgrim badge in his hat, a scrip over his shoulder and probably originally a pilgrim's staff.[63] Piers Plowman describes the typical pilgrim with his distinguishing souvenir badges, and also the continuing popularity of the pilgrimage to Santiago in the later 14th century.[64] An image of St James in the great east window of Gloucester Cathedral, after 1351, shows him in a hat with turned-up brim and a pilgrim badge of the Veronica.[65]

Armfield states that the present figure did not belong here.[66] This could be because the medieval base was taller than the others in Zone D, as other sources show, or he may have had other evidence (he claims the same for the equivalent figure on the north turret buttress). While the presence of the sculpture in earlier sources suggests that he was wrong, the taller console might well indicate that it was inserted after the others. Unfortunately, it has not been possible to assess the niche back for the original fixing, as it is concealed by Redfern's statue, but the figure style would be consistent with a later dating. The shape of the hat and the forked beard might suit the later 14th century. The beard and the fall of the coat are well illustrated by some of the surviving figures of kings from Westminster Hall, c.1385.[67] The fashion in beards is evident also on the tomb of Richard II in Westminster Abbey.[68]

---

166. Deacon Martyr
(St Christopher, St Birinus)[69]
Tisbury/Chilmark stone, with Chilmark additions
Probably 2nd quarter 14th century, with additions of 1866-69
Console: H, 28 cm; W, 56 cm at top; D, 32 cm
Figure: H, 207.5 cm total (c.166 cm, medieval part); W, c.53 cm max; D, 28 cm max
Lower block: H, 56 cm. Upper block: H, c.136 cm

In Zone E, within a flat-backed niche, on a shaft of trefoil section, of 13th-century origin. The canopy head and niche back bear traces of medieval paint (see pp.114-15, pl. VII). The method of fixing the statue is not visible and it is hard to envisage how the medieval hooks-and-ring system found elsewhere at Salisbury could have been installed so close to the wall. The statue may have been refixed in the 19th century. A slight change in the orientation of the console block would also be consistent with this.

---

63 Blum 1996a, p.628. For the pilgrimage, see *Santiago de Compostela: 1000 ans de Pèlerinage Européen*, Europalia 85 España, Centrum voor Kunst en Cultuur, Abbaye Saint-Pierre, Ghent, 1985. For scallopshell badges, see cat. nos. 170–94.

64 W. W. Skeat trans., *The Vision of Piers the Plowman by William Langland*, London, 1931, pp.61 (ll. 126–27), 90 (ll. 524–31).

65 Welander 1985, p.20.

66 Armfield 1869b, p.12.

67 *Westminster Kings*, pp.69–71.

68 *Wilton Diptych*, p.22, fig. 6.

69 Armfield 1869b, p.15, attributing the identification to the sculptor Redfern.

The figure is in two pieces of sandy limestone (of Chilmark type), the lower comprising both the console and the bottom 30.5 cm of the alb. This block seems to be of slightly different colour from the upper piece and has a different decay pattern. Overall, there is weathering to exposed and projecting parts, but the figure is better preserved at the sides. The lost head was replaced by Redfern with that of a mitred bishop. Lower right and left arms lost. A dowel hole, presumably of the 19th century, survives on the stump of the left arm, but the attached attribute is lost (see below).

The console has a moulded profile, framing a central band with groups of three fish to either side and centering a weathered subject at the front, probably a human or animal mask, as there are remains of a surround of hair/fur (fig. 30a). A mask was drawn here by Buckler in 1813.[70] The figure is vested as a deacon, in dalmatic and alb, with a fringed maniple over the left arm. Earlier photographs show that the dalmatic was fringed.[71] However, it is far from clear what garment is falling from the arms in serpentine folds. The sculptor may have misunderstood the vestment, treating it like a chasuble. Shoes emerge from beneath the alb.

The figure's weathered right arm supported an attribute against the right shoulder, a long narrow stem flaring slightly to the top. This was described as a martyr's palm by Cockerell and he was right, the fronds being visible in an early photograph.[72] The left arm was extended almost at right-angles to the body to support an attribute. This had been replaced, to judge from a dowel hole, but is now lost. In the Courtauld photograph, a substantial hand with spread fingers supports an eroded vaguely cylindrical object. The surviving medieval stump suggests that the original attribute was also substantial, rising over 13 cm above the remains of the arm.[73] Behind the face of the stump there remain on the sinister side (below) what could be lumpy drapery folds and (above) a vertical bellows-like structure.

Although Carter and Buckler do not show any definite attribute, Cockerell describes a stone on a

No. 166, Deacon Martyr. CI (A73/1832).

[70] BL, Add. MS 36392, f.85.

[71] CI, copyright Mrs E. L. Green-Armitage.

[72] Cockerell 1851, p.98. CI, copyright Mrs E. L. Green-Armitage.

[73] There could have been a bridge to the medieval body some distance below the arm, as there is a scar partly patched in cement, but this may be just an eroded surface.

napkin and identified the figure, therefore, as St Stephen.[74] This is plausible. The figure was very probably a deacon martyr and clearly not a bishop, like Birinus. One of the first three altars to be consecrated in the new cathedral, in 1225, was dedicated to Stephen.[75] The stoning of the protomartyr is shown in glass of about this date, once in the cathedral but now in Grateley parish church, Hants.; it was probably made originally for the east window of his chapel.[76] Of the other deacon martyrs, Lawrence and Vincent, both with emblems of a gridiron, also had altars in the cathedral.[77]

The strange decoration of the console, with fish and mask, does not correspond to any of these attributions. There was not necessarily a connection between the console subject and the identity of the figure, but it is so specific and unusual that there may have been. There could have been some allusion to the saint's life, as on supports at Wells and Chartres; or the explanation may be found, ultimately, in the rich vocabulary of subject matter in equivalently marginal locations.[78]

The figure is tall with narrow shoulders and swings slightly off the left hip. There is an effective contrast between the bold vertical folds of the vestments, dropping almost unbroken to the ground, and the serpentine hemlines that fall from the arms; the lower block is more wooden in treatment. There is as much undercutting as the relatively thin block allows, especially around the legs, and the figure is flattened off abruptly at the back, with no attempt at modelling in the round. In this respect, it is unlike several figures on the west face, including the prelate in this zone (no. 169). Even allowing for the parlous state of what remains, the style is also slightly less mannered than that of the other surviving figures, and the moulding and decoration of the console beneath is different from the prelate round the corner, all suggesting that the figure may be by another hand.

That said, however, the deacon martyr could certainly be contemporary with the other medieval statues surviving on the front, as the representative of a second distinct hand or team.

The construction of the figure is also different from that of the others. It is just conceivable that parts of two separate figures were combined at some point, but the two pieces were together by 1802,[79] they combine well, and the way in which the join is concealed at the meeting of alb and dalmatic would be tidy for such a repair. The unusual carving of the console and lower body from a single block, unlike any of the other surviving figures, also suggests some different explanation: a failure in the measuring of the niche or in the cutting of the stone at the quarry; or an economy measure, intended to make use of two available pieces of stone of slightly inappropriate size. Such joins are not uncommon in large-scale medieval stone sculpture, being found also on the west fronts of Rochester and Wells (in both cases, a join can be found on the lower legs), as well as the Virgin of the Annunciation (the top of her head) in the Chapter House at Westminster Abbey.[80]

The join is formed with white lime mortar. It was hidden originally by a painted surface. Blue and yellow ochre pigments have been found on the drapery (see p.114). As mentioned above, there are also still traces of paint on the arch mouldings and back of this niche. The possible application of paint over lichen suggests a time lapse between construction and decoration. In the light of the fact that the figure style of the sculpture is later than that of the niche, it seems highly likely that this paint layer was applied contemporary with the erection of the sculpture.

___

167a-168a. Lost Figures

The evidence for these is the survival around both niches of medieval paint traces (see pp.114-15, pl.

[74] Cockerell 1851, p.98.

[75] Wordsworth 1898, p.7; Wordsworth 1913–14, p.560. The cathedral had relics of Stephen by the end of the middle ages: Wordsworth 1901, p.34.

[76] Marks 1993, p.126, fig. 99.

[77] Wordsworth 1913–14, p.563. By the end of the middle ages, the cathedral also had relics of both: Wordsworth 1901, pp.34, 35.

[78] L. Randall, *Images in the Margins of Gothic Manuscripts*, Berkeley/Los Angeles, 1966; G.L. Remnant, *A Catalogue of Misericords in Great Britain*, Oxford, 1969, p.213 (index, fish).

[79] BL, Add. MS 29939, f.39 (no. 1).

[80] Williamson 1995, p.4; Hope and Lethaby 1904, pp.185 (NXXXII), 196 (S22), 203 (N44), 205 (N74); Williamson 1988, p.123.

VII), which have been found elsewhere on the front almost exclusively in relation to the position or likely position of medieval sculptures. The presence of 19th-century figures has made it impossible to assess the existence of original fixings in either niche. The pigment around no. 167 had a white lead ground, more elaborate therefore than that in niches nos. 166 and 168, which may indicate a figure of particular importance. The use of vermilion, prominent in the later decoration of the central porch, might suggest that there was a repainting in the later middle ages.

It is tempting to think that Salisbury's own sainted bishop, St Osmund (d.1099, but canonised only in 1456), appeared somewhere on the front. Although it is hypothesis, niche no. 167 would have offered a suitably prominent location.

---

169. Bishop or Archbishop
(Archbishops Thomas Becket or Stephen Langton, Bishop Bridport)[81]
Tisbury/Chilmark stone, with Chilmark additions
*Probably 2nd quarter 14th century, with additions of
    1866-69*
Console: H, 22 cm; W, 46 cm at top; D (top), c.29 to 30 cm
*Figure: H, 190.5 cm (c.165 cm, medieval part); W, c.64
    cm max; D, c.30 cm max*

In Zone E, within a flat-backed niche and on a shaft of trefoil section, of 13th-century origin, with restored necking. The method of fixing is not visible, as the figure is held close to the wall. Like no. 166, therefore, this figure may have been refixed, perhaps in the late 1860s.

The figure and console are in two different pieces of limestone (of Chilmark type), that for the figure with prominent calcite veins, mostly running diagonally from top left to bottom right, but also a vertical seam down the dexter side. Being harder, the veins now stand proud of the surrounding stone, revealing the depth of the surface loss. Before conservation, the surface was weathering and peeling in exposed areas. The head is lost and was replaced from mid-neck up by Redfern with that of a mitred bishop. Right and left hands lost, the right stump with a slate dowel for a 19th-century replacement and the left with pieced-in hand, supporting metal crosier staff (head lost).[82]

No. 169, Prelate. CI (A73/1831).

[81] Cockerell 1851, pp.97–98; Armfield 1869b, p.13.
[82] Hands and crosier head visible in CI A73/1831 and a print from S. H. Reynolds coll. (NMR, taken 1902).

The console is of irregular section and has a simple bead moulding at the top, different from that beneath no. 166 (fig. 30a). There is a central band of foliage decoration, the trefoil leaves having distinctive volute terminals. Following Scott's principle to be faithful to the surviving fabric, this design was used for the next console but one to the south, and for the equivalent pairs of consoles in the triplets of niches on the north face of the north turret, and on the west and south faces of the south turret.

The figure is relatively thin, but has substantial modelling of folds at the front and is modelled to a degree around the back, in a way not found on the deacon martyr, for example. This is evident not only in the original infulae of a lost mitre, on his shoulders; but also in the drapery, at the sides. These are the best preserved parts of the figure, including diagonal tooling at lower left, which could only have been done *ex situ*, following the usual medieval practice for carving large figures. Traces of paint around the head of the niche suggest that this figure was also originally painted (see p.123).

He is vested for the mass, in chasuble, dalmatic and alb, amice, stole (no fringe, unlike the maniple in no. 166) and buskins on the feet. The infulae of the medieval mitre are carved at the back of the neck. The figure's right arm is raised in blessing and the left arm is angled down slightly, presumably to support a crosier or cross staff, as now. This is, therefore, a bishop or archbishop. There is no sign of a metropolitan's pallium, but this could have been painted on the original figure. No other attribute offers a clue to his particular identity. In the restoration, he was given the new persona of Bishop Bridport of Salisbury (d.1262), as one of a group of 'worthies distinctively belonging to the English Church', but is more likely originally to have been a saint, in the company of the martyr on the north face in this zone.[83]

The bishop has narrow shoulders and sways off the right hip, leaning back and turned slightly to his right, which is apparent both in the shoulders and the position of the feet. Cascading serpentine folds fall from both arms, representing the hemline of the chasuble, which gathers into three substantial pouches across the body, looping rhythmically to left and right. This figure was compared by Prior and Gardner with William of Ireland's statues of Queen Eleanor on the Eleanor Cross at Hardingstone, Northants. (fig. 37).[84] The comparison is generally sound, but the Salisbury figures differ in the degree of sway and the apparent thickness of the drapery.

Among episcopal effigies, the pouchy folds are found on that of Bishop Droxford (d. 1329) at Wells Cathedral. In free-standing English monumental sculpture, the Evangelists around the chancel at Edington Priory, Wilts., *c*.1351-61, offer some similarities (fig. 36), as does a clerical figure from the west front of York Minster.[85] In stained glass, the monumental figures in the choir clerestory at Wells (*c*.1340) are less agitated, but share the pouchy folds.[86] On the Continent, the combination of narrow shoulders, mannered contrapposto and pouchy folds is found in monumental sculpture, both wood and stone, from the Rhineland and Low Countries particularly during the second quarter of the 14th century;[87] and also in northern France.[88] In miniature, it appears on the second seal of Bishop Bury of Durham (1334-35), by a craftsman from the Low Countries (fig. 40), which would be highly influential for future seal design.[89]

The bishop looked to his right, towards the north-west approach to the cathedral. The lost figure on the western buttress of the north turret was also turned in this direction and there is other evidence that the northern side received more attention than the south. A detailed survey of the exposed masonry on the south turret in this zone has revealed no evidence for original fixings on its south face, whereas a deacon martyr survives on the north face of the north turret and may well have been accompanied by other figures (nos. 166-68). This was no doubt to complete the show front, on the north side, almost adjacent to the entrance through the ornate and splendid north porch.

---

83   Armfield 1869b, p.13.
84   Prior and Gardner 1912, pp.345–46.
85   *BoE Wilts.*, p.209; *Romanesque*, no. 33.
86   Woodforde 1946, pl. IV.
87   *Rhin–Meuse*, nos. N5 (Cologne, c.1330), N13 (Liège, c.1330), O7 (Mosan, c.1330–40), O8 (Mosan, 1344).
88   *Fastes du Gothique*, cat. no. 7.
89   *Age of Chivalry*, cat. no. 675.

178a. Lost Figure

Console: Tisbury/Chilmark stone
Console: Probably second quarter 14th century
Console: H, c.25 cm

The console for a figure survives and is decorated with ballflower (fig. 30c), providing a model for many of the new consoles that were carved for this zone during Scott's restoration. It is shown in Fenton's photograph of *c*.1858 and had a pair in niche no. 187. The photograph also reveals that there was a hook set into the back of the niche, for fixing the figure, within a recessed area of stonework. The form is common to many of the other full-scale figures on the front (nos. 19a, 26a, 86, 95, 124, 129), suggesting that they belong to the same campaign. A small area of turquoise green pigment has been located on the roll mouldings of the southern jamb of the niche, providing further evidence that the niches were filled.

At Salisbury ballflower is found also on the central tower and the tomb of Bishop Ghent (d.1315). Becoming popular in the early years of the 14th century, the motif fell out of fashion in the second quarter of the century. Insofar as the surviving figures on the front can be related to this niche, notably in their fixings, it provides a pointer for their possible date (see p.68).

180a-182a. Lost Figures

These niches in the three gables of the central porch probably received sculpture in the 13th century. There are remains of paint in and around niche nos. 180 and 182 (see p.114) and the remains of off-centre fixings for sculpture are visible in these niches in Fenton's photograph of *c*.1858 (fig. 16). The fixings are different from the others on the front and were perhaps to support the shoulders, as on the west front at Wells. The figures had stiff-leaf brackets to support them.

There are other signs of medieval occupation. At the base of niche no. 180, on the dexter side, the stone to the south of the shaft has been worked back along a diagonal line from just beside the shaft at the base to 10 cm south of the southern face of the shaft at its upper bed. This becomes progressively shallower towards the top and the south, suggesting that it was cut to receive the sloping drapery of a kneeling figure, which was turned slightly at the base so that the stone had to be worked back to accommodate it. Adjacent to the dexter shaft on the lower bed of the course below the capitals of niche no. 182, 10 cm north of the northern edge of the shaft, there is a square iron fixing. This might also be associated with a lost medieval figure sculpture, perhaps supporting a censer held by a kneeling angel, for instance.

183a-185a. Lost Figures, including the Virgin Mary

The tympanum of the great west door probably received figure sculpture in the 13th century. It was painted many times in the middle ages and the earliest layers are thought to date from the period of the porch's completion (see pp.113, 129 and pls. II-IV). The central niche was filled with an image of the Virgin by 1467, when a will mentions an 'image of the blessed Virgin Mary adjoining and over the western doors'.[90] No fixings are visible in Fenton's pre-restoration photograph, *c*.1858, but part of a stem for a support is shown to have survived (and still does) beneath the central niche. Above and below this, there are cut away areas, indicating that something has been removed. The survey found signs that an accompanying metal fitting might have been removed from the gable of the central niche. There is further evidence for the use of metal: above and below the capital of the trumeau are bands of a copper alloy. Above the niches, four heads are carved in relief within quatrefoils, the two larger ones displaying the features of the Apostles St Peter and St Paul (tonsure and bald pate). Around the tympanum there was a deeply undercut band, which surviving fragments show to have been inhabited. Fenton's photograph shows that it had been systematically destroyed. This and all of the tympanum sculptures were probably removed after the Reformation, along with other offensive imagery (see no. 204).

187a. Lost Figure

The evidence for a lost figure sculpture is provided both by early visual records and written accounts.[91] Fenton's photograph of *c*.1858 shows a console

[90] Malden 1904, p.29: 'iuxta et super ostia ecclesie cathedralis Sar' in occidente'.
[91] Cockerell 1851, p.97.

decorated with ballflower, like that in niche no. 178, and the lower part of a figure on a separate piece of stone (fig. 16). It shows long robes falling to the ground and protruding feet. Like no. 178a, this sculpture probably dated to the second quarter of the 14th century. There is still slight 'shadowing' on the niche back and there are two patches of Roman cement, perhaps filling holes for post-medieval cramps, to secure the fragment in the niche. The console was apparently discarded in Scott's restoration.

195a. **Lost Figure**

The evidence for this figure is of two kinds. A medieval iron hook is still set into the back of the niche, of the kind that supported many of the other medieval figures (nos. 19a, 26a, 86, 95, 124, 129). Around the niche head there are traces of medieval polychromy (pl. VIII). No console had survived, however, into the age of photography.

201, 206-207. **Lost Figures**

The presence of lead-set iron hooks, within a recessed area of walling suggests that there were also two large medieval figures within the central porch, in the central niche of each triplet of blind arcading on either side of the door. They probably stood on tall bases, as separate iron dog-cramps were let into the wall above the wall bench, to hold them in place. There may have been a third figure in the southernmost niche, where there are remains of another dog-cramp, but the stonework above has been disturbed. The form of the fixings suggests that these figures were added at the same time as other lost and surviving sculptures that used this method, probably in the second quarter of the 14th century.

204. **Lost Figure**
Niche: H, c.84 cm; W, c.51.1 cm
Corbel: H, 14 cm; W, 24.5 cm

The recent survey located the site of a sculpture to the right of the west doorway, on the north-facing wall. At chest height and above, there is an area of disturbed walling (fig. 31), with evenly coursed stones, forming tidy vertical joins with the original masonry. Below, there is a cut-back stone, probably a corbel block, which has been inserted into the 13th-century coursing. At the foot, there is incised a Lombardic letter C, followed by a three-dot word-spacer. To the right are the remains of an iron fixing, lead-set into the wall. This must mark the site of a statue, perhaps within a niche or frame, once neatly inserted into the wall, standing on a corbel block and with an associated feature, perhaps a candle pricket. It may have been the image of the Virgin outside the west door, which is mentioned in Hemingsby's Register of Chapter documents, in March 1341.[92] Oblations of candles were then being made at it.

208. **Lost Figure**
Console: H, 34 cm; W, 38 cm

A console has been inserted into the wall of the blind arch to the right of the south-west door. Set high up, within the arch head, it has a polygonal top that is supported by a feathered angel and must have been for a small statue or group. It is of late medieval date. The sculpture was of distinctive form: to our right, the springing of the arch has been cut away slightly and an iron fixing supplied, suggesting a composition that spread across the arch head in this direction.[93] There is no sign of a fixing in the wall above the console itself. As in other locations where sculpture is or was present, traces of colour have been found (see p.124).

[92] Chew 1963, no. 159: '... super perceptione cere ad ymaginem beate Marie que dicitur gysine, et alteram ymaginem ejusdem ad portam occidentalem, que est extra, ex devocione fidelium oblate ...'

[93] St Michael spearing the dragon might be a possibility, as on the south gable of the west porches at Laon (Sauerländer 1972, p.427), or perhaps St George.

19TH AND 20TH CENTURIES

8. Standing Archangel

Chilmark stone (trough bed); Redfern workshop, ?later 1867
H, 224.5 cm; W, 88 cm; D, 51 cm

No. 8, Archangel.

Massive standing archangel, probably bare headed (hair swept back) and clean shaven, in a frontal, hieratic pose, the tall wings framing the head. It wears a (?hooded) mantle clasped with a circular brooch on the front of the dexter shoulder; long belted tunic with full sleeves to the wrist and round neck. Over this is a strange looping 'belt' or embroidered strip, which falls from the dexter shoulder around the sinister hip, appears again beneath the sinister arm and crosses the body to disappear beside the dexter hand over the top of the dexter thigh. The dexter hand is on the dexter hip and holds a vertical staff, its upper part a separate piece (in a different stone type), the top of which is lost above the dexter shoulder. The sinister hand is held straight out from the body supporting an orb. Armfield states that each archangel bears a globe in his left hand and that the northern one carries a sceptre with a crosspiece derived from the labarum of Roman imperial standards.[94] Echoes of the forms of Redfern's angels may be found in both the text and the illustrations of Jameson's *Sacred and Legendary Art*.[95]

The upper parts of the wings are severely decayed. On both sides they would appear to have been cut back in the 19th century in order to fit the sculpture between the abaci of the niche. There are clear marks of drill-work on the hair and elsewhere on the face, including the cutting of the sinister ear hole, nostrils and tear ducts. The use of trough-bed stone (found also in the Majesty (no. 22b), the first sculpture to be executed) suggests a date very early in the programme, since this variety of Chilmark is found only in the figures of the top tier, the great majority of the sculptures being carved from a finer grained and much less shelly stone.

14. Seated Angel with Harp

Chilmark stone (trough bed); Redfern workshop, ?later 1867
H, 132.5 cm (remaining); W, 69 cm; D, 30 cm

Seated barefoot angel (with no visible seat), facing to sinister and playing a large 'Celtic' harp. The head and top of the dexter (and probably sinister) wing broken away. The angel wears a round-necked belted tunic

with tight cuffs. A harp bag, shown as a large swathe of drapery, is brought around the sinister base of the harp, looping back up over the dexter wrist and falling to terminate in a decorative swag, which appears to end with a ball. As often with Redfern's work at Salisbury, the form of the drapery is not fully resolved, but it seems that the belted tunic was intended to end at mid-shin level and that beneath this an ankle-length under-tunic was worn. The harp, plucked by the right hand, has twelve strings but only seven tuning pegs. The use of trough-bed stone suggests a date early in the carving programme (see no. 8).

No. 14, Seated Angel.

[94] Armfield 1869b, p.7.
[95] Jameson 1857, fig. 24, p.76 and the description on p.74.

19b, 26b. **Angels**

Chicksgrove stone; Jason Battle, 1999-2000

Nos. 19b, 26b, Angels.

As a result of the severely decayed state of two medieval carvings, nos. 19a and 26a, modern replacements have been made, following the Victorian scheme for the front in subject. The head carver Jason Battle was given the commission. Each statue took three months to carve. The first (26b) was installed from the scaffold and the second (19b) was lifted into position by crane and fixed by masons working from a hydraulic platform. The angel on the north buttress (19b) was carved in mid-1999 and fixed into position on 9 November 1999. The angel for the south buttress (26b) was carved in late 1999/early 2000, and fixed into position on 30 March 2000.

22b. **Christ in Majesty**

Chilmark stone (trough bed, but the halo of a finer grained
  Chilmark); Redfern workshop, by October 1867
H, 206 cm; W, 124 cm; D, 54 cm

Seated, the nimbus carved on a separate stone, clothed in an ankle-length, square-necked robe, with voluminous mantle secured across the chest with a wide strap fixed with two circular brooches. The figure is seated on a plain flat-topped bench, its outer edges more or less adjusted to follow the curve of the surrounding mandorla. The arms are outspread, the right hand originally in benediction, the left supporting an orb. The feet are bare, showing the stigmata, and rest upon the frame.

This was the first of the new sculptures to be fixed, in early October 1867, and almost certainly the first to be executed.[96] It is carved from trough-bed stone. The coarseness of this and the exposed position of the figure seem to have led Redfern to produce a sculpture of bold forms and less than normally delicate drapery. The finish is also less complete, with 46 drill marks in the carving of the hair, beard and moustache. These and a number of coarse pointing holes may have been masked originally with a 'filler', subsequently lost. The sides of the head and tops of the shoulders have been roughly reworked and, taken with the fact that the existing halo is a separate piece of stone, this suggests that the position of the halo was altered shortly after completion of the sculpture, from near vertical to angled, in order to accommodate the steep viewpoint from beneath.

The niche bears traces of medieval pigment, strongly suggesting that a medieval sculpture was installed here (see above, no. 22a).

No. 22b, Christ in Majesty.

[96] The maquette must have been agreed with the Dean and Chapter by January 1867, when it was seen by a reporter from *Building News*. It was reported in the *Building News* on 4 October (p. 694) that 'the first statue, the uppermost figure, the Christ in Majesty in the apex of the gable was fixed in place around the beginning of October'.

31. Seated Angel

Chilmark stone (trough bed, but the separate wing of a
finer grained Chilmark); Redfern workshop, ?later 1867
H, 148 cm; W, 61 cm; D, 33 cm

No. 31, Seated Angel.

Choral angel, seated upon a bench that is completely concealed beneath the folds of the robe, facing to dexter and holding a scroll with both hands (the right raised, the left holding the base of the scroll). A round-necked, belted and ankle-length robe is worn (which appears to have voluminous sleeves to just below the elbow). Beneath is a second garment with tight sleeves running down to the wrist. Over these is a mantle, which falls across the lap from the sinister shoulder and covers the knees. The left arm is bridged to the torso, the right has a bridging-block behind both it and the scroll. There is also a fall of drapery (presumably the mantle) from behind the right hand, running down to pass behind the dexter hip. The head is turned to dexter (north), facing the Christ in Majesty. The feet are bare.

Carved in two stones, the sinister wing being a separate block pieced-on (with a red-brown mastic or shellac) behind the shoulder. The main stone appears to be from the trough bed and this suggests that it is among the first sculptures in the campaign (see no. 8), while the left wing is of the more usual greenish Chilmark bed, perhaps indicating an on-site repair to damage in transit.

37. Standing Archangel

Chilmark stone (trough bed); Redfern workshop, ?later 1867
H, 218 cm; W, 84 cm; D, 35 cm

Large frontally posed angel, with curly hair and diadem, dressed in an ankle-length ?unbelted alb, with ?cope over, fastened with a diamond-shaped brooch on the chest. The soft material of the cope is drawn over the flexed arms, the left hand holding an orb, the right upraised but lost. The orphrey of the cope consists of an ornamented band comprising a row of discs, each bearing a cross botonée, separated by single dots in each of the spandrels and edged with bands (about 6 mm wide). The feet are bare. The wings are held in a standard frontal pose, the apices just above the level of the ears.

No. 37, Archangel.

The lost right hand appears to have consisted originally of a separate piece of stone, since the stump of the wrist has a large circular hole cut in its face to receive either a dowel or possibly a stone 'countersink' from the pieced-on hand. The stone appears very similar to that in niche no. 31 and probably derives from the trough bed as used for the Christ in Majesty. As elsewhere, this suggests that the sculpture is from the very first phase of the campaign (see no. 8).

49. King David

Chilmark stone; Redfern workshop, 1869
H, 203.5 cm; W, 59.5 cm; D, 38 cm

David is represented as a standing king, supporting a harp in his left hand, his right holding a fold of the mantle, which is clasped at the neck with a plain oval brooch. The mantle is swept back on the dexter side over the right forearm, whence it curls back under to be caught up by the right hand and fall in a series of zigzag folds. The ankle-length tunic is tied at the waist. The harp is similar to that held by the angel in niche no. 14; the top dexter corner (lost) may have been a separate piece. He stands with his weight on his left foot, the right knee pushed slightly forward and the head turned to sinister as if listening.

Nos. 49 and 50, King David and Moses.

A drawing in the cathedral archive appears to be a draft for the iconography. This and another drawing, indicating donations of sculptures (figs. 55, 58), suggest that the prophets and patriarchs were amongst the last figures to be executed in the main campaign, and point to a date of 1869 for the whole series. Photographic evidence reveals that the figures in niches nos. 49, 50, 65 and 66 were carved before nos. 51-53. Those in niches nos. 61-62 were made later in the 19th century.

50. **Moses**
Chilmark stone (fine grained trough bed?); Redfern workshop, 1869
H, 202 cm; W, 76 cm; D, 31 cm

Moses is represented as balding, with a long beard, 'horns' of radiant light and the tablets of the Law, supported by the right hand and held at mid-height by the left. The numbers of the Commandments are carved, but the text is merely fictive. The form of the garments is exceptionally complex and difficult to

Nos. 51–53, Isaiah, Jeremiah and Ezekiel.

understand. There would appear to be an ankle-length tunic, covered at mid-height by a mantle, pulled across the body from the sinister hip, and falling from the dexter hip in a double swathe. The tunic appears to be unbelted, with a round neck and tight sleeves at the wrist. It falls vertically beneath the mantle, lying over the top of the insteps of the feet (in pointed buskins).

This sculpture appears to owe much to Redfern's (evidently detailed) study of the surviving 14th-century sculptures on the façade. It has the pronounced S-curve of the pose, but the drapery would also seem to owe much to the 14th-century originals here. In general form this sculpture is similar to that of the Prophet Samuel (no. 65).

---

51. Isaiah

Chilmark stone; Redfern workshop, later 1869-70
H, 207 cm; W, 71 cm; D, 41 cm

The prophet is in animated conversation with Jeremiah (no. 52). The strong turn of the head to sinister and the dropping of the left shoulder are balanced by bringing the left arm across the chest and by the thrust of the right knee. He has a low cap with upturned brim, long hair flaring out to dexter and a long beard flowing down on to the sinister shoulder. The brows are furrowed into an almost ferocious frown. The drapery is complex and animated, reflecting the animation of the pose, comprising a more than ankle-length tunic, round-necked and with full-length sleeves. Over this is a mantle (clasped on the dexter shoulder with a brooch), caught up over the sinister forearm and pulled across the front of the body.

The right arm is held beside the body, bridged to it as far as the elbow, but the forearm is free of the remaining stone and bridged back on to the side of the dexter thigh by having it hold a furled scroll. The left arm is bridged to the front of the body throughout its length and brought back horizontally across the chest, with the hand and forefinger raised.

This figure is absent from the pasted-in frontispiece in one copy of Armfield's description of the front (probably taken late summer 1869), but is present in another (perhaps taken shortly after January 1870).

---

52. Jeremiah

Chilmark stone; Redfern workshop, later 1869-70
H, 208 cm; W, 66.5 cm; D, 37 cm

Jeremiah has a more hunched posture than the dynamic Isaiah, swaying slightly away from the companion prophet: the sinister knee pushed forwards and the dexter hip pushed to the side. The dexter shoulder is slightly raised in relation to the sinister, the right hand held up in a gesture of reassurance. The left hand is at waist level and holds a partly rolled scroll. Like the other prophets, he wears a round-necked, long-sleeved tunic of more than floor length, over which is a voluminous mantle, caught back up beneath both wrists and falling in decorative folds over the front of the figure. Like the three (later) sculptures of prophets on the north link-wall, a low pointed cap with an upturned brim is worn. The face has the same exaggerated features and deeply lined forehead as Isaiah, with medium-length hair, but a shorter beard.

This figure is absent from the pasted-in frontispiece in one copy of Armfield's description of the front (probably taken late summer 1869), but is present in another (perhaps taken shortly after January 1870).

---

53. Ezekiel

Chilmark stone; Redfern workshop, later 1869-70
H, 203 cm; W, 66 cm; D, 38 cm

Standing bearded prophet, wearing a pointed cap with deep brim, mantle and tunic – the mantle possibly hooded. In his right hand he holds an open scroll, to which he pointed with his (lost) left hand. There is a slight sway to the pose, the sinister knee brought forward and the head turned sharply to sinister, presumably to animate a pair of figures in conversation, although the companion was never carved. The facial features are deeply carved and somewhat exaggerated, but not as much as those of the other prophets. There are signs of confusion in the drapery over the sinister chest and upper arm, suggesting that the sculptor was not using a draped model but working directly on to the stone (or the plaster of the maquette).

This figure is absent from the pasted-in frontispiece in one copy of Armfield's description of the front (probably taken late summer 1869), but is present in another (perhaps taken shortly after January 1870).

56. **Abraham**

Chilmark stone; Redfern workshop, 1867-69
H, 202 cm; W, 62 cm; D, 37 cm

No. 56, Abraham.

Abraham is represented barefoot and wearing an ankle-length tunic and mantle. The mantle is passed over the top of the head and caught up over both wrists, being gathered on to the top of the left wrist, whence it falls with a characteristic zigzag hem. The left hand is broken off at the wrist; the right hand holds a knife, its point brought across to near centre chest. The head is heavily bearded and turned slightly downwards and to sinister. The eyes are deep set, the face and brows furrowed. The ears and hair within the 'cowl' of the mantle are suggested by an irregular series of (?drill) holes.

This sculpture was conserved in 1982 by Iain Lunn.

59. **Noah**

Chilmark stone; Redfern workshop, 1867-69
H, 202.5 cm; W, 64 cm; D, 40 cm

The standing patriarch with a slight S-curve to the stance, the right knee pushed forward and the weight placed on the left leg. The head is turned to dexter, the face is bearded, the brows frowning. A more than ankle-length robe is worn, falling over the bare feet. Over this is a long mantle, which passes over the top of the head and falls behind the dexter shoulder, to be caught up in a loop across the body and anchored (presumably) beneath the left hand, to fall in U- and V-shaped folds over the upper legs. On the sinister side, the mantle falls vertically down the chest, covering the upper arm, and slips beneath the swathe of mantle from the dexter side, to fall over the sinister forearm in a series of zigzag folds. The right forearm is held horizontally across the chest – the right hand, which was apparently upturned, is lost; the left forearm is held horizontally at the sinister side, the hand supporting a model of the Ark.

This sculpture is similar to that of Abraham and was presumably

No. 59, Noah.

designed with it, perpetuating the 14th-century tradition of pairing figures on the central buttresses.

61. **Job**

Chilmark stone; unknown sculptor, after 1870
H, 205 cm; W, 63 cm; D, 42 cm

A standing figure holding a scroll in the left hand, inscribed with his name, the right raised. The head is bearded, with a bushy moustache and very pronounced cheek bones. The nose is damaged, but was probably hooked, with overhanging eyebrows and deeply recessed eyes. The ears are just visible beneath the long hair, which falls on to the shoulders; the head is balding across the brow. While the head is not unlike those of Redfern's prophets, it is smaller, the features are finer, and the treatment of the hair and beard is softer.

Job wears an ankle-length tunic, belted at the waist; and a mantle caught up over his left wrist and falling outside it, with the folds brought taughtly

Nos. 61 and 62, Job and Daniel.

across from the dexter side. The treatment of the multiplicity of delicate folds is quite different from that normally associated with Redfern's stylistic vocabulary, lacking the sinuous falls of the hems in which Redfern delights, with stiff rather than sinuous blocks of drapery caught up over the sinister wrist. The vertical falls of the drapery of the mantle on the sinister side are square in profile, while the folds of the tunic towards the feet, in addition to being square in profile, are hollowed on their faces. The prophet stands upon a small two-legged dragon, its ridged, rather dog-like head turned back from the dexter side and looking back up towards Job, its tail curling back on to the plinth block from the sinister end.

There are no pointing holes on the stone and the tool marks remaining in the folds run across the axis of the fold, rather than along it, as is usual in Redfern's work. The figure is also cramped to the wall in a different way. The stylistic and technical differences, plus the fact that it does not appear in either of the photographs in Armfield's book of 1869, strongly suggest that it is not by Redfern's workshop.

62. Daniel

Chilmark stone; unknown sculptor, early 20th century
H, 198 cm; W, 98 cm; D, 50 cm

Standing prophet holding an open book in the left hand, the right arm upraised, the hand lost. The left foot is pushed forward and from behind the right leg appears the front of a rather imperial lion. The head is bearded and windswept. The cheekbones and folds of the cheek above the moustache are pronounced, the brows are furrowed. Daniel is dressed in a tunic and mantle of heavy material, the tunic falling in wide folds to ankle level and bunched up over the mantle where it is drawn across the midriff.

The fold forms and the weight of the material represented are quite unlike those in the carvings by Redfern – though the facial features are not dissimilar, if coarser. The width of the sculpture and the drama of its pose are also untypical of Redfern's work. The fixing system is different from that of both the Redfern sculptures and the later figure of Job. There is a mastic or mortar repair in the outer face of the drapery below the left wrist. The sculpture is not

Nos. 65 and 66, Samuel and King Solomon.

shown in a photograph by Carl Norman and Co. (in White 1898, facing p.1), suggesting that it was carved in the last decade of the 19th or the first decade of the 20th century. It was installed before nos. 168 and 172. In this case, as with the earlier figure of Job, some attempt was made to follow Armfield's iconographical scheme. Armfield's drawing in the cathedral archive shows Enoch (no. 61), Job (no. 62), David (no. 63; an inadvertent repetition, since he also occupies niche no. 49, as now) and Jeremiah (no. 64).[97]

65. Samuel

Chilmark stone; Redfern workshop, 1869
H, 208.3 cm; W, 86 cm; D, 33 cm

A standing figure with a pronounced curve to the stance, similar to that of the remaining 14th-century sculptures. Samuel's head is turned to dexter and looks slightly downwards. He wears a cap with upturned brim. His long beard falls almost to waist level. The left hand holds the beard on the front of the chest, while the right is upraised and held out to dexter. Samuel wears an ankle-length round-necked tunic, with a few flat folds across the upper torso disappearing beneath the mantle, which swings across the body from the top of the sinister shoulder, beneath the dexter armpit. This falls in elegant flat folds with the typical sinuous Redfern hemline on the dexter side, and to a lesser extent on the sinister.

There is a small workshop repair fixed with red mastic on the forward-facing upturned brim of the cap.

66. King Solomon

Chilmark stone; Redfern workshop, 1869
H, 180.3 cm (head missing); W, 75 cm; D, 31.5 cm

King, dressed in tunic, undertunic and mantle, the head lost. The tunic is restrained at the waist with a heavy decorated belt, from which hangs a large purse supported upon twining strings passed through a ring

---

[97] The figures nominated for these niches in his book were Melchisedec and Enoch (Armfield 1869b, p.16), with Job and Daniel in niches nos. 63–64.

Nos. 79–82, St Jude, St Simon, St Andrew, St Thomas.

which closes the bag, hanging centrally at the level of the knees. The mantle is caught up beneath each wrist and clasped at the centre of the chest with a circular brooch, its outer rim decorated with a series of drill holes. The right hand holds a trefoil-headed sceptre, while the left held a square-backed object (now mostly lost), which Armfield identifies as a church 'to designate him as the Founder of the Temple'.[98]

79. St Jude
Chilmark stone; Redfern workshop, 1867-69
H, 201 cm; W, 61 cm; D, 41 cm

The long-haired, bearded Apostle wears a more than ankle-length tunic and mantle, the head tilted slightly to dexter, giving an air of quizzical assertion. The hands are held in front of the chest slightly to sinister, in an attitude of prayer, and behind is the shaft of a halberd, its base resting on the plinth. The mantle is brought forward over both shoulders and caught up over both wrists, disappearing behind the figure at

[98] Armfield 1869b, p.8.

knee-level to dexter and at the level of the upper thigh to sinister. Beneath, over the central part of the figure to knee level, falls what appears to be a third garment, which ends in a curved hem, almost like a chasuble. The arrangement of drapery may again have been unclear in the mind of the sculptor.

80. St Simon
Chilmark stone; Redfern workshop, 1867-69
H, 201.5 cm; W, 58.5 cm; D, 42 cm

The standing Apostle holds with both hands a tall saw, which rests on top of the plinth beside his foot. He wears a more than ankle-length round-necked tunic. Brought forward over both shoulders is a voluminous mantle, which wraps around the front and is pulled in taught curves down the sinister side. The head has medium-length hair and a long beard falling on to the chest.

The treatment and stone are very similar to the figure in niche no. 79, the stone again being a shelly block with plentiful diagonal calcite veining running downwards from sinister to dexter at approximately 45 degrees. It seems probable – in view of the care with which Redfern designed the 11 Patron Saints of Christendom as a tableau (see below) – that groups of sculptures, such as this set of four Apostles, were conceived, designed and executed together, so that their draperies enhanced, echoed or contrasted with each other.

81. St Andrew

Chilmark stone; Redfern workshop, 1867-69
H, 206 cm; W, 68 cm; D, 40.5 cm

The almost scowling figure of St Andrew, his head turned somewhat to sinister, has hair of medium length and a long flowing beard falling on to the chest. He holds a diminutive saltire cross, which is supported from beneath by the left hand and held by the right. He wears a more than ankle-length tunic, which is round-necked with a collar, apparently unbelted and falling in vertical folds, which sweep to sinister from the knee downwards. Like the figures in niches nos. 79 and 80, the mantle is brought forwards over both shoulders and caught up over the wrists. Down the front of the figure hangs an intricate zigzag hem of the type so often employed by Redfern, while beneath the sinister forearm is a series of gradually elongating V-shaped folds. Both feet are shown. Their positions are dictated by the pose, with the left knee pushed forwards, the right leg straight, turning the lower part of the body somewhat to the north, contrasting with the southward turn of the head.

This block has a shelly and chert-rich bed.

82. St Thomas

Chilmark stone; Redfern workshop, 1867-69
H, 210.5 cm; W, 65 cm; D, 38 cm

The standing Apostle holds a builder's square in both hands across his chest. He wears a round-necked full-length tunic, with mantle brought forwards over both shoulders and with both ends brought up into the left hand and falling in a dividing swathe of drapery down the front of the sculpture. The feet are large and bare. The head is also bare, with a ring of short curls above the ears and across the forehead. Short

beard and moustache. The figure is turned slightly to dexter, in conversation with St Andrew. The hand gestures also bring the two figures into communication.

There are 6 mm diameter drill marks at the centres of the hair curls. The stone is sufficiently similar to that of the other three Apostles in this group to suggest that they were carved together or in close sequence.

89. St Mark the Evangelist

Chilmark stone; ?Redfern workshop, 1870 or later
H, 183 cm; W, 57 cm; D, 43.5 cm

The Evangelist holds a book in his left hand, in which he writes with a quill. He is lightly bearded and wears a mantle which falls over the fronts of both shoulders, is caught up over the dexter forearm, falls down over the sinister elbow, and is brought back across the body in a wide swathe which has the appearance of being continuous with the fall over the dexter shoulder – thus the arrangement of this garment is somewhat illogical. Beneath the mantle is worn a floor-length tunic, quite loose at the neck and falling in parallel folds, beneath which the toes appear. The weight is placed on his left foot, the right being placed slightly forwards and with the dexter knee slightly protruding. Appearing from beneath the drapery on the dexter side are the forequarters of a lion.

No. 89, St Mark the Evangelist.

Numerous stylistic and technical anomalies suggest that this figure was not executed in Redfern's atelier. However, it is so similar in design to Redfern's St Mark on the south

5   St Mark the Evangelist, south porch, Gloucester Cathedral.

porch of Gloucester Cathedral (commissioned 24 June 1870) that it seems certain to have been designed by him (Catalogue fig. 5).[99] The sculpture may have been executed by another carver working from a maquette by Redfern. One technical feature that might support this conclusion is the fact that the pointing holes which remain on the figure were cut with a flat-ended drill-bit rather than the pointed drills universally used by Redfern and his carvers.

This sculpture was not specified by Armfield in either his original drawing for the iconography (which suggested angels with Symbols of the Passion for the six niches around the west windows) or in his 1869 publication. Neither this nor St Matthew is shown in the later version of the photographic frontispiece to Armfield's guide (1869), although the two Evangelists on the south side had been installed.

90. St Matthew the Evangelist

Chilmark stone; ?Redfern workshop, 1870 or later
H, 242 cm; W, 72.5 cm; D, 43 cm

Matthew stands with his left knee thrust forward and his right leg pushed back, to accommodate the small figure of a winged man, his Evangelistic symbol. The Evangelist is a large, loose-limbed figure, dressed in tunic and mantle, his long head turned to sinister. In his right hand he holds a quill pen, its nib apparently a (lost) separate piece, and with his left hand he supports a box with a large trefoil clasp (alluding to

his career as a tax gatherer). The angel has its dexter knee on the ground and the sinister raised. It holds a large open book and the head is turned up towards Matthew, framed by flame-like locks of hair. It wears a full-length tunic, with a circular orphrey at the collar; its right wing held (conventionally) behind it, the left raised with the tip flying upwards against the dexter side of the saint. The face is cursorily drawn (though weathering has erased some detail), the mouth slightly open, the eyes partly erased beneath arching brows.

This carving possesses many of the traits of the figure in niche no. 89 (St Mark), including those that separate the latter from the Redfern workshop. The loose gathers at the neck of the tunic are the same as those on St Mark and the overall lack of finish is even more pronounced, especially at the sides of the head.

No. 90, St Matthew the Evangelist.

There is little similarity between this figure and Redfern's St Matthew on the south porch of Gloucester Cathedral (1870). The figure has an exceptional number of pointing holes, 113 compared with 100 on Wyon's Bishop Ken (no. 177) and 83 on St Christopher (no. 137), which is the highest number for a Redfern workshop sculpture. Not only is this the largest number on any figure, but many are on surfaces that were usually scrupulously cleaned, such as the face. No use of the drill, a hallmark of Redfern's work at Salisbury, has been seen on either Matthew or Mark. The carving is absent from both the earlier and later versions of the frontispiece in Armfield's guide (1869).

[99]   Gloucester Cathedral, Chapter Act Book, 24 June 1870.

91. St Luke the Evangelist

Chilmark stone; ?Redfern workshop, late 1869-70
H, 187 cm; W, 64 cm; D, 37 cm

A standing figure of St Luke, his head turned slightly to dexter and downwards, holding a pen (a separate piece of zinc) in his raised right hand (bridged to the chest), and a book with two clasps in the left. The sinister knee is pushed forward and behind the leg appears the front of an ox, his Evangelistic symbol. Luke wears a round-necked tunic with a collar and a voluminous mantle, which is wrapped across the body and thrown over the sinister shoulder. The head is narrow and long, the beard full and forked at the chin, with symmetrical locks falling on to the chest. The left foot is fully carved, but the right may have been left smoothly roughed out. The ox looks up towards the saint. It has short horns and tubular ears, heavy brow, a short muzzle with the square teeth shown, and large nostrils probably partly worked with the drill. The hanging dewlap has flat chisel work, and the flat chisel has been used on the side of the face to suggest the hide.

The stone is slightly different from that normally used, in being almost free of calcite veins and showing almost no sign of the bedding. At the centre of the top of the saint's head is a circular cement patch approximately 2.5 cm in diameter, which would seem to be the capping of a vertical dowel; this is almost certainly associated with a horizontal mastic joint that runs around the head just below the nose and ears. The plinth is on a separate stone, the joint running immediately beneath the feet. There is little sign of the use of the drill in the working of the stone; and the most typical tool marks are those of flat chisels, rather than the characteristic claw chisels usually found on Redfern's sculptures. However, the general form of drapery, the pose, the positions of the hands and the facial features are all reminiscent of Redfern's style. Redfern's figure of St Luke on the south porch of Gloucester Cathedral has a more widely forked beard, lacks the fringe of hair and has a more exaggerated pose.

This sculpture is absent from the first version of the frontispiece in Armfield's guide of 1869, but present in the second.

No. 91, St Luke the Evangelist.

92. St John the Evangelist

Chilmark stone; Redfern workshop, late 1869-70
H, 238.5 cm; W, 69 cm; D, 37 cm

John stands in a relaxed pose, his head in profile to dexter, wearing an ankle-length tunic and a hooded mantle, clasped at the throat with a diamond-shaped brooch and caught up across the body into the left hand. This supports a chalice from which emerges a winged demon. The right hand holds a large clasped book. The head is youthful and clean shaven, the medium-length hair swept back and centrally parted. Beneath his feet is a large eagle, his Evangelistic symbol. This spreads both wings and turns to look upwards towards the saint, over its dexter shoulder. The detail is finely carved.

The stone, like that in niche no. 91, is almost free of calcite veins and shows little sign of the bedding. The pointing holes are light and fine, similar to those found elsewhere on Redfern's carvings. The sculpture appears to have been broken on two occasions. An almost horizontal break across the figure, a little above

No. 92, St John the Evangelist.

Nos. 99–102, St James the Less, St James the Great, St Bartholomew, St Matthias.

elbow level, has been repaired with red mastic or shellac, and there are two small refixings in the same material probably associated with this on the dexter elbow and forearm. At shin level there is a second break, this time repaired with Portland cement, and two vertical cramps, which look more like a repair carried out by masons during fixing.

This sculpture is absent from the earlier version of the frontispiece in Armfield's guide of 1869, but present in the second. At Gloucester Cathedral the south porch carving of St John (commissioned in June 1870), at the sinister edge of the composition, stands frontal, but with the head turned to dexter and the face in full profile, his left hand raised and the right at his side, exactly as at Salisbury (fig. 56). The face is very similar, youthful, clean-shaven, with medium-length wind-blown hair, straight nose and strong chin.

99. St James the Less

Chilmark stone; Redfern workshop, 1867-69
H, 208 cm; W, 64 cm; D, 40 cm

Standing figure with short beard and long hair, wearing a belted tunic with loose sleeves folded back at the cuff and hooded mantle. The latter appears to be physically joined (rather than clasped) at the front of the sinister shoulder (cf no. 100) and falls over the dexter forearm, where it is caught up over the left wrist and the handle of the fuller's club, his distinguishing attribute. The club is held in the sinister hand and its large heavy end rests between the feet. The surfaces show a distinct lack of finish, with coarse and medium claw-chisel marks remaining over large areas (cf no. 100).

100. St James the Great

Chilmark stone; Redfern workshop, 1867-69
H, 201 cm; W, 64 cm; D, 37 cm

Standing figure, bearded and with medium-length hair, in a full-length tunic (falling over bare feet), hidden from knee to lower chest by a voluminous hooded mantle, which divides just below the neck but is caught up from both sides into the left hand. The right hand holds a pilgrim's staff, bridged at its top to the dexter side of a wide-brimmed hat. There is no scrip and any hat badge would have been lost in the general decay of the front of the head.

The two St Jameses almost form a pair in conversation: St James the Less (no. 99) turning slightly to the south and the head of St James the Great inclined and turned slightly to the north. The lack of finish noted on the figure in niche no. 99 is also found here, suggesting that both may have been executed in haste, perhaps to meet a deadline for the partial striking of scaffolding.

101. St Bartholomew

Chilmark stone; Redfern workshop, 1867-69
H, 203 cm; W, 67 cm; D, 35.5 cm

A standing figure wearing an under-tunic that falls over bare feet, an unbelted over-tunic with loose sleeves, round neck and broad round collar, and an unclasped mantle, which is caught up over the dexter forearm, its sinister side held in the left hand. The right hand holds the flaying knife, this Apostle's attribute. The head has medium-length curly hair, a long moustache and a beard that leaves the centre of the chin clean-shaven.

This figure is considerably better finished than the two adjacent Apostles to the north.

102. St Matthias

Chilmark stone; Redfern workshop, 1867-69
H, 203 cm: W, 66 cm; D, 33 cm

The head of the Apostle is strongly turned to dexter, balding and with a long beard falling in two forks, the brows furrowed and the eyes deep set. A long loose tunic is worn, falling over the bare feet, the neck loose, with a vertical 'gather' behind the shaft of his attribute the lance (tip lost), similar to that on the figures of St Matthew and St Mark to the north of the central windows (nos. 90, 89). The mantle is wrapped around the shoulders, the sinister side tucked under the dexter, which is caught up into the crook of the right wrist. The sinister side also passes around beneath the sinister forearm to be caught up in the left hand, falling in long sinuous folds on both sides of the figure.

There is a workshop repair in the upper face of the dexter shoulder, a squared insert 1.3 x 4.5 x 14 cm deep.

116. St Patrick

Chilmark stone; Redfern workshop, after 1869
H, 208 cm; W, 61.5 cm; D, 36 cm

St Patrick is dressed as an archbishop vested for mass, with mitre, crosier and pallium. He stands in contrapposto, looking down and slightly backwards to dexter, in the general direction of the serpent that he tramples beneath his right foot. His left hand holds a crosier, the head of which rises beside his left ear, the foot pressing against the snake; it is bridged to his dexter knee, rises across the body and is freestanding above the hand. The right hand is brought across the body and points to sinister in a gesture of dismissal. The head is heavily bearded, four wavy locks falling on to the chest.

The head (and perhaps the original head of the crosier) appears to have been accidentally broken off and refixed with a ?mastic repair and vertical dowel. The upper shaft of the crosier consists of a zinc tube and the head is a simple curved piece of ?stone. There are signs that the carving was finished rapidly. The dexter half of the amice has been accidentally omitted; the pallium has been represented only by incised lines, rather than as a raised vestment (as elsewhere); there is a distinct lack of finish on the top of the mitre; there are a great many more unerased tool marks than is usual.

The fineness of this block and the slightly yellow (rather than grey) calcite veins suggest a different origin from the rest of the carving block. This would be commensurate with a slightly later date for this sculpture, which is indicated by its absence from the list of completed figures in Armfield's guide of 1869. The characteristic use of the drill in the execution of the sculpture, however, confirms the stylistic impression that this figure is from the workshop of James Redfern.

No. 116, St Patrick.

Nos. 119–22, St Ambrose, St Jerome, St Gregory, St Augustine of Hippo.

THE FOUR LATIN FATHERS (NOS. 119-22)

An engraving in Mrs Jameson's *Sacred and Legendary Art* (facing p.280), taken from Antonio Vivanni, together with her text, seems to have provided Redfern with inspiration for his representation of the Four Latin Fathers, both here and on the porches of Gloucester and Bristol Cathedrals.

119. St Ambrose

Chilmark stone; Redfern workshop, 1867-69
H, 211 cm; W, 65 cm; D, 44.5 cm

Depicted as a bearded bishop with medium-length hair, head raised and turned to dexter, wearing mitre and vested for mass (maniple and stole omitted). The dalmatic is not split at the sides, nor is there any

decoration on its hem, and this austerity extends also to the chasuble and amice, both being quite plain. The sleeves of the dalmatic are long and pendulous, terminating in tassels. The left hand holds the shaft of a pastoral staff and the right holds a scourge with three knotted thongs against the dexter shoulder.[100] The feet are bare.

There is a probable original repair to the lower part of the shaft of the pastoral staff. The front face of the staff precisely follows the vertical line of the bedding of the stone.

120. St Jerome

Chilmark stone; Redfern workshop, 1867-69
H, 214 cm; W, 66 cm; D, 41.5 cm

Jerome, with long forked beard, wears under-tunic, tunic and hooded mantle, with a cardinal's hat over,

---

[100]   Armfield describes 'the staff of a Bishop': Armfield 1869b, p.10.

its long tasselled strings tied at the waist and crossing again below. The under-tunic falls over the shoes, with a mid-shin-length tunic and a hooded mantle, clasped at the throat. Supported on the right hand is a small stylised church; in his left, he holds a clasped book, spine inwards.[101]

Like St Ambrose, the garments are plain and undecorated. Whereas the latter looks up and to dexter, Jerome looks down and to sinister. The rear dexter part of the cardinal's hat may have been broken during installation. The facial features strongly resemble those on Redfern's sculpture of the same saint on the south porch of Gloucester Cathedral.

121. St Gregory

Chilmark stone; Redfern workshop, 1867-69
H, 213 cm; W, 71 cm; D, 43.5 cm

Clean-shaven and slightly fat-faced (following the description given by Jameson),[102] St Gregory turns his head to dexter towards a dove with outspread wings that is perched on his dexter shoulder, referring to the dictation by the Holy Spirit of his homilies on the Book of Ezekiel.[103] He wears a papal tiara with triple crown and is robed in processional vestments, the cope caught up over the forearms, with more of this garment being gathered up in the left hand; the orphreys are decorated with lozenges and circles separated by groups of four small jewels, and the cope is clasped with a richly decorated morse. There is some confusion in the forms of the drapery over the sinister arm. The right hand (largely gone) was probably held up in benediction, the left holds a book, from behind which the shaft of the pastoral cross appears.[104]

This sculpture is very similar to that on the south porch of Gloucester Cathedral, in the facial features and drapery. The morse fixing the cope is almost identical.

122. St Augustine of Hippo

Chilmark stone; Redfern workshop, 1867-69
H, 211 cm; W, 67 cm; D, 42 cm

Augustine is represented as a standing bishop, vested for mass and holding a flaming heart in his right hand (which is covered by the chasuble), while his left (now lost) held a book.[105] In the crook of the wrist of this hand is supported the crosier, which rises to be bridged to the mitre. The maniple and stole are absent. The face is clean-shaven and heavily lined, the suggestion of age also present in the narrow ligaments of the neck.

The heart may have been broken and refixed at some date using Portland cement.

125. St Remigius of Reims

Chilmark stone; ?Redfern workshop, c.1873
H, 213 cm; W, 64 cm; D, 43.5 cm

A standing bishop in mass vestments (the mitre with free-standing infulae; no maniple), his right hand raised in benediction, his left holding a book, which rests open on the palm, while secured in the crook of his left arm is a crosier. The shoulders sway slightly to sinister, with the weight placed on the right leg, the head turned to dexter and looking slightly downwards. The face is clean-shaven and relatively unlined, giving an impression of youth turning to middle age. The mitre, amice and sides of the dalmatic are decorated, and the head of the crosier appears to have been a stylised serpent head. The wide sleeves of the dalmatic are pendulous and terminate in tassels. Gloves may have been intended on the hands.

Across the upper surface of the book is a deep groove, running from sinister to dexter, probably to drain water from the sloping pages before it could gather against the chest and form a runnel down the drapery.

---

[101] Armfield describes him 'with a church in his right hand and the volume of Holy Scripture [The Vulgate] which he translated in the left': Armfield 1869b, p.10.

[102] Jameson 1857, p.317. Also Armfield 1869a, p.68.

[103] Armfield 1869a, p.69.

[104] Armfield 1869b, p.10: 'the pastoral staff with a double cross, and the volume of his theological writings in his hand.'

[105] Armfield 1869b, p.10: 'a burning heart in his right hand, the pastoral staff of a Bishop supported by his left arm, and a volume in his left hand indicative of his vast contributions to the theology of the Church.'

No. 125, St Remigius of Reims.

This may be one of two sculptures known to have been fixed in 1873.[106] The authorship is disputed. The zigzag hem on the front fall of the chasuble beneath the dexter wrist is characteristic of Redfern, but the drapery forms are less deep and complex than those on many of his bishops from the first campaign at Salisbury. The tasselled end of the dalmatic cuff and the absence of the maniple are also typical of Redfern. However, no pointing holes were observed. If this figure is not by Redfern, then the unknown carver has made a careful study of his work – could it be by a member of his workshop working solo? This sculpture was found to bear traces of the 19th-century preservative layer, which may indicate a date for the application of this in 1873 or later.

THE PATRON SAINTS OF CHRISTENDOM AND FOUR VIRGIN MARTYRS (NOS. 132-42)

The 11 sculptures in the prominent niches above the central west porch are recorded on a diagram in the cathedral archive as the gift of Revd C.B. Bicknell, Rector of Stourton (fig. 58). The total cost is given as £583. Redfern conceived the group of the seven patron saints of Christendom, flanked by the four virgin martyrs (both groups defined by Jameson), as a single tableau centred upon the Christ Child borne by St Christopher. The child occupies the apex of the central niche and this is the natural focus of the entire group. To each side are three patron saints and, flanking these, two virgin martyrs. In the position of honour to the north is St George (with whom the patriotic Jameson begins her group). According to Armfield's original iconographic scheme, he was initially intended to have the central place. The poses of the figures emphasise the centrality of the St Christopher group, since all but Sebastian (his eyes raised to heaven) and Cosmas (in conversation with his brother Damian) are turned towards the central image. This turn is slight in St George and progressively greater in St Nicholas and St Roch, until St Barbara's head is almost in profile.

132. St Barbara
Chilmark stone; Redfern workshop, ?1868
H, 203.5 cm; W, 69 cm; D, 40.5 cm

Barbara's turn to sinister is emphasised by the way in which the weight is placed upon her left leg, allowing the right knee to project slightly, and by the lean of the upper torso, which balances the book that is held at the sinister side. She wears a long gown falling over the feet, with a mantle clasped centrally at the throat and brought back across her body, to be tucked beneath the sinister elbow. In her left hand she holds an open book;[107] in her right a martyr's palm. From behind her right leg appears the Gothic castle of her legendary imprisonment. She wears a low four-peaked cap or coronet, beneath which her hair falls in coiled locks on to the shoulders. It is tied just below ear level. The hair has been roughed out using a 6 mm diameter drill. The face is almost pre-Raphaelite.

The back of Barbara's head is now missing, having apparently been a workshop repair. The remaining surface appears to have been worked to a fine flat finish, rather than being a natural shear-plane in the stone, and in several places there are patches of a reddish brown mastic (or shellac?).

---

[106] *The Times*, 22 September 1873, reports that these were 'the gifts of private munificence'.
[107] Armfield 1869b, p.11: 'suggestive of her studious habits'.

Nos. 132–42, Patron Saints of Christendom and four Virgin Martyrs.

133. St Katherine

Chilmark stone; Redfern workshop, ?1868
H, 208.5 cm; W, 65 cm; D, 38 cm

St Katherine, situated one niche closer to the centre than St Barbara, has a less extreme turn to sinister, but the sharp turn of the head is again accentuated by the pose. In this Redfern seems to be consciously imitating the 14th-century poses. The saint wears a long gown and a mantle thrown loosely over the shoulders, falling over the dexter forearm and the sinister elbow. In her right hand she holds the hilt of a long sword, her attribute, which rests upon the ground beside her right foot; in her left, she holds a martyr's palm. Behind her right leg appears part of the wheel of her martyrdom. The cap is of the same form as that worn by the other female martyrs, with a lozenge-shaped pyramidal jewel in each peak.

The face is typical of Redfern's female saints, though the eyes are somewhat more open and less heavily lidded. The eyebrows are nearly horizontal, rather than highly arched, as on the other female figures. It is an altogether simpler sculpture than the St Barbara, with little in the way of projecting or free-standing elements, both arms being fully bridged to the body, and the drapery elementary and vertical. The

execution could safely have been entrusted to a workshop assistant and there are some signs of this, such as the over-drilling of the pointing marks, the untypical weight of the cloth of the mantle and the unusual treatment of the left hand, which is almost like relief sculpture. The face, however, was probably finished by Redfern himself.

134. St Roch

Chilmark stone; Redfern workshop, ?1868
H, 210.5 cm; W, 65 cm; D, 39 cm

St Roch (the sculpture indebted to Jameson's text and illustration, fig. 54)[108] stands facing to sinister, holding a staff at his sinister side with his right hand. His left arm pulls back the hem of his tunic, exposing the plague spot on his thigh; the hose on this leg is rolled down around the ankle. At his feet a small dog is seated, leaning back and upwards to lick the saint's leg. Roch is garbed as a pilgrim, wearing a mid-shin-length tunic with a cowl, narrow cuffed gauntlets, a round hat with a scallop-shell badge and, hanging from a strap over the sinister shoulder, a scrip. There is an outer, wide-sleeved hooded garment, worn over an inner tight-sleeved garment of similar length.

[108] Jameson 1857, p.429, fig. 106, from a representation by Carotto.

The short beard shows plentiful signs of drill-work, as does the moustache running down to frame the mouth and beard. The nose is decayed but appears to have been relatively short and slightly hooked.

135. St Nicholas

Chilmark stone; Redfern workshop, ?1868
H, 207.5 cm; W, 65.5 cm; D, 42 cm

St Nicholas is represented as a standing bishop vested for mass, wearing amice, chasuble (with a Y-shaped orphrey), dalmatic with richly decorated hem, stole, alb and a richly decorated mitre with infulae (the maniple is absent). Supported on his right hand (over which the chasuble falls in graceful curves) is a clasped book, resting flat upon which are the three golden balls of his legend. The left hand (now largely lost) once held a pastoral staff, which has itself been lost from approximately 50 cm below the hand – that is, the point at which it was last bridged to the drapery. He stands with a slight sway to the sinister hip, the head turned to sinister and inclined slightly downwards. The head is bearded, but the saint is represented as only a little over middle aged.

Reliance upon the drill is evident in the carving of the face – particularly in the beard, where each of the curling locks is centred upon a drill hole – but the

nostrils, pupils, ears and tear ducts are also cut with drills of various diameters; the pupils clearly having been cut with at least two holes of relatively narrow diameter, and then opened up either with a larger drill or the chisel.

136. St George

Chilmark stone; Redfern workshop, ?1868
H, 214.5 cm; W, 67 cm; D, 39.5 cm

St George's head is turned only slightly towards the centre. His brow is slightly furrowed, but the face is youthful. He is depicted in full mail, the coif apparently over a steel cap. The knee-length surcoat is short-sleeved, tied at the waist and slit at the front. The left hand emerges from beneath a shield that is charged with a raised cross, hanging from a guige over his right shoulder, and holds the hilt of a sword, the tip of which rests upon the back of a slain dragon. The right hand, hanging down the dexter side, holds the dragon's head. The right foot rests upon the neck of the dragon, which curls back up behind the middle of the shin and disappears, so that it is unclear whether the head which the saint holds has been severed or is merely held up. The dragon has one wing beneath the saint's left foot and the other upraised between his legs, forming a bridging structure between them that adds strength to the lower part of the sculpture.

---

137. St Christopher

Chilmark stone; Redfern workshop, ?1868
H, 234 cm; W, 74 cm; D, 47.5 cm

The St Christopher was probably inspired by an illustration in Jameson's *Sacred and Legendary Art* (fig. 53).[109] Set above the central gable, it forms the centrepiece to this group of 11 sculptures. The saint carries the Christ Child on his left shoulder and leans to dexter, supported upon a massive palm bough, which he holds in his right hand. His left arm is flexed, the hand resting on the sinister hip, providing support for the seated child above. He is represented as a large and heavily muscled man, bearded and with swept back hair (slightly balding), wrapped in a single loose garment, which appears over his right shoulder and is brought back and pinned on the sinister hip by his hand. The Christ Child is seated upon the sinister shoulder, the head turned to dexter and inclined slightly downwards, his right hand upraised in benediction (the elbow bridged to the saint's head), the left supporting an orb. The head is nimbed. The Child appears to wear a single garment, which forms broad plain sweeps of drapery across the legs and busier, more complex folds on the chest and right arm. Folds around the neck make it appear that it has a cowl.

The head of the Christ Child has been broken off and refixed using a red mastic. Part of the upper dexter quadrant of the halo has been broken off and refixed with the same material. The nimbus is decorated with a raised cross, the slightly sunken panels between the arms being framed by a narrow incised fillet parallel to the rim. The head is more to Victorian taste than modern, with fat cheeks and a chin crying out to be chucked. The hair flies back in flame-like forms around the face, and there is evidence of prolific drilling in the cutting of the locks. The orb (the cross now lost) also appears to have been broken off at some point, since there is a very fine joint running across the top of the knee, up beneath the base of the thumb and underneath the orb over the top of the hand.

[109] Jameson 1857, p.446, fig. 111.

Not only were the hair and features of Christopher roughed out with a drill, but deep points between the bifurcation of two folds in the drapery were often treated similarly. This can be seen also in other areas of undercutting – particularly behind the left leg to the sinister side and to dexter of the left knee. A further line of drill holes runs along the dexter margin of the dexter shin, and beside the palm adjacent to his right leg, where it pierces through beside the drapery. The pointing holes are particularly numerous: 83 have been noted. However, this sculpture is considerably larger than the others on the façade and, furthermore, comprises two figures. The majority of the holes are in protected positions: on the side of the Christ Child (almost completely hidden from view); at the base of the chest muscles; and down the angle between the dexter knee and the staff.

---

138. St Sebastian

Chilmark stone; Redfern workshop, ?1868
H, 204.5 cm; W, 66.5 cm; D, 35 cm

St Sebastian stands with his right foot forward and his wrists tied behind his back, presumably to the dead tree beside him to dexter. His head is inclined slightly to dexter and looks slightly upwards. He is pierced by three arrows. From behind his left leg appears the inside surface of a shield. From beneath his left shoulder appears an otherwise irrelevant piece of drapery, which loops across the lower torso and is tucked through the binding ropes that slope down from the saint's waist, to fall demurely over the upper thighs. Sebastian is represented as youthful and clean-shaven, his medium-length hair windblown across the forehead from sinister to dexter. The face is unlined, in early middle age.

The sinuous curve of the pose resembles, but is more subtle than that of the 14th-century sculptures. A fine crack runs around the head, from the hair locks above the dexter temple, across his right eye and nose, over the sinister cheek, on to the sinister ear lobe, and thence around the back of the head. This is a break in the stone, which, at the sinister side, can be seen to contain a red mastic, indicating an original workshop repair. It may have occurred along a natural line of weakness, which the bridging of the head to the branch of the tree in this area was intended to reinforce.

139. St Cosmas

Chilmark stone; Redfern workshop, ?1868
H, 209.5 cm; W, 74 cm; D, 43 cm

Cosmas and his brother Damian (no. 140) are represented in conversation. The design of Cosmas is derived partly from an original by Bicci di Lorenzo, illustrated in Jameson's book.[110] His weight is planted on his left foot, the left hip pushed across, and the torso sways slightly to dexter, as he turns his head towards his brother. The sway of the torso is balanced by the thrust of the sinister elbow, the arm being brought down on to the sinister hip and holding the leading edge of the mantle. The relationship with Damian is stressed not only by their pose, but also by their facial similarity and clothing: both wear round caps with drapery falling behind the neck (Cosmas's being fur-lined), fur-lined over-garments clasped at the throat and knee-length tunics. In his right hand Cosmas holds a cube-shaped ointment box; the left holds the hem of the coat and, according to Armfield, also a surgical instrument, as he was a patron saint of doctors.[111] The face is youthful and clean-shaven, similar to that of St Sebastian (no. 138), with an unlined brow.

There are two workshop repairs, fixed with red mastic, on the left hand. The main one comprises the whole of the back of the hand, the fingers and the object they held, and incorporates the leading edge of the front hem of the coat to 17 cm below the underside of the hand. In addition a smaller piece of stone within it has also been re-adhered, comprising the knuckle of the middle joint of the forefinger.

140. St Damian

Chilmark stone; Redfern workshop, ?1868
H, 209 cm; W, 67 cm; D, 42.5 cm

Damian stands in a relaxed pose, right leg crossed over left, the whole body turned to dexter, facing his brother Cosmas. The right hand is raised in a gesture of exposition; the left holds a mortar and pestle, representing his trade as a physician. His dress is similar but not identical to that of his brother, including a round cap with attached drapery, but without a fur lining. Instead of a fur-lined coat with

[110] Jameson 1857, p.435, fig. 107
[111] Armfield 1869b, p.11.

its own sleeves, Damian wears a fur-lined mantle, falling over the outside of the dexter forearm and caught up underneath the left wrist. His tunic has a broad belt and the hem is slightly shorter, ending just above the knee. The facial features are also similar but not identical. Damian appears slightly younger.

The middle finger of the right hand, from just below the middle joint, has been broken off and refixed with red mastic or shellac. There is an original workshop repair to the handle of the pestle, where a 5 mm diameter round-sectioned copper dowel has been drilled along the handle into the body of the stone and the joint has been made with red mastic or shellac. There is a small workshop repair beneath the dexter elbow on the lining of the mantle. Here a small area 3.5 cm wide x 1 cm high appears to have been refixed using the bright red shellac/mastic, the area at its sinister end covered with a darker material, possibly a residue of dirt, but equally likely to be either a cement or discoloured plaster patch.

From the top of the thigh downwards the fur lining of the mantle is absent. It would appear from this and other evidence that the carving remains unfinished. It displays tool marks, several areas lacking finish (such as the dexter side of the face and the mantle over the right forearm) and many front-facing surfaces retaining relatively coarse claw-chisel work. Large diameter drill holes, from the initial opening up of the carving, remain in deep corners of the drapery and there are numerous pointing holes on the surfaces. There is an area of accidental over-cutting on the dexter fall of the mantle above the right forearm. This sculpture may, therefore, represent the last of the 11 figures in this group to be executed.

141. St Margaret of Antioch

Chilmark stone; Redfern workshop, ?1868
H, 210 cm; W, 61 cm; D, 39 cm

St Margaret stands upon a dragon, swaying slightly, with her left hip thrust out and right knee slightly forward. Her head is turned to dexter and looks slightly downwards towards the dragon. She wears a long gown with parallel vertical folds, waisted but not belted, its round neck visible within the neck of the mantle (the latter perhaps intended to be hooded), which is held with a wide strap fixed with two round brooches. It has an additional cord tie knotted between the breasts, with tasselled ends hanging down the front of the gown. As with the corresponding figure of St Katherine (no. 133), the mantle falls over the dexter arm and the dexter side of the chest, whilst to sinister it is pulled back across the left upper arm to fall vertically and disappear behind the figure. In her right hand she holds a martyr's palm, in her left a zinc alloy cross. She wears a low plain cap of the same type as that worn by St Barbara and St Katherine, and pointed shoes. Beneath the feet is the curling body of the dragon, its head rising vertically at the dexter side. It is similar to that associated with St George, but less detailed and smaller.

The front 4 cm of the wing along the front face of the plinth is a workshop repair: the joint being fine and straight and, where it is not obscured, a fine line of red mastic can be seen. The piece is held on with two 5 mm copper alloy dowels set in grey-brown Portland cement, in holes of approximately 1.05 cm diameter. The dexter side of the hair and other areas of the head have been left with a mass of drill-holes from the initial stage of the carving. The underside of the tassels of the mantle cord are also worked with a drill. There are numerous pointing holes (fifty to sixty) and some signs of rapid finish at lower sinister.

142. St Ursula

Chilmark stone; Redfern workshop, ?1868
H, 205 cm; W, 70 cm; D, 40 cm

Like St Barbara at the opposite end of this series, Ursula turns her head in full profile towards the centre of the screen, the upper torso swaying to sinister, her right hip pushed out to dexter, giving the pose a strong S-curve, similar to that employed by the 14th-century sculptors. Like the northern pair, this outer figure of the southern pair has rich complex drapery, but the inner figure much simpler vertical folds, illustrating the way in which Redfern was planning the entire set as a symmetrical series.

Unlike the other three virgin martyrs Ursula is crowned. She carried in her (lost) right hand a martyr's palm and in her left an arrow, the instrument of her martyrdom. The shaft is a zinc alloy tube, painted black, and the flights are also of zinc. She wears a mantle with a circular collar, fastened at the centre of

the throat with a simple circular brooch, and a long gown loosely belted at the waist. The mantle falls behind the dexter forearm, the hem zigzagging down the dexter side. On the sinister side, it passes around the outside of the left elbow and is then caught back up and tucked underneath the loose belt of the tunic, whence it falls down the outside of her left leg. The double hemline of the gown suggests that two garments are worn, but only one cuff is shown at the wrists. Her hair is unbound and her features are smooth and youthful, the eyes large and fully open.

150b. St Stephen

Chilmark stone; Redfern workshop, late 1869 or early 1870
H, 203.4 cm; W, 67.5 cm; D, 34 cm

Stephen is represented as a clean-shaven deacon, in alb, amice, dalmatic and maniple, but without the stole. The vestments are richly decorated. His right hand holds the stones with which he was martyred. The left originally held a martyr's palm, of which all that remains is the lower stem beneath the hand, while above the hand is a copper dowel, fish-scaled to secure the upper part of the palm (perhaps a workshop repair). The pose is frontal, with the weight thrown on to his left leg and the right brought forward, breaking the monotonous vertical fall of the drapery. This gives a very slight sway to dexter and the head is also turned slightly to dexter.

No. 150b, St Stephen.

In addition to the normal copper alloy hooks-and-ring fixing, there appears to be a slate dowel between the ashlar of the niche and the back

Nos. 152–55, St Lucy, St Agatha, St Agnes, St Cecilia.

of the figure. The sculpture had not been installed when the first version of Armfield's frontispiece was taken (1869), but is present in the second, showing that it was carved late in 1869 or very early in 1870.

THE FOUR VIRGINS (NOS. 152-55)

152. St Lucy

Chilmark stone; Redfern workshop, 1867-69
H, 197.3 cm; W, 60 cm; D, 34 cm

There is a slight S-curve to Lucy's pose, together with a slight backward lean. Like many of Redfern's female sculptures, the face is almost pre-Raphaelite in character. She wears a low cap or coronet and her long hair falls loose behind her shoulders. She wears a long round-necked gown with relatively tight cuffs and the folds of the hem fall over her shoes, with their diamond diaper. Over the gown is a mantle, clasped at the centre, a little below the neckline of

the gown, open across the chest and falling over the forearms. On the sinister side, this is caught up beneath the left wrist and then falls vertically down. On the dexter side, it is brought back underneath the elbow and then across the body a little above waist level, and again caught beneath the left wrist, whence it falls in sinuous folds. The right hand holds a lamp, while the left holds the dagger of her martyrdom.

The right hand had been refixed with two copper alloy dowels set in Roman cement, probably shortly after the installation of the figure in the niche.

153. St Agatha

Chilmark stone; Redfern workshop, 1867-69
H, 198.3 cm; W, 64 cm; D, 42 cm

The head is slightly downcast and turned to sinister, the hair concealed beneath the mantle. There is a slight backward sway to the head and upper torso. The voluminous mantle is passed over the top of the head, where it is held in place by the cap that Redfern's female martyrs wear. The two sides are brought forward, cross below the throat, pass beneath the wrists and are then caught up into her left hand, at the centre of the chest, from where they fall in tubular folds, to part and disappear behind the figure a little below knee level. The weight is placed on the left leg, the right knee slightly protruding, and the long gown falls over the feet. The right hand holds a large pair of pincers, the traditional instrument of her martyrdom.

---

154. St Agnes

Chilmark stone; Redfern workshop, 1867-69
H, 194 cm; W, 59 cm; D, 34 cm

St Agnes wears a round-necked gown of full length, which falls over plain shoes and has relatively narrow cuffs. In the crook of her right arm she supports a lamb, her attribute, its forelegs to dexter, its head turned back and slightly upwards to sinister, the saint's left hand resting on its back. Partly concealing the rear legs is the fall of the mantle, which drops vertically from the shoulder, falling across the left arm. The dexter fall of the mantle is caught up in the fingers of her right hand, whence it falls vertically beneath the folds of the sinister side of the cloak. The weight is placed on the left leg, the right knee pushed slightly forward. The head is downcast and turned very slightly to sinister, the long hair falling loose behind the shoulders. A cap of similar design to that of the other female virgins is worn. Like St Agatha the eyes are heavily lidded.

The diagonal hem of the mantle may have been conditioned by the angle and direction of the calcite veins in the stone.

---

155. St Cecilia

Chilmark stone; Redfern workshop, 1867-69
H, 197.8 cm; W, 62 cm; D, 49 cm

Cecilia wears a long gown, its lower hem falling over the feet, but mostly concealed beneath an over-garment with a wide round collar and split sides, the sinister side being partly laced over the sinister upper arm, with the toggles for further lacing on this side visible in the opposing hems beneath the sinister arm. The weight is placed on the right leg, the left knee

slightly protruding. As the patron saint of music, she carries a small portative organ, suspended on a strap over the dexter shoulder. Her left hand rests on the keyboard, while the right is beneath, blowing the instrument with a small bellows. Cecilia's long hair is in plaits. Her head is tilted slightly to sinister, as if listening. She wears a cap of identical design to that of St Agnes.

There are two workshop repairs (the fixing material not certainly identified but probably red mastic or shellac): the larger comprises the sinister elbow and part of the drapery beneath it; the smaller being in the fall of drapery from the dexter elbow.

167b. St Etheldreda

Chilmark stone; ?Redfern workshop, after 1869
H, 207.7 cm; W, 71.5 cm; D, 41 cm

Etheldreda is depicted as a royal foundress, standing with her right knee slightly forward, head turned slightly to dexter and downwards; holding a stylised model of the convent church of Ely in her right hand, and with her left supporting the shaft of a pastoral staff (upper part lost). The swaying pose and the forms of the drapery consciously imitate those of the medieval figure to the east (no. 166). The under-gown is of full length, falling over the toes and concealing all but the tip of the right foot. The over-gown ends at 'dalmatic height', echoing the form of the medieval figure, and the fall of the mantle beneath the right wrist is similar to that beneath the left wrist of the earlier sculpture.

She wears a crown of four fleurons, beneath which is a veil, whose decorated hem is visible on the sinister shoulder, but whose leading edge appears to merge into the mantle on the dexter side. Beneath the veil and the mantle the chest appears to be covered by a short garment almost like a tippet, with a horizontal decorated hem at the level of the left wrist. The mantle is caught up beneath the dexter wrist but passes over the left forearm and falls in a single wide flat area. The hem of the mantle is again decorated. On the dexter side this decoration appears to have been left incomplete. The hem of the over-gown is richly decorated with a single wide band, divided into three horizontal registers.

The upper part of the crosier is broken and lost, below an original repair, since there is the indentation

Nos. 166–168b, St Birinus (as restored by Redfern), St Etheldreda, King Henry VI.

left by the base of a dowel in the break surface. The decorated section of the staff beneath the hand is also a separate piece, probably a second workshop repair. The nave of the model church had a western finial which is now lost, exposing a small wood dowel of 4 mm square section. Another possible workshop repair is present on the sinister side of the plinth.

This figure is not listed by Armfield in his guide, so its authorship remains unproven, but stylistically and technically it resembles Redfern's work. Etheldreda was included in Armfield's programme for the lowest tier (the drawing in the archive indicates a position in niche no. 179). The sculpture is present in photographs taken before the installation of the figure in niche no. 168.

168b. **King Henry VI**
Chilmark stone; unknown sculptor, ?early 20th century
H, 222 cm; W, 73 cm; D, 43 cm

The clean shaven and youthful figure of King Henry stands with his weight on his right leg, left foot forward and left knee slightly bent. He holds a fleur-de-lis headed sceptre in his right hand and an orb (the cross lost) in his left. He wears a belted floor-length tunic, the hem falling over the pointed shoes, and a heavy mantle with an ermine tippet. The mantle is fastened at the centre of the chest and above its collar is the collar of the tunic with a stiffened and decorated hem, bearing a lozenge pattern. Henry has long hair, falling to the level of the jaw, and wears a high crown with large trefoil fleurons alternating with smaller Maltese crosses. There was a copper dowel at the apex to fix a lost finial. There appears to be a joint between the fleur-de-lis head and the shaft of the sceptre.

The sculptor appears to have made an error in carrying out the decoration of the hem of the mantle, where this bears a 7 cm high band containing square quatrefoils with pierced centres. This exists not only on the mantle to dexter, but is also carried on to the prominent fold of the tunic over the dexter foot.

There are numerous divergences from Redfern's style, suggesting that this sculpture is not from his workshop. In general, the folds are heavier and less faceted. In particular, the form of the tunic where it

Nos. 169–71, Bishop Bridport (as restored by Redfern), Bishop Poore and King Henry III.

bags over the belt is unusual. Whereas Redfern favoured swags of S-shaped folds, the opportunity to deploy them in the drapery at the base of the dexter fall of the mantle is not taken. While Redfern often shows one knee projecting, he seldom forms the folds into ridges around it, as here. Unusually, the shaft of the sceptre is bridged throughout its length, with a thin projection of stone running from the body of the stone to support it. The form of the crown would also be unique in Redfern's oeuvre. There are two technical differences. Rather than using the hooks-and-ring system for fixing sculptures to the niches (which Scott copied from the medieval arrangement), this sculpture is fixed using a square copper alloy bar into the back of the sinister shoulder, fixed into the ashlar with lead. No certain pointing holes have been located, suggesting that the sculptor may have been working directly on the stone.

This figure is not present in a photograph taken around 1900, when Daniel (no. 62) had already been fixed.

170. **Bishop Poore**

Chilmark stone; Redfern workshop, 1868-69
H, 207.5 cm; W, 76.5 cm; D, 40 cm

Standing bishop with medium-length beard and relatively short hair, vested for mass, wearing mitre with infulae, amice, chasuble, maniple, dalmatic without split sides and alb (no stole); the chasuble with an odd T-shaped central orphrey, the maniple, dalmatic and amice undecorated. The weight is placed on the right leg, the left foot projecting beyond the corner of the plinth, the leg bent and the knee slightly protruding. In his right hand he supports a model of Salisbury Cathedral (lacking tower and spire), the easternmost part of which is a separate piece, probably fixed with red mastic. In his left hand he holds the shaft of a crosier, the foot and upper half of which are lost. The head was originally bridged to the shoulder, but this was apparently broken (probably in the course of installation) and refixed with a heavy copper armature.

The back of this sculpture is accessible within the recess of the stair-well window and appears to represent the rough surface of the bed of the stone as drawn from the quarry, with little or no secondary reworking. In order to fix the sculpture it was necessary for Scott's contractor to insert a new stone across the head of the window behind the shoulders.

171. King Henry III

Chilmark stone; Redfern workshop, 1868-69
H, 204 cm; W, 78 cm; D, 39+ cm

King Henry is shown in middle age, with short forked beard and medium-length hair, wearing a low crown with fleurons at the cardinal points. He stands with his right elbow thrust outwards, left hand raised and the weight on his left leg. The right hand holds a sceptre, the head broken away, and the left is lost at the wrist. A mantle, clasped on the dexter shoulder with a circular brooch, all but envelops the body. S-shaped folds run down on both sides. An ankle-length round-necked tight-sleeved tunic is visible only at the feet, down the sinister side of the leg and over the right arm. Pointed shoes appear beneath the hem of the tunic, the right toe being broken. The whole composition derives from the gilt-metal effigy of the king on his tomb in Westminster Abbey.

The sculpture is remarkably well finished, with almost no traces of tool marks, although there are traces of very fine claw-chiselling on a few of the folds.

172. St Edmund of Canterbury

Chilmark stone; unknown sculptor, early 20th century
H, 187.5 cm; W, 62 cm; D, 45 cm

Uniquely the base bears the raised letters of the saint's name. Standing figure of an archbishop in processional vestments: highly decorated mitre with infulae, amice, alb with decorated orphrey between the feet, fringed cassock or dalmatic ending at mid-shin level, with the stole ends appearing beneath it, fringed pallium, and cope secured with a decorated strip across the upper chest with a pair of lozenge-shaped brooches. The vestments are richly decorated, with crosses on the pallium, foliage on the orphreys of the cope, and flowers on the amice and on the orphrey of the alb – even the shoes bear embossed crosses. The right hand is raised in benediction

(middle finger with a ring), the left holds the staff of a processional cross. The head is finely detailed, wide swathes of hair sweeping back from the temples, with a heavy moustache and a full beard, the hair lines cut with claw chisels and flat chisels over the lower forks (rather than the drill-work favoured by Redfern).

The niche was empty when Daniel (no. 62) was installed late in the 19th century. No pointing holes have been located and the sculpture is very finely finished, with few traces of toolmarks. It is possible that the head has been broken away at the neck and refixed with a vertical dowel, although the suspected joint line may be no more than a prominent calcite vein. A large blob of Roman cement on the sinister

No. 172, St Edmund of Canterbury.

hair may have been part of the refixing of the head of the processional cross. The same material is found between the shoulders and the niche back and almost certainly dates from the installation of the figure.

173. Bishop Odo of Ramsbury

Chilmark stone; Redfern workshop, 1867
H, 195.5 cm; W, 64 cm; D, 39 cm

Standing, clean-shaven bishop in alb and cope; the latter of soft material wrapped around the body and held at the neck with a hexagonal morse. The decorated amice is shown rising over the neck of the cope, and the mitre (with rich decoration) has infulae falling on to the shoulders. The right hand is held up, the fingers and dexter half of the hand being lost. The left holds a chalice, within which a host wafer stands

No. 173, Bishop Odo of Ramsbury.

upright.[112] The weight is placed on the left foot, the right leg being flexed with the knee projecting slightly. The head is tilted downwards and turned slightly to sinister. The cope is treated as if it were a cloak. The mechanics of the drapery are difficult to interpret and it may be that, as on other figures, Redfern was less concerned with the precise details of the structure than with overall effect.

Standing on the south-west corner of a projecting buttress, this sculpture has been exposed to the worst of the weather and has suffered accordingly. The front of the alb from sinister centre all the way to the dexter edge has lost its surface; the sinister side of the body being likewise decayed; and the face and dexter side of the head being in a state of advanced powdering and exfoliation. So great is the decay that this sculpture has occasionally been identified as a medieval survival.

---

177. **Bishop Ken**
?Clipsham stone; Allan Wyon, c.1930-31
H, 213 cm; W, 97.5 cm; D, 49 cm

Standing figure of a bishop, clean-shaven, with long hair and head inclined to dexter and downwards, the right hand in benediction, the left holding a tall crosier. The bishop is vested for mass, wearing a mitre with infulae, amice, chasuble, dalmatic, stole and alb, the maniple hanging from the left wrist, and the toes of

pointed shoes appearing beneath the lowest hem. The mitre, amice, outer orphrey of the chasuble, dalmatic and maniple are all decorated, the front of the dalmatic with an overall lozenge pattern, the remainder with foliate designs; the dalmatic (cuffed), infulae and maniple have fringed ends. The multiple folds of the hem of the 'alb' appear crimped, as if a 17th-century cassock has been conflated with this garment.

The features are large and somewhat coarsely cut. The head is brought forward and bent downwards towards those entering or leaving by the north door, presumably to effect a dignified interaction between the sculpture and the viewer. Unfortunately the result is a hunched pose and a facial expression avuncular to the point of imbecility.

The yellow grey limestone is partly oolitic, coarse but consistent and shows little sign of its bedding. While lightly weathered, it shows little decay. The nature of the carving block may well have conditioned the coarseness of the carving. Despite the stone, the finish is excellent, with few tool-marks. There is no sign of drill-work, other than in the numerous pointing marks (totalling 123), which are found on all surfaces except the face. This indicates that the sculpture has been worked from a maquette, presumably from a model that had been agreed with the commissioning donors. The sculpture is secured in the niche using two copper alloy cramps leaded into the niche back and the shoulders. The head of the crosier appears to be a separate piece. It has been independently fixed with cement to the niche back using copper alloy wire.

This sculpture was commissioned by Bishop St Clair Donaldson as a memorial for his son; it was approved by the Dean and Chapter in 1930 and installed in 1931. Wyon was also responsible for the monuments to Bishop Ridgeway (d.1921) and Bishop St Clair Donaldson (d.1936) in the cathedral, both incorporating bronze portrait reliefs.[113]

178b. **St Osmund**
Chilmark stone; Redfern workshop, ?1868
H, 207.5 cm; W, 65 cm; D, 39 cm

---

[112] Armfield 1869b, p.13: 'the bleeding wafer of the statue commemorates a legendary miracle whereby he exhibited the transubstantiation of the Sacrament.'
[113] RCHME 1999, pp.143, 146 (no. 9), 152 (no. 14).

No. 178b, St Osmund.

Bishop Osmund is shown as an old man, with furrowed brow, medium-length hair, beard and moustache. He is depicted standing, head inclined to dexter and slightly downwards, holding two books in his right hand[114] and the staff of a crosier (head lost) in his left. He wears a mitre, decorated and with infulae, and full mass vestments, including amice, chasuble with pallium-like orphrey, maniple, dalmatic with split sides and decorated hem, stole and alb, pointed buskins and plain gloves with wide cuffs.

The sculpture is similar in form to that of Bishop Brithwold (no. 187b) in the corresponding position on the southern buttress, but with a lower collar to the amice and a decorated band above the lower hem of the dalmatic. In May 1868 W. H. Poynder of Rowhill, near Chippenham, gave 'the two statues to fill the niches on each side of the great doors of the West Front'.[115] A drawing in the cathedral archive labels this and the figure in niche no. 187 '2 New figures, cost £106. Mr Poynder's donation' (fig. 58). The sculpture was conserved in 1982.

The bulk of the upper stone of the console is medieval. A medieval sculpture is known from documentary and physical evidence to have been located here (see no. 178a).

180b. Angel of the Annunciation

Chilmark stone; Redfern workshop, late 1869 (installed January 1870)[116]
H, 89.5 cm; W, 46.7 cm; D, 18 cm

No. 180b, Angel of the Annunciation.

The standing figure of the Archangel, wings outspread, seems arrested in mid-stride, his right hand held up to his chest in benediction, his left holding a lily stem with three flowers. He is represented as a bareheaded clean-shaven youthful male, his hair swept back in flame-like curls, with a cusped nimbus flat against the wall. He wears a full-length tunic, with round neck and collar. Both the tunic (which falls over the bare feet) and the garment worn over it are caught up at the waist by a tie, which is entirely concealed by the upper garment. The precise form of this upper garment is difficult to determine, but it seems to exist only beneath the waist. The feathering of the wings has a softer, more downy appearance than that of the censing angels within the porch.

---

[114] Armfield 1869b, p.13: 'the two volumes which he compiled and for which his name was famous – the Portiforium and the Consuetudinarium, which may be called respectively a Prayer Book and a Regulation Book.'
[115] *Salisbury and Winchester Journal*, 10 May 1868, p.5.
[116] *Salisbury Standard*, 8 January 1870.

No. 181b, Standing Virgin Mary.

No. 182b, Virgin of the Annunciation.

At the base of the dexter wing there is a workshop repair, refixing a piece 8.3 cm high and 4 cm wide at the tip of the wing, on a straight joint made with a dark red material, possibly shellac. There was a medieval figure in this niche and the others in the gables (see above, nos. 180a-182a).

181b. Standing Virgin Mary

Chilmark stone; Redfern workshop, late 1869 (installed January 1870)[117]
H, 132.8 cm; W, 45.5 cm; D, 27 cm

Standing Virgin with nimbus, tight-fitting cap or fillet, and long hair falling behind the shoulders. There is a strong S-curve to the pose, similar to that found in the 14th-century sculpture on the façade. The face is typical of Redfern's female figures, with long nose, small mouth and slightly protruding chin. The neck is very long and the head is slightly tilted to sinister

and angled downwards, so as to bring it into direct communication with the spectator on the ground.

A long round-necked gown is worn, the folds falling over the pointed shoes. A mantle falls from the sinister elbow and vertically down the sinister side, and is brought up from beneath the dexter arm to be wrapped around the body. The lost right hand held a flowering lily stem, the flowers of which remain bridged to the dexter shoulder. The left hand rests on the centre of the chest, with the elbow thrust outwards above her left hip. The side of the sculpture has been roughly cut back at the base to sinister, perhaps by the fixers, to locate it directly above the side of the medieval stiff-leaf console beneath.

182b. Virgin of the Annunciation

Chilmark stone; Redfern workshop, late 1869 (installed January 1870)[118]
H, 83 cm; W, 42 cm; D, 18.5 cm

[117] *Salisbury Standard*, 8 January 1870.
[118] *Ibid.*

Nos. 183b–185b, Virgin and Child flanked by censing angels.

Seated on a cushioned stool or bench, the Virgin is turned to dexter, her body in three-quarter profile and the head in full profile. She is bare headed, with a nimbus flat to the wall. She wears a full-length gown, with round neck and collar, falling to the floor and leaving only the tip of the pointed left shoe visible. A hooded mantle, restrained by a band across the chest, is brought across from sinister over the lap. The index finger of the right hand rests upon the mantle strap, while the left holds a closed book with decorated cover.

There have been major repairs to the junction between the head and the nimbus, suggesting that it was broken away, probably during carving or fixing. There is a red (?shellac) joint line between the nimbus and the dexter side and top of the head, and the dexter shoulder and mantle, indicating that the joint has been neatly made along the junction between the head and the nimbus. This is suggestive of a repair during carving. On the back of the Virgin's head there is a roughly square patch, which appears to have been made up with a small piece of inserted (?)stone, held in

position with red mastic and then painted over with a stone-coloured paint. This may conceal a cramp or other fixing between the nimbus and the back of the head. A second and more major refixing apparently holds the two halves of the sculpture together at the waist, as indicated by a hairline crack filled with red mastic.

183b. Censing Angel

Chilmark stone; Redfern workshop, late 1869 (installed January 1870)[119]
H, 120.2 cm; W, 50.8 cm; D, 21 cm

The kneeling angel holds a censer, and is dressed in a belted robe and a long mantle, fixed with a circular brooch. The face is considerably more masculine than Redfern's female figures and is clean shaven. The head is nimbed, the sinister wing upraised, the dexter behind the back. The figure is turned in profile towards the Virgin and Child, the hair flowing back

[119] *Salisbury Standard*, 8 January 1870.

in the same flame-like locks as Gabriel's (no. 180b). The carving of the irises and pupils shows that the gaze is directed upwards towards the Virgin, rather than towards the Child. The main garment is tied at the waist, though the form of the tie is concealed by the bagging of the material. The crinkled drapery across the front of the chest is unusual in its form for Redfern, but well realised – it suggests a 15th-century model. The censer has a stylised cruciform church for a lid.

While the front faces of the sculpture are fairly well finished to a smooth surface, the sides – particularly at the base and the sides of the wings, and the dexter side of the head and halo – were left very roughly worked. This may be partly the result of haste in completing the work to a pre-determined deadline. The trimming at the base may be the result of cutting back to install the sculpture in its niche.

184b. Virgin and Child

Chilmark stone; Redfern workshop, late 1869 (installed January 1870)[120]
H, 133 cm; W, 60 cm; D, 35 cm

Seated Virgin and Child, her head inclined forwards and slightly to sinister, with nimbus; wearing a long round-necked gown, with a mantle over and a veil falling across the brows and on to the shoulders. The stool upon which she sits is concealed by gown and mantle, the only suggestion of its form being the oval plinth beneath the feet. The Child is seated upon his mother's lap and her hands support his outstretched arms, the right in a gesture of benediction, the left holding an orb. He has a decorated nimbus with cross arms and is dressed in a single long tunic with round neck.

The mantle is brought forward over both shoulders, but has no sign of any securing device. On the dexter side, the fabric falls below the right wrist before rising above it to fall in decorative folds beside the figure. On the sinister side, the mantle sweeps over the left forearm and is caught back across the lap, its hem falling across the legs in deep V-shaped folds. The drapery dies out at the sides of the figure of the Virgin. The unresolved forms here may be signs that

Redfern's workshop was under pressure to complete the work, although the figures in the porch were the lowest and easiest to install.

There are three representations of Christ on the west front, twice as a child (here and in niche no. 137 (St Christopher)) and once in Majesty (no. 22b). In all three instances he holds the right hand aloft in benediction and carries an orb in the left. Both here and in the central gable, the arms are outspread; while in no. 137 the left hand and orb rest upon the knee. There must be a conscious imitation of the Christ in Majesty here; it is also probable that the sculptor was intending, in the outspread arms, to evoke the Crucifixion.

185b. Censing Angel

Chilmark stone; Redfern workshop, late 1869 (installed January 1870)[121]
H, 118.5 cm; W, 49.5 cm; D, 22 cm

A censing angel, forming a pair with that in niche no. 183, kneeling upon clouds, facing inwards and, like the latter, with its gaze fixed upon the Virgin. The similar execution of the wings, the haloes, the censers, the facial characteristics and the swept back hair also serve to relate the sculptures stylistically. The pose is not a complete mirror image, however. The censers are held differently and here the forward lean of the torso has brought both wings vertically above the head. The drapery is simpler and smoother, forming long curves, in sharp contrast to the angular folds of the other angel – even the folds over the lower part of the body are curved rather than angular. The tunic is round-necked and tied at the waist, but the rest of the figure is swathed in the voluminous mantle.

Below the right hand, the chains of the censer have been heavily repaired using a white or pale buff plaster(?), incorporating several broken pieces of original carving. Evidently the stone here had broken into a number of pieces, probably during installation. In making the repair, any pretence of rebuilding the form of the rear chain was abandoned. A similar patch of buff mortar or plaster exists on both sides of the sinister wing, centred 19 cm down from the wing tip. This patch rests against the niche wall and there is a

---

[120]   *Salisbury Standard*, 8 January 1870.
[121]   *Ibid.*

pale line across the wing at this height, running almost horizontally but slightly down from sinister to dexter. It seems likely that the wing tip was broken off during installation and refixed with the sculpture in the niche.

187b. Bishop Brithwold

Chilmark stone; Redfern workshop, ?1868
H, 202 cm; W, 65 cm; D, 34+ cm

A standing bishop vested for mass, wearing a jewelled mitre with infulae, amice, chasuble, dalmatic, stole and alb (no maniple), holding a crosier (the head lost) in his left hand, the greater part of the right hand lost.[122] The head is slightly inclined to sinister. The hair is relatively short and the face clean-shaven. Like no. 178 the lining of the face suggests a man of advanced years. Both hands were gloved and the feet shod in pointed buskins. The weight is placed upon the left foot, with the right knee slightly flexed and pushed forwards against the shaft of the crosier. The splits in the sides of the dalmatic are wide and pronounced; the drapery of the chasuble is bold, with curved hems typical of Redfern's style at the sides.

No. 187b, Bishop Brithwold.

There is a dowel hole in the broken face of the right wrist, suggesting that this break may have occurred early, possibly even in the workshop. The break plane is clean and flat and follows the line of the bedding. There is a second dowel hole in the face of the sinister shoulder (with copper staining around the rear half of the hole), which presumably served to secure the head of the crosier. This was originally bridged to the chest and was presumably broken in carving or (more likely) fixing. There is a possible (lost) workshop repair low on the shaft of the crosier.

The fragment of a medieval sculpture survived here until at least *c*.1858, when it appears in Fenton's photographs (see no. 187a). In May 1868 W.H. Poynder of Rowhill, near Chippenham, gave the 'two statues to fill the niches on each side of the great doors of the West Front', the present nos. 178b and 187b, as confirmed by a drawing in the cathedral archive.[123] The figure was conserved by Nicholas Durnan in 1994, at the beginning of the current programme of works.

---

192. St Alban

Chilmark stone; Redfern workshop, 1867-69
H, 200 cm; W, 67.5 cm; D, 34+ cm deep

Alban is shown as a youthful, clean-shaven, standing figure with long hair, wearing a pyramidal cap with an upturned brim. He wears 'Roman' armour, with a heavy mantle clasped over the front of the dexter shoulder with a circular brooch. His right hand is lost, but held a sword; the left holds a cross-headed sceptre.[124] The head is turned to sinister following the stance of the body – the left foot is somewhat forward of the right. The ?hooded mantle falls vertically to the right foot.

No. 192, St Alban.

---

[122] Armfield 1869b, p.14: 'with his staff in his left hand and with the right hand in the attitude of benediction.'

[123] *Salisbury and Winchester Journal*, 10 May 1868, p.5.

[124] Armfield 1869b, p.14: 'holding sword and cross in his character of knight and martyr.'

Nos. 194–96, St Alphege, St Edmund the Martyr, St Thomas of Canterbury.

On the sinister side, it is drawn tightly across the chest and pulled beneath the left wrist, whence it falls beside the leg. Much of the forward-facing detail has been lost in a catastrophic lamination of the stone, but the chest and midriff were covered with scale armour, there was a belt decorated with discs and beneath this a knee-length fabric skirt. The knees, fronts of the legs and feet were encased in plate armour.

On the dexter side of the chest at the front is a squared recess, which is either a partially lost stone repair or an anchoring point for the sword that was held in the right hand.

194. St Alphege
Chilmark stone; Redfern workshop, 1867-69
H, 208 cm; W, 68.5 cm; D, 43 cm

The archbishop is standing, his head inclined and tilted slightly to dexter. He is represented as an old man, with a heavily lined smiling face, clean shaven

and with medium-length curly hair. He is in mass vestments, the chasuble and end of the pallium being drawn up to accommodate five stones, the instruments of his martyrdom by the Danes. Two more stones are affixed in a rather unlikely fashion: one to the dexter side of the amice and the other to the dexter brim of the mitre. His hands hold the chasuble, the shaft of the pastoral staff (head lost) passes inside the sinister wrist. The pallium, maniple and stole all have fringed ends; the dalmatic has a decorated hem following the lines of the split sides, and tasselled ends to the cuffs. The mitre is richly jewelled. Otherwise the vestments are plain.

195b. St Edmund the Martyr
Chilmark stone; Redfern workshop, 1867-69
H, 206 cm; W, 72.5 cm; D, 42 cm

Edmund has a strong face, with a heavy moustache, no beard and long hair falling on to the shoulders.

He wears an eight-pointed crown with sloping sides. The form of the main garments is obscure, but there is a short tunic to just above the knee, with a heavy belt and armoured midriff, over which is a full-length mantle clasped on the front of the sinister shoulder with a circular brooch; the legs are in cross-tied hose. The dexter fall of the mantle is pulled back across the chest by the right hand to reveal a dagger thrust into the side of the chest; the mantle is then caught up over the right forearm and falls behind the figure.

The fixing consists of the normal hooks-and-ring assembly, common to both the medieval and Redfern sculptures. Both the hook in the figure and the ring are of copper alloy, but the hook in the wall is of iron and likely to be the medieval original from a lost sculpture (a hook is visible in the *c*.1858 Fenton photograph). Paint exists on the canopy and niche back indicating that it was decorated in the 13th or 14th century (see no. 195a).

---

196. St Thomas of Canterbury

Chilmark stone; Redfern workshop, 1867-69
H, 203 cm; W, 64 cm; D, 34 cm

Standing archbishop vested for mass, holding a cross-headed pastoral staff in his gloved left hand, the right raised in benediction. The head is turned to sinister and slightly downcast, looking out from the corner of the building towards the spectator on the ground. A broken sword or dagger is thrust through the head from dexter to sinister. The weight is placed on the left leg, with a distinct sway to dexter in the upper torso.

The vestments are slightly unusual. A second collar is visible beneath the decorated amice. There is a second hem beneath the dalmatic, which is presumably intended for the tunicle. There is a vertical 'fold' beneath the left wrist which appears to represent the unfinished maniple – unless this vestment has been misinterpreted by the workshop assistant working from Redfern's maquette, or by Redfern himself during the adaptation of a drawn model. The pallium is worn, but the stole omitted. In numerous instances, garments merge or separate in illogical ways in Redfern's sculpture at Salisbury. It appears that he was not working from draped models in making his maquettes and that he was working at such speed that mistakes of this sort could pass unnoticed into the finished stone sculpture.

Numerous toolmarks remain over the sides and lower vestments and, taken with the possibly unfinished state of the maniple, this suggests that the sculpture may have been hurriedly completed.

Bibliography

Age of Chivalry — *Age of Chivalry, Art in Plantagenet England 1200-1400*, exhibition catalogue, Royal Academy of Arts, London, 1987

Allan and Blaylock 1991 — J. Allan and S. Blaylock, 'The Structural History of the West Front', in *BAA Exeter*, pp.94-115

Andersson 1949 — A. Andersson, *English Influence in Norwegian and Swedish Figuresculpture in wood, 1220-1270*, Stockholm, 1949

Armfield 1869a — Revd H. T. Armfield, *The Legend of Christian Art Illustrated in the Statues of Salisbury Cathedral*, Salisbury/London, 1869

Armfield 1869b — Revd H. T. Armfield, *Guide to the Statues in the West Front of Salisbury Cathedral, being a chapter from the Legend of Christian Art*, Salisbury/London, 1869

Atterbury and Wainwright 1994 — P. Atterbury and C. Wainwright eds., *Pugin: A Gothic Passion*, New Haven/London, 1994

Ayers 1994 — T. Ayers, 'Fragments of Sculpture from the West Wall of the Cloister', unpublished report for the Dean and Chapter, Salisbury Cathedral, 1994

Ayers 1996 — T. Ayers, 'The Painted Glass of Wells Cathedral, *c.*1285-1345', unpublished PhD thesis, Courtauld Institute of Art, London University, 1996

Ayers 1998 — T. Ayers, 'The Medieval Figure Sculpture on the West Front of Salisbury Cathedral', unpublished report for the Dean and Chapter, Salisbury Cathedral, 1998

Aylmer and Cant 1977 — G. E. Aylmer and R. Cant, eds., *A History of York Minster*, Oxford, 1977

BAA Exeter — British Archaeological Association Conference Transactions (1985), XI, *Medieval Art and Architecture at Exeter Cathedral*, 1991

BAA Gloucester and Tewkesbury — British Archaeological Association Conference Transactions (1981), VII, *Medieval Art and Architecture at Gloucester and Tewkesbury*, 1985

BAA Lichfield — British Archaeological Association Conference Transactions (1987), XIII, *Medieval Archaeology and Architecture at Lichfield*, 1993

BAA Salisbury — British Archaeological Association Conference Transactions (1991), XVII, *Medieval Art and Architecture at Salisbury Cathedral*, 1996

Barham 1976 — F. Barham, *The Creation of a Cathedral*, Truro, 1976

Bilson 1928 — John Bilson, 'Notes on the Earlier Architectural History of Wells Cathedral', *Archaeological Journal*, 85, 1928, pp.23-68

Binski 1995 — P. Binski, *Westminster Abbey and the Plantagenets, Kingship and the Representation of Power, 1200-1400*, New Haven and London, 1995

Binski 1996 — P. Binski, *Medieval Death, Ritual and Representation*, London, 1996

Birch 1887-1900 — W. de G. Birch, *Catalogue of Seals in the Department of Manuscripts in the British Museum*, 6 vols. London, 1887-1900

Blair 1975 — W. J. Blair, 'The Consecration-cross Indents of Salisbury Cathedral', *Transactions of the Monumental Brass Society*, xii, I, 1975, pp.16-20

Blum 1969 — P. Z. Blum, 'The Middle English Romance "Iacob and Iosep" and the Joseph Cycle of the Salisbury Chapter House', *Gesta*, viii, 1969, pp.18-34

Blum 1986 — P. Z. Blum, 'Liturgical Influences on the Design of the West Front at Wells and Salisbury', *Gesta*, xxv/1, pp.145-50

Blum 1991 — P. Z. Blum, 'The Sequence of the Building Campaigns at Salisbury', *The Art Bulletin*, lxxiii, no. 1, 1991, pp.6-38

Blum 1996a — P. Z. Blum, 'Sculpture', in the entry for Salisbury Cathedral, *Dictionary of Art*, ed. J. Taylor, 27, London, 1996, pp.628-29

Blum 1996b — P. Z. Blum, 'The Sculptures of the Salisbury Chapter-house', in *BAA Salisbury*, pp.68-78.

BoE, Dorset — J. Newman and N. Pevsner, *The Buildings of England, Dorset*, Harmondsworth, 1972

BoE, Wilts. — N. Pevsner, *The Buildings of England, Wiltshire*, Harmondsworth, 1963

Bony 1979 — J. Bony, *The English Decorated Style, Gothic Architecture Transformed, 1250-1350*, Oxford, 1979

BoW, Powys — J. Newman, *The Buildings of Wales, Powys*, London, 1995

Brakspear 1922 — H. Brakspear, 'St Mary Redcliffe, Bristol', *Transactions of the Bristol and Gloucestershire Archaeological Society*, xliv, 1922, pp.271-92

Britton 1836 — J. Britton, *Historical and Descriptive Account of the Cathedrals of Salisbury, Norwich, and Oxford*, vol. II of *The Cathedral Antiquities ...*, London, 1836

Brodrick 1993 — A. Brodrick, 'Painting Techniques of Early Medieval Sculpture', in *Romanesque*, pp.18-27

Burges 1859 — W. Burges, 'The Iconography of the Chapter-House, Salisbury', *The Ecclesiologist*, cxxx, February 1859, pp.109-14, 147-62

Cal. Close — *Calendar of the Close Rolls preserved in the Public Record Office*, HMSO

Cennini — C. D'A. Cennini, *The Craftsman's Handbook , The Italian 'Il Libro dell'Arte'* , trans. D. V. Thompson, New York, 1960

Chew 1963 — H. M. Chew ed., *Hemingsby's Register*, Wiltshire Archaeological and Natural History Society, Records Branch, XVIII, 1963

Coales 1987 — J. Coales ed., *The Earliest English Brasses: Patronage, Style and Workshops 1270-1350*, London, 1987

Cobb 1980 — G. Cobb, *English Cathedrals, The Forgotten Centuries, Restoration and Change from 1530 to the Present Day*, London, 1980

Cochrane 1971 — G. L. Cochrane, *Salisbury Cathedral, The West Front*, Salisbury, 1971

Cockerell 1851 — C. R. Cockerell, *Iconography of the West Front of Wells Cathedral, with an Appendix on the Sculptures of Other Medieval Churches in England*, Oxford/London, 1851

Colchester 1982 — L. S. Colchester, ed., *Wells Cathedral, A History*, Shepton Mallet, 1982

Cook 1947/1968 — G. H. Cook, *Mediaeval Chantries and Chantry Chapels*, London, 1947 (1968 edn)

Coulson 1982 — C. Coulson, 'Hierarchism in Conventional Crenellation', *Medieval Archaeology*, xxvi, 1982, pp.69-100

Crook 1993 — J. Crook ed., *Winchester Cathedral, Nine Hundred Years, 1093-1993*, Chichester, 1993

CVMA, GB, III, 1 — T. French and D. O'Connor, *York Minster, A Catalogue of Medieval Stained Glass*, 1, *The West Windows of the Nave wI, wII, nXXX, sXXXVI*, CVMA, Great Britain, III, Oxford, 1987

Dewick 1908 — E. S. Dewick, 'Consecration Crosses and the Ritual Connected with Them', *Archaeological Journal*, lxv, 1908, pp.1-34

Dodsworth 1814 — W. Dodsworth, *An Historical Account of the Episcopal See, and Cathedral Church, of Sarum, or Salisbury*, Salisbury and London, 1814

Draper 1996 — P. Draper, 'Salisbury Cathedral: Paradigm or Maverick?', in *BAA Salisbury*, pp.21-31

Edwards 1949 — K. Edwards, *The English Secular Cathedrals in the Middle Ages*, Manchester/New York, 1949 (1967 edn)

Ellis 1986 — R. H. Ellis, *Catalogue of Seals in the Public Record Office, Monastic Seals. Volume I*, London, 1986

EMA — J. Harvey, *English Mediaeval Architects*, London, 1954; revised edn, Gloucester, 1984

English Romanesque Art — *English Romanesque Art 1066-1200*, exhibition catalogue, Hayward Gallery, London, 1984

Erlande-Brandenburg 1994 — A. Erlande-Brandenburg, *The Cathedral. The Social and Architectural Dynamics of Construction*, Cambridge, 1994 (first published 1989)

Erlande-Brandenburg 1995 — A. Erlande-Brandenburg, 'The Building of Lincoln Cathedral by Bishop Hugh', trans. C. Gaston, in *Cathedral Builders of the Middle Ages*, London, 1995, pp.131-34

Erskine 1981/1983 — A. M. Erskine ed., *The Accounts of the Fabric of Exeter Cathedral, 1279-1353*, Parts 1 and 2, Devon and Cornwall Record Society, n.s. 24, 26, 1981, 1983

Fastes du Gothique — *Les Fastes du Gothique, le siècle de Charles V*, exhibition catalogue, Grand Palais, Paris, 1981-82

Fletcher 1927 — J. M. J. Fletcher, *The Statues on the West Front of Salisbury Cathedral*, Salisbury, 1927

Frere 1898/1901 — W. H. Frere ed., *Use of Sarum. I. The Sarum Customs as set forth in the Consuetudinary and Customary, The Original Texts Edited from the MSS*, Cambridge, 1898; *II. The Ordinal and Tonal*, Cambridge, 1901

Gardner 1937 — A. Gardner, *A Handbook of English Medieval Sculpture*, Cambridge, 1937

Gillerman 1994 — D. Gillerman, *Enguerran de Marigny and the Church of Notre-Dame at Ecouis*, Pennsylvania State University, 1994

Golden Legend — J. de Voragine, *The Golden Legend, Readings on the Saints*, trans. W. G. Ryan, 2 vols., Princeton, 1993

Green 1968 — R. B. Green, 'Virtues and Vices in the Chapter House Vestibule in Salisbury', *Journal of the Warburg and Courtauld Institutes*, xxxi, 1968, pp.148-58

Greenway 1996 — D. E. Greenway, '1091, St Osmund and the Constitution of the Cathedral', in *BAA Salisbury*, pp.1-9

Gunnis 1964 — R. Gunnis, *Dictionary of British Sculptors 1660-1851*, London, 1964 edn

Hannavy 1975 — J. Hannavy, *Roger Fenton of Crimble Hall*, London, 1975

Hardy 1996 — E. Hardy, 'James Frank Redfern and George Gilbert Scott's Restoration of the West Front of Salisbury Cathedral', unpublished report for the Dean and Chapter, Salisbury Cathedral, September 1996

Harris 1984 — R. A. Harris, 'A Survey of Medieval Repairs to the Fabric of the West Front', unpublished typescript, Wells Cathedral Library, 1984

Harvey 1975 — J. Harvey, *Mediaeval Craftsmen*, London/Sydney, 1975

Hassall 2000 — C. Hassall, 'Salisbury Cathedral: West Doors', unpublished report for the Dean and Chapter, February 2000

Hastings 1997 — A. Hastings, *Elias of Dereham, architect of Salisbury Cathedral*, Salisbury, 1997

Henry 1991 — A. Henry, 'The Iconography of the West Front', in *BAA Exeter*, pp.134-46

Hewett 1985 — C. A. Hewett, *English Cathedral and Monastic Carpentry*, Chichester, 1985

Hirschhorn 1977 — R. E. Hirschhorn, 'The Chapter-Room Doorway at Rochester Cathedral', unpublished MA Report, Courtauld Institute of Art, London University, 1977

HKW — H. M. Colvin ed., *The History of the King's Works, The Middle Ages*, 2 vols., London, 1963

HMC — Historical Manuscripts Commission, *Calendar of the Manuscripts of the Dean and Chapter of Wells*, I, ed. W. H. B. Bird, 1907; II, ed. W. Paley Baildon, 1914

Hope and Lethaby 1904 — W. H. St John Hope and W. R. Lethaby, 'The Imagery and Sculptures on the West Front of Wells Cathedral Church', *Archaeologia*, lix, 1, 1904, pp.143-206

Howard 1996 — H. Howard, 'Salisbury Cathedral: Scientific Examination of Samples from the West Front', unpublished report for the Dean and Chapter, Salisbury Cathedral, 1996

Howard, Manning and Stewart 1998 — H. Howard, T. Manning and S. Stewart, 'Late Medieval Wallpainting Techniques at Farleigh Hungerford Castle and their Context', in *Painting Techniques. History, Materials and Studio Practice*, ed. A. Roy and P. Smith, Contributions to the Dublin Congress, International Institute for Conservation, 1998, pp.59-64

Hulbert 1987 — A. Hulbert, 'Notes on the Techniques of English Medieval Polychromy on Church Furnishings', in *Recent Advances in the Conservation and Analysis of Artifacts*, ed. J. Black, University of London Institute of Archaeology Press, 1987, pp.277-79

Jameson 1857 — Mrs [A.] Jameson, *Sacred and Legendary Art*, 2 vols., 3rd edn, London, 1857

Jansen 1996 — V. Jansen, 'Salisbury Cathedral and the Episcopal Style in the Early 13th Century', in *BAA Salisbury*, pp.32-39

Jones 1995 — H. A. Jones, 'Salisbury Cathedral: Interim Archaeological Report on Nave South Clerestory External Wall (Major repair area 17 - Phase 1)', unpublished report for the Dean and Chapter of Salisbury Cathedral, October 1995

Katz 1998 — M. Katz, 'The Medieval Polychromy of the Majestic West Portal of Toro, Spain: Insight into Workshop Activities of Late Medieval Painters and Polychromers', in *Painting Techniques. History, Materials and Studio Practice*, ed. A. Roy and P. Smith, Contributions to the Dublin Congress, International Institute for Conservation, 1998, pp.27-34.

Katzenellenbogen 1959 — A. Katzenellenbogen, *The Sculptural Programs of Chartres Cathedral*, New York, 1959

Kendall 1998 — C. B. Kendall, *The Allegory of the Church, Romanesque Portals and Their Verse Inscriptions*, Toronto, 1998

Kennerley 1991 — P. Kennerley, *The Building of Liverpool Cathedral*, Preston, 1991

Kimpel and Suckale 1985 — D. Kimpel and R. Suckale, *Die gotische Architektur in Frankreich 1130-1270*, Munich, 1985

Knight 1998 — H. Knight, *William Russell Sedgfield - Pioneer Photographer*, 2 vols., University of Otago, Dunedin (NZ), 1998

Kowa 1990 — G. Kowa, *Architektur der Englischen Gotik*, Köln, 1990

Leland — *The Itinerary of John Leland*, ed. L. Toulmin Smith, 5 vols., London, 1907, reprinted 1964

Lepine 1995 — D. Lepine, *A Brotherhood of Canons Serving God, English Secular Cathedrals in the Later Middle Ages*, Woodbridge, 1995

Lexicon 1994 — *Lexicon der Christlichen Ikonographie*, 8 vols., Rome/Freiburg/Basel/Wien, 1994 edition

Lindley 1987 — P. G. Lindley, 'Figure-Sculpture at Winchester in the Fifteenth Century: A New Chronology', in *England in the Fifteenth Century*, Proceedings of the 1986 Harlaxton Symposium, ed. D. Williams, Woodbridge, 1987, pp.153-66

Lindley 1990 — P. G. Lindley, 'Sculptural Discoveries at Winchester Cathedral', *Proceedings Hampshire Field Club and Archaeological Society*, 46, 1990, pp.101-11

Lindley 1991 — P. Lindley, 'Romanticizing Reality: The Sculptural Memorials of Queen Eleanor and their Context', in *Eleanor of Castile, 1290-1990, Essays to Commemorate the 700th Anniversary of her Death: 28 November 1290*, ed. D. Parsons, Stamford, 1991

Lindley 1995 — P. Lindley, *Gothic to Renaissance, Essays on Sculpture in England*, Stamford, 1995

McAleer 1984 — J. P. McAleer, *The Romanesque Church Facade in Britain*, New York/London, 1984

McAleer 1988 — J. P. McAleer, 'Particularly English? Screen Façades of the Type of Salisbury and Wells Cathedrals', *Journal British Archaeological Association*, cxli, 1988, pp.124-58

McNeilage 1999 — R. McNeilage, 'Salisbury Cathedral: The Pulpitum. Polychrome Survey, Condition Report and Recommendations', unpublished report for the Dean and Chapter, Salisbury Cathedral, 1999

Malden 1904 — A. R. Malden, 'A Salisbury Fifteenth Century Death Register', *The Ancestor*, ix, 1904, pp.28-35

Martin 1997 — E. Martin, 'Some Improvements in the Techniques of Analysis of Paint Media', *Studies in Conservation*, 22, 1997, pp.63-67

Merrifield 1999 — M. P. Merrifield, *Medieval and Renaissance Treatises on the Arts of Painting*, London, 1999 (first published 1849)

Mâle 1913 — E. Mâle, *Religious Art in France, XIII Century*, London/New York, 1913

Marks 1993 — R. Marks, *Stained Glass in England during the Middle Ages*, London, 1993

Marks 1996 — R. Marks, 'The Thirteenth-Century Glazing of Salisbury Cathedral', in *BAA Salisbury*, pp.106-20

Meredith 1881 — R. F. Meredith, 'Salisbury Cathedral', in 'Correspondence', *The Antiquary*, iv, 1881, p.278

Middleton 1885 — J. H. Middleton, 'On Consecration Crosses, with some English examples', *Archaeologia*, xlviii-2, 1885, pp.456-64

Morgan 1982/1988 — N. Morgan, *Early Gothic Manuscripts [I and II], 1190-1285*, A Survey of Manuscripts Illuminated in the British Isles, 4, 2 vols., London, 1982 and 1988

Morgan 1991 — N. Morgan, 'Texts and Images of Marian Devotion in Thirteenth-century England', in *England in the Thirteenth Century*, Proceedings of the 1989 Harlaxton Symposium, ed. W. M. Ormrod, Stamford, 1991, pp.69-103

Morgan 1992 — N. Morgan, 'Old Testament Illustration in Thirteenth-century England', in B. S. Levy ed., *The Bible in the Middle Ages: Its Influence on Literature and Art*, Binghamton (NY), 1992, pp.149-98

Morris 1974 — R. K. Morris, 'Tewkesbury Abbey, the Despencer Mausoleum', *Transactions Bristol and Gloucester Archaeological Society*, xciii, 1974, pp.142-55

Morris 1985 — R. K. Morris, 'Ballflower Work in Gloucester and its Vicinity', in *BAA Gloucester and Tewkesbury*, pp. 99-113

Morris 1993 — R. K. Morris, 'The Lapidary Collections of Lichfield Cathedral', in *BAA Lichfield*, pp.101-108

Morris 1994 — R. K. Morris, 'The Lost Cathedral Priory Church of St Mary, Coventry', in *Coventry's First Cathedral*, ed. G. Demidowicz, Stamford, 1994, pp.17-66

Morris 1996 — R. K. Morris, 'The Style and Buttressing of Salisbury Cathedral', in *BAA Salisbury*, pp.46-58

Nilson 1998 — B. Nilson, *Cathedral Shrines of Medieval England*, Woodbridge, 1998

Nonfarmale and Rossi-Manaresi 1987 — O. Nonfarmale and P. Rossi-Manaresi, 'Il restauro di "Portal Royal" della cattedrale di Chartres', *Arte Medievale*, ii, series 1, 1987, pp.259-75

Norton 1993/94 — C. Norton, 'Klosterneuburg and York: Artistic Cross-currents at an English Cathedral, c. 1330', *Wiener Jahrbuch für Kunstgeschichte*, xlvi/xlvii, 2, 1993/94, pp.519-32

Norton, Park and Binski 1987 — C. Norton, D. Park and P. Binski, *Dominican Painting in East Anglia, The Thornham Parva Retable and the Musée de Cluny Frontal*, Woodbridge, 1987

Noyes 1913 — E. Noyes, *Salisbury Plain, its Stones, Cathedral, City, Villages and Folk*, London, 1913

Oosterwijk and Norton 1990 — S. Oosterwijk and C. Norton, 'Figure Sculpture from the Twelfth Century Minster', *Friends of York Minster*, 61st Annual Report, 1990, pp.12-30

Osmond 1880 — W. Osmond Jnr, 'Memorandum of mason's work done at the Cathedral, Salisbury', c.1880, Salisbury Cathedral Archive

Die Parler — *Die Parler und der Schöne Stil, Europäische Kunst unter den Luxemburgern*, exhibition catalogue, 3 vols., Schnütgen Museum, Cologne, 1978

Policy 1995 — N. Durnan (Consultant Conservator) and M. Drury (Cathedral Architect), 'Salisbury Cathedral, Policy for the Conservation & Repair of the West Front', unpublished report for the Dean and Chapter, Salisbury Cathedral, March 1995

Polychromy Report 1994 — E. Sinclair, 'Salisbury Cathedral: West Front Polychromy - Polychromy Report', unpublished report for the Dean and Chapter, Salisbury Cathedral, June 1994

Polychromy Report 1995 — E. Sinclair, 'Salisbury Cathedral: Current Assessment of Salisbury Cathedral West Front Polychromy', unpublished report for the Dean and Chapter, Salisbury Cathedral, September 1995

Polychromy Report 1997 — E. Sinclair, 'Salisbury Cathedral West Front Central Porch: Polychromy Report', unpublished report for the Dean and Chapter, Salisbury Cathedral, 1997

Powicke and Cheney 1964 — *Councils and Synods, with other Documents Relating to the English Church*, II, 1-2, ed. F. M. Powicke and C. R. Cheney, Oxford, 1964

Prior and Gardner 1912 — E. S. Prior and A. Gardner, *An Account of Medieval Figure-Sculpture in England*, Cambridge, 1912

RCHME 1987 — Royal Commission on the Historical Monuments of England, *Churches of South-East Wiltshire*, London, 1987

RCHME 1993a — Royal Commission on the Historical Monuments of England, *Salisbury: The Houses of the Close*, London, 1993

RCHME 1993b — Royal Commission on the Historical Monuments of England, T. Cocke and P. Kidson, *Salisbury Cathedral: Perspectives on the Architectural History*, London, 1993

RCHME 1999 — Royal Commission on the Historical Monuments of England, S. Brown, *Sumptuous and Richly Adorn'd, The Decoration of Salisbury Cathedral*, London, 1999

Read 1982 — B. Read, *Victorian Sculpture*, New Haven/London, 1982

Réau 1955-59 — L. Réau, *Iconographie de l'art chrétien*, 3 vols., Paris, 1955-59

Report, Phase 1 — J. Sampson, 'Salisbury Cathedral, The West Front: Phase 1, Report on the archaeological recording on the west front of Salisbury cathedral: S spirelet, S and E faces of Southern Stair-Turret, and E face of link wall', unpublished report for the Dean and Chapter, Salisbury Cathedral, 30 August 1995

Report, Phase 2 — J. Sampson, 'Salisbury Cathedral, The West Front: Phase 2, Report on the archaeological recording on the west front of Salisbury Cathedral: W elevation, from SW corner of south-centre buttress to SW corner of south stair turret', unpublished report for the Dean and Chapter, Salisbury Cathedral, 6 March 1996

Report, Phase 2 (Polychromy) — J. Sampson, 'Salisbury Cathedral, The West Front: Phase 2, Polychromy Survey', unpublished report for the Dean and Chapter, Salisbury Cathedral, 29 September 1995

Report, Phase 3a — J. Sampson, 'Salisbury Cathedral, The West Front: Phase 3, Report on the archaeological survey of the west nave wall above the roofs of the central porch together with its flanking buttresses', unpublished report for the Dean and Chapter, Salisbury Cathedral, 24 October 1998

Report, Phase 3a (Polychromy) — J. Sampson, 'Salisbury Cathedral, The West Front: Phase 3a, Polychromy Survey', unpublished report for the Dean and Chapter, Salisbury Cathedral, 14 May 1999

Report, Phase 3b — J. Sampson, 'Salisbury Cathedral, The West Front: Phase 3B - Report on the archaeological recording ... Central West Porch', unpublished report for the Dean and Chapter, Salisbury Cathedral, 5 June 1999

Report, Phase 3b (Polychromy) — J. Sampson, 'Salisbury Cathedral, The West Front: Phase 3 - West Porch Polychromy', unpublished report for the Dean and Chapter, Salisbury Cathedral, 8 May 1999

Report, Phase 4/5 — J. Sampson, 'Salisbury Cathedral, The West Front: Phase 4/5 - Report on the archaeological survey of the northern west elevation and the north stair turret', in preparation

Report, Phase 4/5 (Polychromy) — J. Sampson, 'Salisbury Cathedral, The West Front: Phase 4-5 - Polychromy Survey', unpublished report for the Dean and Chapter, Salisbury Cathedral, 11 May 1999

Reynolds 1881 — H. E. Reynolds ed., *Wells Cathedral: its Foundation, Constitutional History and Statutes*, Leeds, 1881

Rhin-Meuse — *Rhin-Meuse, Art et Civilisation 800-1400*, exhibition catalogue, Kunsthalle, Cologne and Musées Royaux d'Art et d'Histoire, Brussels, 1972

Roger Fenton — V. Lloyd, *Roger Fenton - Photographer of the 1850s*, exhibition catalogue, Hayward Gallery, London, 1988

Rogers 1987 — N. J. Rogers, 'English Episcopal Monuments, 1270-1350, Parts I to III', in Coales 1987, pp.8-68

Romanesque — *Romanesque Stone Sculpture from Medieval England*, exhibition catalogue, Henry Moore Sculpture Trust, Henry Moore Institute, Leeds, 1993

Rossi-Manaresi and Tucci 1984 — R. Rossi-Manaresi and A. Tucci, 'The Polychromy of the Portals of the Gothic Cathedral of Bourges', *ICOM Committee for Conservation Preprints*, 7th Triennial Meeting, Copenhagen, 1984, 84.5.1-84.5.4

Rushforth 1936 — G. McN. Rushforth, *Medieval Christian Imagery, as illustrated by the painted windows of Great Malvern Priory Church, Worcestershire*, Oxford, 1936

Sampson 1992 — J. Sampson, 'Bath Abbey West Front: Report on the Early Restorations', unpublished report for Bath City Council and English Heritage, 1992

Sampson 1998 — J. Sampson, *Wells Cathedral West Front, Construction, Sculpture and Conservation*, Stroud, 1998

Sampson 1999 — J. Sampson, 'Salisbury – The Poultry Cross: The Archaeological Survey 1994/9', unpublished report for Salisbury City Council, 1999

Sandler 1983 — L. F. Sandler, *The Psalter of Robert De Lisle, in the British Library*, London, 1983

Sandler 1986 — L. F. Sandler, *A Survey of Manuscripts Illuminated in the British Isles, V, Gothic Manuscripts 1285-1385*, 2 vols., London, 1986

Sauerländer 1972 — W. Sauerländer, *Gothic Sculpture in France 1140-1270*, London, 1972

Scott 1866 — Sir G. G. Scott, 'Specification of Works to West Front of Nave', unpublished specification for the Dean and Chapter, Salisbury Cathedral, Salisbury Cathedral Archive, 10 August 1866

Scott 1879 (1995 edn) — Sir G. G. Scott, *Personal and Professional Recollections, A Facsimile of the Original Edition with New Material and a Critical Introduction*, ed. G. Stamp, Stamford, 1995 (first published 1879)

Simpson 1996 — G. Simpson, 'Documentary and Dendrochronological Evidence for the Building of Salisbury Cathedral', in *BAA Salisbury*, pp.10-20

Sinclair 1991 — E. Sinclair, 'The West Front Polychromy', in *BAA Exeter Cathedral*, pp.116-33

Sinclair 1992 — E. Sinclair, 'Exeter Cathedral: Exterior Polychromy', in *The Conservator as Art Historian*, United Kingdom Institute of Conservation, 1992, pp.7-14

Sinclair 1995 — E. Sinclair, 'The Polychromy of Exeter and Salisbury Cathedrals: A Preliminary Comparison', in *Historical Painting Techniques, Materials and Studio Practice*, Leiden University (NL), The Getty Conservation Institute, 1995, pp.105-10

Spencer 1990 — B. Spencer, *Salisbury Museum Medieval Catalogue, Part 2. Pilgrim Souvenirs and Secular Badges*, Salisbury, 1990

Spring 1979 — R. Spring, *The Stained Glass of Salisbury Cathedral*, 2nd edn, Salisbury, 1979

Spring 1987 — R. Spring, *Salisbury Cathedral*, New Bell's Cathedral Guides, London/Sydney, 1987

Spring 1991 — R. Spring, *Salisbury Cathedral: A Landmark in England's Heritage*, Salisbury, 1991

Stalley 1971 — R. A. Stalley, 'A Twelfth-century Patron of Architecture, A Study of the Buildings Erected by Roger, Bishop of Salisbury, 1102-1139', *Journal British Archaeological Association*, xxxiv, 1971, pp.62-83

Stone 1955 — L. Stone, *Sculpture in Britain, The Middle Ages*, Harmondsworth, 1955

Stroud 1984 — D. Stroud, 'The Cult and Tombs of St Osmund at Salisbury', *Wiltshire Archaeological and Natural History Magazine*, 78, 1984, pp.50-54

Tatton-Brown 1989 — T. Tatton-Brown, *Great Cathedrals of Britain*, London, 1989

Tatton-Brown 1991a — T. Tatton-Brown, 'The Archaeology of the Spire of Salisbury Cathedral', in *BAA Salisbury*, pp.59-67

Tatton-Brown 1991b — T. Tatton-Brown, 'Building the tower and spire of Salisbury Cathedral', *Antiquity*, 65, 1991, pp.74-96

Tatton-Brown 1994 — T. Tatton-Brown, 'Salisbury Cathedral Cloisters: Some provisional notes', unpublished report for the Dean and Chapter of Salisbury Cathedral, December 1993, revised January 1994

Tatton-Brown 1995 — T. Tatton-Brown, 'The Tombs of the Two Bishops who Built the Tower and Spire of Salisbury Cathedral', *Wiltshire Archaeological and Natural History Magazine*, 88, 1995, pp.134-37

Tatton-Brown 1996 — T. Tatton-Brown, 'The Pulpitum Screen, Salisbury Cathedral; some provisional notes', unpublished report for the Dean and Chapter of Salisbury Cathedral, June 1996

Tatton-Brown 1998 — T. Tatton-Brown, 'The Building Stone for Salisbury Cathedral', in *Building with Stone in Wessex over 4000 Years*, ed. T. Tatton-Brown, Hatcher Review, v, 45, 1998, pp.39-47

Thompson 1956 — D. Thompson, *The Materials and Techniques of Medieval Painting*, London, 1956

Thurlby 1986 — M. Thurlby, 'The North Transept Doorway of Lichfield Cathedral: Problems of Style', *RACAR*, xiii, 2, 1986, pp.121-30

Tracy 1987 — C. Tracy, *English Gothic Choir-Stalls, 1200-1400*, Woodbridge, 1987

Tristram 1955 — E. W. Tristram, *English Wall Painting of the Fourteenth Century*, London, 1955

Tudor-Craig 1982 — P. Tudor-Craig, 'Wells Sculpture', in Colchester 1982, pp.102-31

Vauchez 1999 — A. Vauchez, *Saints, prophètes et visionnaires, Le pouvoir surnaturel au Moyen Age*, Paris, 1999

Walcott 1877 — M. E. C. Walcott, *The Early Statutes of the Cathedral Church of the Holy Trinity, Chichester*, London, 1877

Waylen 1857 — J. Waylen, 'Who destroyed the Images at the west end of Salisbury Cathedral?', *Wiltshire Archaeological and Natural History Magazine*, iii, 1857, pp.119-24

Webb 1956 — G. Webb, *Architecture in Britain. The Middle Ages*, Harmondsworth, 1956

Weeks 1998 — C. Weeks, 'The Portail de la Mère Dieu of Amiens Cathedral: Its Polychromy and Conservation', *Studies in Conservation*, 43, 1998, pp.101-108

Welander 1985 — D. Welander, *The Stained Glass of Gloucester Cathedral*, Gloucester, 1985

Werckmeister 1972 — O. K. Werckmeister, 'The Lintel Fragment representing Eve from Saint-Lazare, Autun', *Journal of the Warburg and Courtauld Institutes*, 35, 1972, pp.1-30

Westminster Kings — *Westminster Kings and the medieval Palace of Westminster*, British Museum, Occasional Paper 115, London, 1995

White 1898 — G. White, *Salisbury Cathedral*, London, 1898

Whittingham 1970/1979 — S. Whittingham, *A Thirteenth-century Portrait Gallery at Salisbury Cathedral*, Salisbury, 1970; 2nd edn, 1979

Whittingham 1974 — S. Whittingham, *Salisbury Chapter House*, Friends of Salisbury Cathedral, 1974.

Wickham Legg 1916 — J. Wickham Legg, *The Sarum Missal Edited from Three Early Manuscripts*, Oxford, 1916

Williamson 1988 — P. Williamson, 'The Westminster Abbey Chapter House Annunciation group', *The Burlington Magazine*, cxxx, February 1988, pp.122-24.

Williamson 1991 — P. Williamson, 'Sculpture of the West Front', in *Exeter Cathedral - A Celebration*, ed. M. Swanton, Exeter, 1991

Williamson 1995 — P. Williamson, *Gothic Sculpture 1140-1300*, London/New Haven, 1995

Willis 1845 — R. Willis, *The Architectural History of Canterbury Cathedral*, London, 1845

Wilson 1986 — C. Wilson, *Westminster Abbey*, New Bells Cathedral Guides, London, 1986

Wilson 1990 — C. Wilson, *The Gothic Cathedral, The Architecture of the Great Church 1130-1530*, London, 1990

Wilton Diptych — D. Gordon *et al.*, *Making and Meaning, The Wilton Diptych*, National Gallery Publications, London, 1993

Winston 1849 — C. Winston, 'Painted Glass at Salisbury', Report of the Archaeological Institute's Meeting at Salisbury (1849). Reprinted in *Memoirs Illustrative of the Art of Glass Painting*, London, 1865, pp.106-29

Woodforde 1946 — C. Woodforde, *Stained Glass in Somerset 1250-1830*, London, 1946

Wordsworth 1898 — C. Wordsworth, 'On the Sites of the Mediaeval Altars of Salisbury Cathedral Church', *Proceedings Dorset Natural History and Antiquarian Field Club*, xix, 1898, pp.1-24

Wordsworth 1901 — C. Wordsworth, *Ceremonies and Processions of the Cathedral Church of Salisbury*, Cambridge, 1901

Wordsworth 1913-14 — C. Wordsworth, 'List of Altars in Salisbury Cathedral, and Names of Kings of whom there were Representations there about the Year 1398', *Wiltshire Archaeological and Natural History Magazine*, xxxviii, 1913-14, pp.557-71

Wordsworth 1917 — C. Wordsworth, 'Elias de Derham's Leadenhall in Salisbury Close 1226-1915', *Wiltshire Archaeological and Natural History Magazine*, xxxix, 1917, pp.433-44

Wordsworth and Macleane 1915 — C. Wordsworth and D. Macleane eds., *Statutes and Customs of the Cathedral Church of The Blessed Virgin Mary of Salisbury*, London, 1915

Index

Illustrations are denoted by page numbers in *italics*. The letter n following a page number indicates that the reference will be found in a note.

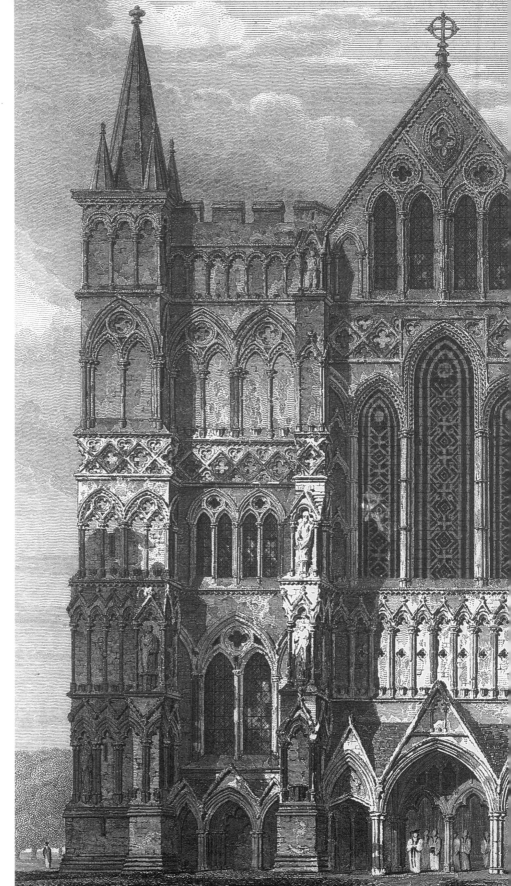

The West Front, drawn by
F. Mackenzie and engraved
by J. Le Keux, from Britton
1836, pl. V.